TERM 1
VSP - week ③

SC HOO. NTAL AND AFRICAN STUDIES
sity of London

before the last date shown

ONE WEEK LOAN

be renewed up to 10 times
be renewed
This book is due for return no later than rdue items
A fine will be charged for late

tron fo
h e)

17 OCT 2001

2 0 JUL 2005

- 8 NOV 2006

1 2 JUN 2002   2 3 OCT 2003

2 4 NOV 2006

1 0 OCT 2002   2 7 JAN 2004

0 7 MAY 2003   2 2 JUL 2002   2 3 FEB 2004

                                      1 2 OCT 2004
3 0 MAY 2006   1 7 OCT 2002

                                      1 5 DEC 2004

2 5 NOV 2002   14 APR 2005

                    2 1 MAR 2005
1 5 OCT 2003   - 4 MAY 2005

        1 0 OCT 2005

Edited by
Anthony Jackson

Anthropology at Home

Tavistock Publications
London and New York

First published in 1987 by
Tavistock Publications Ltd
11 New Fetter Lane, London EC4P 4EE

Published in the USA by
Tavistock Publications
in association with Methuen, Inc.
29 West 35th Street, New York,
NY 10001

© 1987 Association of Social
 Anthropologists

Typeset by Keyset Composition,
Colchester

Printed in Great Britain at the
University Press, Cambridge

British Library Cataloguing in
Publication Data

Anthropology at home.
– (ASA monograph; 25)
1. Ethnology – Europe
I. Jackson, Anthony, *1926–*
II. Series
306'.094 GN308.3.E85

ISBN 0-422-60560-3 Pbk

Library of Congress Cataloging in
Publication Data

Anthropology at home.
(ASA monographs ; 25)
A selection of papers presented at the
ASA Conference, held at the University
of Keele, England, in March 1985.
Bibliography: p.
Includes indexes.
I. Anthropology – Congresses.
I. Jackson, Anthony, Ph. D.
II. Association of Social Anthropologists
of the Commonwealth.   III. ASA
Conference (1985 : University of Keele)
IV. Series: A.S.A. monographs ; 25.
GN3.A753   1987   306   86-14407

ISBN 0-422-60560-3 (pbk.)

Contents

vi   Contents

List of contributors

Edwin Ardener is University Lecturer in Social Anthropology, Fellow of St John's College, Oxford.

Angela Cheater is Associate Professor of Social Anthropology, University of Zimbabwe.

Tamara Dragadze was formerly Lecturer in Social Anthropology, University of Leeds.

Chris Hann is Assistant Lecturer in Social Anthropology, University of Cambridge.

Kirsten Hastrup is Professor of Social Anthropology, University of Aarhus.

Anthony Jackson is Senior Lecturer in Social Anthropology, University of Edinburgh.

Orvar Löfgren is Lecturer in European Ethnology, University of Lund.

Maryon McDonald is Lecturer in Social Anthropology, Brunel University.

Stella Mascarenhas-Keyes is a PhD student, School of Oriental and African Studies, University of London.

Judith Okely is Lecturer in Social Anthropology, University of Essex.

Martine Segalen is Directeur de Recherches at the Centre National de la Recherche Scientifique and Director of the Centre d'Ethnologie Française, Paris.

Marilyn Strathern is Professor of Social Anthropology, University of Manchester.

Shalva Weil is Senior Researcher, School of Education, Hebrew University of Jerusalem.

Françoise Zonabend is Maître-assistant at the Ecole des Hautes Etudes en Sciences Sociales, Laboratoire d'Anthropologie Sociale, Paris.

Preface

This volume results from the ASA conference held at the University of Keele in March 1985. It is not a complete record of the proceedings since only a third of the thirty-nine papers presented can be published here owing to the economic stringencies of publishing today. As may be imagined, it has been difficult to choose between these papers and I have opted to give a representative selection which I hope will appeal to the widest cross-section of readers. The theme of *Anthropology at Home* was, really, an experiment to tap the expertise of anthropologists working in different countries around the world, and it succeeded in attracting more interest from paper-givers and participants than had ever been anticipated. It was decided to hold a 'grand' conference in order to allow the widest possible hearing from workers in this relatively new field but to restrict their presentation-time since most of the papers had already been pre-circulated.

The totality of the conference papers showed how differently one could interpret anthropology at home, yet it served to indicate the scope and quantity of work being done at 'home'. Not surprisingly, there were no standard methodologies or theoretical approaches employed in the various pieces of research. However, the conference acted as a good sounding-board for future meetings where more specific issues can be taken up on a smaller scale.

The articles published here are arranged in a quite different order from the one in which they were presented at the conference and this reflects only my view about their mutual coherence. I have grouped the selected papers into four consecutive and undivided sections:

1. Basic problems: M. Strathern, E. Ardener, J. Okely.
2. West European research: O. Löfgren, K. Hastrup, M. Segalen and F. Zonabend, M. McDonald.
3. East European research: C. Hann, T. Dragadze.
4. Non-European research: A. Cheater, S. Mascarenhas-Keyes, S. Weil.

The basic problems that are discussed are not concerned exclusively with anthropology at home but with doing social anthropology in the modern world. The grouping of the papers by research area is to show how different methodologies are used as one proceeds away from the UK. It will be clear that the theoretical perspectives are also dissimilar.

My introductory essay does not attempt to weave that magical scarlet thread that is supposed to link up all the papers since I am sceptical about such *post facto* devices. The papers have to stand on their own as individual and subjective contributions to the problems we face when we come 'home' to do research.

My essay is a separate contribution in which I reflect upon the present state of our art besides our professional relationships with colleagues who are very much 'at home'. If I appear to be unduly critical of archaeologists and sociologists it is because they almost wilfully distance themselves from us on the pretext that their disciplines are more 'scientific' than ours. If we are to do anthropology at home then we must learn how to accommodate and to include these colleagues in a common enterprise.

The success of the conference was due to the efforts of many people in keeping up a lively debate on a wide range of topics. I should like to thank all the paper-givers for their contributions. My thanks are also due to the chairmen: Paul Bellaby, Ronnie Frankenberg, Marilyn Strathern, Maryon McDonald, Judith Okely, Edwin Ardener, Leo Howe, and Raymond Firth, and to the respondents: Liz Hart, Richard Whipp, Judith Sidaway, Reg Byron, Tony Cohen, Stella Mascarenhas-Keyes, Tim Ingold, and Parminder Bhachu for, respectively, keeping order both chronologically and intellectually in the discussions. Special thanks are owing to Jonathan Benthall for his initiative in organizing the RAI event and for his translation of Martine Segalen and Françoise Zonabend's paper.

We were all grateful to the University of Keele which hosted the conference and very warm thanks go to Ronnie Frankenberg who made all the local arrangements and provided us with such good cheer!

Anthony Jackson
December 1985

Anthony Jackson

1 Reflections on ethnography at home and the ASA

It is now forty years since the ASA was founded by Radcliffe-Brown, Evans-Pritchard, Firth, Forde, and Fortes and a dozen others from Britain: such was the small scale of the enterprise, yet these figures were to dominate the anthropological scene for the next twenty years, up to the appearance of the very first ASA volumes in 1965. These four publications arose out of the Association's meeting in Cambridge in 1963, as a direct result of Firth's suggestion that American anthropologists should be invited to the annual gathering. The membership had then grown to 150 and some forty-odd people were attending the meetings instead of the previous dozen.

This particular volume arose out of a suggestion of mine at the decennial meeting at Cambridge in 1983. The ASA membership had soared to 450, of which nearly 300 are based in Britain. The Keele conference attracted almost a third of this membership and was privileged to have Raymond Firth as an active participant – thus lending the meeting an essential continuity with the foundation of the Association. Indeed, Firth (Firth and Djamour 1956) was one of the early pioneers of studying at home, as were Gluckman, Krige, Kuper, and Schapera. The theme of *Anthropology at Home* was meant to attract contributions from around the world and it did, for the conference heard about researches from Oceania, India, North and South America, Africa, the Middle East, the Soviet Union, and Western Europe.

Unfortunately, it has not proved possible to reproduce all those papers here and so a balance had to be struck between Europe and the rest of the world. If this sounds like sheer ethnocentrism, let me explain that it is not. A majority of ASA members are Europeans and so would be disqualified from this theme if they talked about anything other than Europe. Second, a third of the younger members are interested in European research. Third, it was agreed at Cambridge that Europe should figure at the Keele conference. In fact, nearly two-thirds of the papers given there were about Europe, but since this volume is not devoted solely to European research it means that many have had to be excluded.

In a curious way, anthropology has come full circle in the last one hundred years, since it was established in 1884 as Section H of the British Association for the Advancement of Science. Some eight years after this event the Anthropological Institute, the Society of Antiquaries, and the Folklore Society met to discuss making an *Ethnographic Survey of the United Kingdom*. This unlikely combination of experts was not, of course, undertaking what is currently meant by ethnography: they wished to ascertain the anthropomorphic, archaeological, and customary traces of the various *races* that have inhabited these isles. What is interesting today is why this grand scheme collapsed. The proposed merger of the Anthropological Institute and the Folklore Society was called off because they disagreed on fundamentals. Folklorists were not interested in the endless arrays of skulls collected by anthropologists – they wanted to know what went on inside those skulls. On the other hand, the anthropologists thought that their evidence was much more scientific and objective than that gathered by folklorists. This, remember, was the period when it was thought possible to integrate different types of information into a comprehensive ethnography of mankind along evolutionary lines; see Urry (1984) for more details.

It is an irony of fate that physical anthropologists – the front-runners in 1900 – are a back-number today, while folklorists never achieved academic recognition in Britain. A similar situation obtained in France. Yet in Germany and Scandinavia (which followed the German system) there has been a thriving academic tradition in material culture and folk-life studies which was only displaced by social anthropology in the 1960s. One reason for this was the fact that *ethnological* studies of different races were centred on museums which, naturally, collected *things*. Indeed, it is the 'invention' of museums that created that unholy triple alliance of physical anthropologists, folklorists, and archaeologists. Even today, the archaeologists are basically museum-folk since their prize exhibits are there on open display – in serried rows, too often, alas.

There was a time in the nineteenth century when folklore claimed to be a science (*Wissenschaft*). Social anthropologists are now becoming somewhat coy about claiming their discipline as a science, even a *social* science. However, many archaeologists still hold that their discipline is a science – exact and objective – using the latest scientific techniques for finding and dating objects with a precise and accurate measurement of where *things* are found. It is, therefore, somewhat ironic that most departments of archaeology are to be found in arts faculties – a sub-department of the history of the human race. This clinging to nineteenth-century scientific ambitions is all the more curious when one considers that some of the most astonishing discoveries of past cultures made by archaeologists were a matter of chance. Few people regard history as a science in this sense – it is an *interpretation* of the past – yet many archaeologists refuse to speculate about the societies whose artefacts they are digging up. Their passion for objectivity is a hindrance rather than a help in understanding the past: thus anthropologists part company with the old-fashioned archaeologists. However, anthropologists are reaching an understanding with folklorists and historians as anthropologists research their own societies, for their evidence is helpful in making sense of particular communities. The oral and written accounts of the past may be part of the collective memory of the people one is studying.

Yet why was it that folk-life studies did not really flourish in England and France but did so in Germany and Scandinavia? Folklore and folk-life studies are essentially part of that scholarly endeavour devoted to preserving the last remnants of a disappearing world. In this respect, these sentiments are not that dissimilar to the aims of current anthropology – hence, possibly, their mutual convergence today which is also aided and abetted by the interest that certain historians are showing in both anthropology and folklore, especially with regard to minority groups. Examples of such historical research are the works of Le Roy Ladurie (1978) and Thomas (1971).

If simple note is taken of the fact that folk-life studies in Western Europe are of the *greatest* concern to the Celts – Bretons, Cornish, Irish, Welsh, and Scots – then one may understand those similar Teutonic concerns in Germany and Scandinavia with their own racial origins and separate identities, excepting the Finns, who are singularly obsessed with their own Finno-Ugric origins. The common denominator, oddly enough, is that old nineteenth-century concept of 'race', the original spur to that ill-fated British ethnographic survey. A very simple reason why the English and French opted out of such research is that they knew very well that they had no such racial 'purity'. The English were admitted mongrels, from all over Europe, while the French were in no better a situation because their nation was not really of Gaulish origin anyway; it was perhaps better to avoid the subject entirely and concentrate upon the present. After all, in 1900, Britain and France had the largest empires ever known in the world. They were obviously the superior races and did not have to go back to the past to prove it. What they could do was to research their own empires and show what benefits they could bring to less fortunate races. After all, most of the classical anthropological research was done in these empires up until the 1960s – discounting the internal research conducted in India and America.

Ethnology, as such, collapsed as a serious academic study in Britain after the retirement of Perry from University College, London, just before the Second World War. His extravagant diffusionist claims had a greater popular appeal than Malinowski's ideas on savage society. In a way both sets of writings were sensationalist in that they appealed to the public's curiosity about people who were distant in time and space. The 'hard' factual evidence for the ethnological study of racial movements was drawn from a combination of physical anthropology and material culture research. The material culture included both archaeological artefacts and ethnographic objects, and they were often to be found in the same department or, more likely, the same museum, e.g. at Cambridge and Oxford. It was thought that material culture formed a seamless web whereby one artefact was replaced by a better-designed one. Here is Pitt-Rivers' concept (Penniman 1965) of a museum that showed the *evolution* of different tools, weapons, and so forth. Hence it is permissible to mix ethnographic objects and archaeological finds if they form part of the same sequence. It is an undisputed fact that the West improved its technology over the centuries. The question is how? Do similar objects in different areas show that it was people (races) or ideas that moved? That was the core of the diffusionist debate. Folklore (now part of folk-life studies) was also part of ethnology since it provided a mental gloss on the use of objects in the recent past, besides helping to trace the diffusion of tales, myths, and songs. It is easy to see how Frazer (1922) slips into this scene with his accounts of magic and religion from around the world. Such interlinkages explain the apparently cohesive structure of ethnology when Malinowski entered upon the stage of anthropology.

The basic question is: why was ethnology so popular with the general public? The flip-side of that question is why social anthropology is not. One clue may be that those close colleagues of anthropology (in the 1890s) are *still* popular – archaeology and folklore (and folk-life studies) attract widespread interest up and down the country. The answer probably lies in the continuingly powerful nineteenth-century academic quest for *origins* that is labelled today as 'roots', a desire not wholly unconnected with the industrial revolution, patriotism, and feelings of being cut off from one's past. After all, what is the appeal of popular archaeology in Britain except to know more about the past and where the British came from? That interest can range from one's own kin to mankind at large. This quest for the past satisfies some people's desires to belong to something. While this may be true, professional archaeologists are likely to deprecate such motives in favour of dispassionate scholarship; yet if there was *not* that popular support they would hardly get a penny of state support. Folklorists, being less expensive since they are usually dedicated amateurs and hence not so well organized professionally, have found it difficult to be accepted into the academic community, although their material readily finds a market in the innumerable local histories and regional descriptions that pour from the publishers every year.

Perry's extreme brand of ethnology, which stated that *all* civilizations stemmed from Egypt, was being increasingly called into doubt during the 1930s as archaeological researches into ancient civilizations around the world showed that his chronologies were quite wrong and his simple schema collapsed. Diffusionism got a bad press, and so did physical anthropology after the Piltdown Man scandal. Social anthropology, at the time, lacked popular Western appeal precisely because it concerned iself with small exotic societies and with *other* peoples' 'roots'. The situation has been utterly transformed today with the advent of universal television coverage of world-wide news and documentary programmes on tribal societies.

This disquisition on the relative fates of the triple alliance between anthropology, archaeology, and folklore may seem miles away from the Keele conference theme, yet this old alliance was the very first experience that participants had. The conference was presented with an ethnographic film on the Potteries, an anthropological report on factory life, and a reconstruction of past conditions based upon folklore, besides a trip to the industrial archaeological museum of the Potteries. This is not quite the turn of the wheel that was mentioned earlier but it comes close since all three disciplines are studying *man at home*. In other words, anthropology has returned home to its roots at Keele. Yet, even so, these three disciplines are not at all of one mind today. Why?

Archaeologists from Europe go all over the world digging up different 'pasts', just like European anthropologists explore the world looking at 'present' indigenous folk. The former are rewarded with grants and public acclaim, the latter struggle single-handedly with little public recognition. Now whose fault is that? At one time, archaeologists and anthropologists collaborated because the joint enterprise was to be the understanding of mankind, *tout court*. Things fell apart when anthropologists started to deconstruct that trinity of race, culture, and language and began to regard these as three interesting, but different, aspects of man. Anthropologists had moved from regarding culture (or civilization) as being a unity to being a plurality – and that step spelled the beginning of diffusionism and relativism. Gradually, under Malinowski and Radcliffe-Brown (both originally diffusionists), anthropologists renounced interest in hypothetical pasts and settled for synchronic studies in the here and now. Anthropologists became relativists in all but name. The search for patterns concentrated on looking for comparative social structures in different societies. The old unities had disappeared.

One wonders whether archaeologists have truly questioned that trinity of race, culture, and language since they come across skeletons, material objects, and occasional writings on the same site. They also compare their 'assemblages' and give them distinctive names on the basis of some characteristic feature of their material culture or the site itself, e.g. the Beaker culture, the La Tène culture, etc. The aim has not changed since the nineteenth century – the tracing of the movements of the Beaker *folk* by plotting similar *material* finds on maps. Archaeologists have become their own physical anthropologists and do their own measuring of skulls. So there still remains that trinity of concepts which identifies race, objects, and language. The archaeologists' 'culture' (assemblages of artefacts) is like the anthropologists' notion of material culture but wholly dissimilar to the anthropologists' 'culture' (social practices and beliefs). What, after all, is the connection, if any, between things and social organization?

Archaeologists are rightly suspicious of ethnographic 'parallels' since not only is there a time-gap between their finds and contemporary peoples but there are too many possibilities to choose between. So what are they to do?

Some go on quietly digging in the hope that, one day, their careful measure-ments may be explained. Others inductively 'create' an appropriate society that would have been responsible for the assemblages, along evolutionary lines. Few wish to talk to anthropologists – an exception being Colin Renfrew (1984) who, enthusiastically, is pursuing what he calls 'social archaeology' which aims to explain culture change by reconstructing the social organization of past societies. Renfrew's use of mathematical models in explaining change can be applied to ethnographic societies as well as prehistoric societies.

The rather tenuous relationship that exists between anthropology and archaeology becomes a liability when anthropologists do research at home, because it becomes important to enquire what people think about their local history. The European landscape, in particular, is strewn with remnants of the past and these form part of the experience that Europeans have of them-selves. Ruins betoken continuity with their ancestors – literally and symbo-lically – yet, simultaneously, ancient ruins denote a cultural separation from the present. However, preserved historic buildings serve as ideal object-lessons for displaying continuity in space with distance in time from our ancestors. Such contrasts make them great tourist attractions, as witness to the long European past. Prehistoric remains also have this kind of charisma and exercise a like charm on both local inhabitants and curious visitors to such monuments. It is the task of the archaeologist to explain the past and the social anthropologist to explain the local folk models of the past: the two are interrelated. Nowadays, anthropologists are very willing to talk to historians and folklorists about past European society, so why should anthropologists not extend an invitation to archaeologists to talk things over? This has not been done by this Association so far. Is it not time that this happened?

Anthropological research in Europe has shown that anthropologists can learn something from folklorists, since both students come across similar remnants of past beliefs. A case in point is Hastrup's discussion (in this volume) of ghosts and *huldufólk* (wee folk) in modern Iceland, which are experienced as continuing realities and not just as the old beliefs of previous generations. Similar beliefs still exist in the Faroe Islands, the Western Isles, and Ireland besides on the mainland in Brittany, Holland, Germany, and Scandinavia. A closer inspection might reveal that they exist all over Europe. Although this might not astonish anthropologists it does suggest that *The Golden Bough* (Frazer 1922) could still tell anthropology more about today's beliefs than it ever did about the past. Frazer's theories may be discredited but ancient rituals are still practised – not including those that have been recently reinvented. Such old rituals, e.g. at 'wishing' wells – not a hundred miles from Keele – must have a past of several thousand years that carries one beyond history into the territory of archaeology. The important point is that anthro-pologists should cease looking at folklore simply as a tale about a world that has been lost, and should regard it as a possible source of present-day enquiry. What it actually says about the past is another matter.

It is noteworthy that anthropologists working in their own countries, e.g. Africa, India, Brazil, and North America, have, until the recent collapse of sociology's credibility, referred to themselves as sociologists. By contrast, anthropologists and sociologists in Europe have striven hard to distinguish themselves from each other in terms of theory and methodology when examining their own societies; this is a recent phenomenon, however, since most anthropologists still hanker after the more romantic, unexplored parts of the world–if they can get there and stay there. One obvious reason why the term 'anthropologist' is so unwelcome is that it is associated with colonialism (and the preservation of tribalism – the anathema of all modern states), while the label 'sociologist' denotes a scientific examination of one's own society *for its own good*, since sociology is closely linked to notions of social welfare and progress – misplaced as this notion may be.

This leads on to an enquiry of why it is that social anthropologists are so keen on finding ever more new and unknown societies to investigate. Why do they never even bother to re-examine the societies that have already been studied? This would surely be the procedure for natural scientists to follow: repeat the experiment. However, anthropologists rarely do this. Are they afraid that they will 'lose' another society that is about to become extinct? Are anthropologists simply, then, the conservers of cultures – like folklorists? This curious reluctance of anthropologists to re-examine societies already studied suggests one of two things:

1. Anthropologists are extremely 'possessive' about 'their' societies and regard them as simply an expression of themselves, of their personal knowledge and credit-worthiness for a job – far removed from 'their' people.
2. Anthropologists are simple romantics at heart who only wish to contribute their own individual coloured chip of knowledge to that kaleidoscope of different human societies that constitutes mankind.

Both such views receive a dusty answer if one is to examine one's own society since one can neither claim absolute rights nor novelty since there have been others there before. Hence anthropologists have generally taken themselves off abroad if they could. Why stay at home, then? There are several reasons for this, but a significant feature may have been the failure of sociologists, in recent years, to explain their own societies: this has given rise to the hope that micro-studies by anthropologists might do better.

Messerschmidt (1981: 7) points out that there was no real discussion in his book about the relations of anthropology to sociology. There is certainly very little relationship today. Anthropologists have abandoned the idea of a universal theory about the evolution of human societies, but sociologists fear to do so, since it would undermine the whole rationale of their existence. Sociologists are wedded to the notion that all societies can be explained in terms of some universal law of human development. Sociology is premised on its claimed ability to predict the course of social change – if it had not done so then it would be no different from history. This claim, however, has never been sustained and disillusionment has set in.

Anthropologists have always been conscious of social change but they have not been too eager to offer any forecasts about it. When, in the late 1920s, anthropologists gave up speculative history, they devoted themselves to synchronicity and disavowed diachronic studies – not simply about the past but also about the future. After all, anthropologists were not contemporary historians but simply 'antiquarians' interested in 'primitive' life *before* the Western intrusion. There was no question then of 'concern' about the peoples themselves – only their culture was of interest, and they did not want it changed. One reason why early anthropologists sought island communities and other remote areas was to find societies unaffected by Western culture – a somewhat vain hope. Nevertheless, few anthropological monographs ever acknowledge the existence of a state or political authorities when discussing societies. Maybe there was little interaction between the people and government in these places. This cannot, however, be the case when one does research in the West. It is all very well for anthropologists to adopt a synchronic view about societies that were themselves ahistorical and lacking writing, but this will hardly do in modern societies which have extensive records about the past, besides an immense amount of detailed legislation that governs most aspects of citizens' lives.

It is possible to say, quite unkindly, that the basic difference between sociologists and anthropologists is a love of and a distaste for modern society. Anthropologists try to escape it, along with folkloristic and archaeological colleagues, by going to the remotest parts of the world it is possible to find – in imagination, if not in fact. It is also noticeable that anthropologists are rapidly abandoning their formerly strong interest in social organizations in favour of studying ritual, symbolism, and classification – a complete return to the major interests of the nineteenth century. This suggests that anthropologists do not really like the present but prefer the past. In essence, anthropologists are the folklorists of the exotic. Look carefully at these papers and reflect for yourselves. The exotic might be only five miles away – it is, indeed, all around one. It was a grave mistake to think that the distant 'savage' had more to give to anthropologists than one's local 'compatriot'; they simply have different types of information to impart.

Some of the other factors affecting anthropological research recently that pull one 'home' are:

1. Decreased funding.
2. Increased student numbers.
3. Objections by many new states to research into what they call 'tribalism' and a suspicion of neo-colonial intellectual imperialism.
4. The discovery of large areas of ignorance about one's own society.

5. The current interest shown by historians in using anthropological insights to interpret past records.

6. The ease of access to one's own society and a reduction of the time and money needed to 'enter' the field.

It is a matter of debate whether conferences actually reflect burning current issues since they have to have considerable support from the majority of members if they are ever to see the light of day. Some issues are only the intense concern of a few. Perhaps it was significant that by 1963 the membership of the ASA had suddenly doubled, as many younger people joined the Association in the wake of the Robbins report. The theme of that conference, significantly enough, was 'New approaches in social anthropology' (Banton 1965a/b, 1966a/b), since it was just before the old guard handed over power to their successors. It should be noted that even at this early date Frankenberg was recommending a study of British community studies. Looking back, one can see that there were really very few *new* approaches but a lot of doubt was being expressed about the old approaches: structural-functionalism was in deep trouble.

The following ASA conferences showed anthropologists anxiously searching for new ideas in the study of myth, economics, history, socialization, witchcraft, language, kinship, ethnicity, medicine, law, the body, cults, sex and age, ecology, work, folk models, religious experience, semantics, Malinowski, and back again to 'new approaches' in 1983. What has characterized the last ten years has been, perhaps, a *turning away* from other academic disciplines such as politics, economics, history, linguistics, medicine, law, and (implicitly) sociology in favour of a greater concern about what anthropologists themselves are doing and *how* they are doing it. There has been a going back to basics to see how anthropologists are treating sex, age, work, folk-models, etc.

Putting it another way, one can faintly detect three cycles in anthropological thinking since the Malinowskian period (1925–40): (1) post-war structural-functionalism that was quite content with its own ethnographic fieldwork (1945–60): (2) a search for *new* theoretical inputs from *other* disciplines and typified by Epstein's *The Craft of Social Anthropology* (1967) which was published halfway through this period (1960–75); (3) an introspective look at what anthropologists, themselves, are doing as a discipline in terms of theory and methodology (1975–90?). Such fifteen-year cycles are purely hypothetical, of course, but may there be something behind these swings of opinion? What causes them? Obviously, changing political situations in the world have affected the collective attitudes of anthropologists. As Kuper (1983) shows, via Kappers' analysis of the interests of ASA members (broken down into ten-year cohorts), there have been radical shifts over the years between the cohorts. Are these shifts reflected in and by conference themes? Broadly speaking, anthropologists seem to have moved from an objective ('social scientific') stance towards a more subjective ('intuitive') and self-questioning position, to judge by the recent conferences of the ASA.

Leach (1984), in a typically provocative article, pours scorn on the idea that the 1946 anthropological 'power map' (Kuper 1983: 125) had any *real* power in academic political circles: they were all outsiders. Certainly in Britain anthropology has, since the 1960s, always been the poorer cousin of sociology in universities, and this may reflect upon the incompetent advocacy of anthropology as a discipline. However, there were other contributory factors concerning 'relevance' to the needs of society. Another interesting point made by Leach is that ethnographical monographs are all subjective and *not* objective – they are simply an extension of the personality of the anthropologist. That is a thought to conjure with.

It is unlikely that the youngest cohort of ASA members (1945 onwards), who matured during the student 'troubles' of the 1960s and 1970s, had their personalities changed as a result but their outlook must have been altered by these events and not by changes in anthropological theory. The question is, why did they choose to read anthropology in the first place – their personality? It was, after all, a period when students were experimenting with alternative life-styles. Social anthropology has that unique attraction that it is basically a voyage of *self-discovery* mediated through other, exotic, people. Yet there was a moral debt to be repaid for all this and it took the form of increased interest in applied anthropology and ecology: nearly half the younger cohort opted for that. They wanted to use their knowledge constructively for those others – that is where their personality comes into their writings.

It was a chance remark made by Marilyn Strathern at the 1983 ASA conference in Cambridge that led to the theme of the Keele meeting in 1985. She mentioned that one was about to see the first indigenous anthropologist going into the field in Papua New Guinea – seventy years after Malinowski. What would be *his* problems in looking at his own society? Would he see it differently from the way that outsider anthropologists saw it? Would it be easier or more difficult?

Now these are not new problems, because anthropologists in India, Africa, Brazil, and North America have been doing research upon their own societies for decades. However, as there has been a recent growth of anthropological research within Europe the time seemed ripe to investigate the problems and results that ASA members have found both at home and abroad in their researches. It should be pointed out that there was an early efflorescence of social anthropological research in Britain in the 1950s, especially under Little at Edinburgh. Some of the most famous publications of that school were those by Goffman (1959) and Littlejohn (1964).

The North Americans have recently published their own thoughts on this theme, at length, in Messerschmidt's *Anthropologists at Home in North America* (1981). It has the significant subtitle *Methods and Issues in the Study of One's Own Society*. By 'issues' they seem to refer to matters of social concern – a kind of 'rescue' anthropology. That is not the immediate objective of this volume, although such matters do concern some of the ASA members. The aim is to tackle more general problems of theory and methodology in the discipline of social anthropology itself, not of society.

As already indicated, the Keele conference was basically a self-reflective affair where the majority of the speakers were from the younger cohort of anthropologists. They were concerned about their responsibilities to their informants, and about how to reconcile their methods 'at home' with traditional approaches in anthropology. What was the difference, if any? This was the first major opportunity they had had to discuss their own particular problems with each other – doing anthropology 'at home'. The chief topic of interest, not surprisingly, was methodology: how was it done?

If one holds with Leach that the pursuit of social anthropology is really personal and subjective then one is admitting that it is not 'scientific' and cannot contribute to any form of cumulative record or to the discovery of 'laws'. The sociological criticism of rural sociology (basically, anthropology at home) is thus justified: the studies are discrete and idiosyncratic; they are of no use to grand sociological theory. A good account of such studies as were done in Britain is given in Frankenberg (1966), who had himself conducted work in Wales (1957). The sociologists' conclusion was that these studies should therefore be discontinued as useless – which they mainly were. There was a blight on such work until the 1970s when Newby (1977, 1979) began his own sociological researches into agricultural life. This was also the time that anthropologists again started to look at life in rural Britain.

The results of these new researches were not revolutionary but they revealed aspects of life at home which were not that unique to the fieldwork sites. It awakened new interest in the 'taken-for-granted' acceptance of things in small communities and their perceived problems. It taught other researchers new things to look for, stimulating them to approach their subjects in different ways. Personal insight was heightened for the researchers, and while this could not help to validate the more mechanistic theories of society put forward by sociologists and anthropologists, it did spread understanding about people: others and oneself.

If Leach's view of the subjective nature of ethnographies is correct it applies to *all* anthropologists (both at home and abroad) and, by the same token, to sociologists as well. This could explain why sociology has now fallen from official favour since it could *never* deliver what it promised about understanding social problems. The same financial fate could threaten archaeologists as well if they persist in claiming they have an objective 'science' – but with results which seem to lead nowhere.

Applied anthropology has never had a happy history, and it is unlikely that anthropologists are any better at helping to formulate social policy matters than other social scientists. The problems about policy research are detailed in Okely's paper (this volume, pp. 55–73), as well as in Messerschmidt's book (1981).

The story of the *Ethnographic Survey of the United Kingdom* has been used as a peg upon which to hang several observations about doing research at home:

1. The close relationship that existed a century ago between anthropology, folklore, and archaeology no longer obtains, and this needs explaining.

2. Their common concern to trace the indigenous *races* of the UK contrasts with current anthropological concerns to investigate non-indigenous 'ethnic' groups in British society. In point of fact, Little (1948) was one of the earliest social anthropologists to have pursued ethnic research in Britain, upon Negroes. The Keele conference papers included research on Armenians, Gypsies, Pakistanis, Poles, and Sikhs in the UK, but they could not all be published here.

3. The failure to produce that survey, and any other since, by sociologists and anthropologists has been blamed on the lack of an adequate theory. Such a view, that there must first be a unitary, comprehensive theory, was also typical of the Victorian evolutionists. The data were simply to be slotted into place but, be it noted, such nineteenth-century theories and views are still around today. However, things may not be that simple, for there is no guarantee that such a theory is possible, desirable though it may be. Time slips by and societies change.

4. The 'scientific' aspirations of the triple alliance have now largely evaporated, except for the archaeologists, who still maintain high standards of careful and methodical *observation* which, in the natural sciences, is the essential basis for the testing of any theory. The irony is that archaeology has no scientific *theory* about human societies to test – except for old-fashioned nineteenth-century evolutionary and diffusionist theories. It is the old story of methodology in search of a theory to justify its own activities.

   Anthropologists have given up the search for such a theory and hold that their discussions about people are interesting in their own right. It would be hard to argue that archaeological finds and their meticulous description are similarly interesting *in their own right*. Artefacts are meaningless without a human context but archaeologists will not speculate because that would *not* be 'scientific'.

5. Now that anthropology has returned home after its century-long flirtation with exotic fieldwork, it might well think of taking up its former relations with folklore and archaeology, if it wants to look again at local 'communities'. The old joint concern with ethnological 'race' has vanished, but there are still the problems of 'roots' and identity (basically, the same *emotional* idea in modern dress).

6. Maybe anthropologists should now join hands with other local experts 'at home', such as social and economic historians, and sociologists (of the more pragmatic kind). There is a *need* to co-operate since there is no overarching theory and all ethnographic accounts are subjective. The discussion would be at the personal level – a good thing – since such social interaction could be mutually beneficial in changing anthropological perspectives, if not their weakly held theories.

7. Social anthropology abroad will, of course, continue, but it is clear that 'anthropology at home' is here to stay from now onwards. There is a need to develop this line of investigation so that there is an interchange between anthropologists at home and abroad. It is, perhaps, fortunate that many who do research 'at home' have also done work overseas, but that will not always be the case. It would be fatal if the Association fell into two separate groupings, home and abroad; there is a need for the *mixture as before*.

This introduction has touched on several aspects of anthropological research and that of others with the deliberate intent of provoking a discussion about the present role of anthropologists *vis-à-vis* other academic colleagues. If anthropologists are now to share a common social field then an agreement must be reached about what the respective responsibilities are. The main distinctive characteristic of anthropology as a discipline is that the fieldworkers go and *live* with the people under investigation. It is not just a question of simple participant-observation, which only means seeing what people do at specific times, according to the sociological usage of this method which sociology has borrowed from anthropology. Moving into one's own society is not always so easy since there is so much to know beforehand about the general background; more difficult to get to know is the *local* knowledge since this is rarely written down, yet it can be vast.

If it can take several generations before one can be accepted as a 'local', then how does one characterize the localized, *real* existing population? Strathern's (1981) description of the Elmdoners is a case in point. Modern Western society is more mobile than it ever was before, in every sense. So what should one be looking for – today's, tomorrow's, or yesterday's community?

It is this instability of population, in both urban and rural areas, that creates a problem in discussing local communities (local social structures?) since it is always hoped that there is *some* continuity over time, somewhere. One feels a need to 'find' a bounded unit – even if it is illusory – since local people can always find dividing lines between themselves. The nature of these units is the real subject of anthropological enquiry. Such problems of local mobility do not always strike the overseas anthropologist with quite the same force as they do 'at home' where there is abundant proof – through the census reports, electoral rolls, medical registers, etc. The ignorance of the fieldworker abroad about the true mobility of people is compounded by lack of records and the limits of people's memories.

This is not the place to discuss such problems in detail as they are well known to most researchers at home. The point is that there is a different series of problems to be faced when doing research at home, as opposed to doing it abroad, even if it is, apparently, so much easier to enter the field. The contrast may be likened to the difference between undergraduate dissertations based upon personal fieldwork (that are quite unique but, typically, personal) and those based upon library research (that are common knowledge but are *so much more difficult to master*). Greater credit is still given to the *experiences* of the fledgling anthropologist rather than to the far more demanding intellectual *struggles* of the lone student in the library. It could be pointed out, however, that some experienced field anthropologists (e.g. Goody 1983; Macfarlane 1970) have made scholarly contributions to the historical understanding of past societies through intensive library research. As the papers in this volume show, doing anthropology at home is of benefit when the researcher has prior experience of fieldwork abroad before turning homewards, since this aids the 'distanciation' process that is necessary if *we* are to see ourselves as others see *us*.

References

BANTON, M. (ed.) (1965a) *The Relevance of Models for Social Anthropology*. ASA Monographs 1. London: Tavistock Publications.
— (ed.) (1965b) *Political Systems and the Distribution of Power*. ASA Monographs 2. London: Tavistock Publications.
— (ed.) (1966a) *Anthropological Approaches to the Study of Religion*. ASA Monographs 3. London: Tavistock Publications.
— (ed.) (1966b) *The Social Anthropology of Complex Societies*. ASA Monographs 4. London: Tavistock Publications.
EPSTEIN, A. (1967) *The Craft of Social Anthropology*. London: Tavistock Publications.
FIRTH, R. and DJAMOUR, J. (1956) *Two Studies of Kinship in London*. London: Athlone Press.
FRANKENBERG, R. (1957) *Village on the Border*. London: Cohen & West.
— (1966) *Communities in Britain*. Harmondsworth: Penguin.
FRAZER, J. (1922) *The Golden Bough*. London: Macmillan.
GOFFMAN, E. (1959) *The Presentation of Self in Everyday Life*. New York: Doubleday.
GOODY, J. (1983) *The Development of the Family and Marriage in Europe*. Cambridge: Cambridge University Press.
KUPER, A. (1983) *Anthropology and Anthropologists* (revised edn). London: Routledge & Kegan Paul.
LEACH, E. (1984) Glimpses of the Unmentionable in the History of British Social Anthropology. In B. Siegel *et al.* (eds) *Annual Review of Anthropology*. Palo Alto: Annual Reviews Inc.
LE ROY LADURIE, E. (1978) *Montaillou*. London: Scolar Press.
LITTLE, K. (1948) *Negroes in Britain*. London: Routledge & Kegan Paul.
LITTLEJOHN, J. (1964) *Westrigg*. London: Routledge & Kegan Paul.

MACFARLANE, A. (1970) *Witchcraft in Tudor and Stuart England*. London: Routledge & Kegan Paul.

MESSERSCHMIDT, D. A. (ed.) (1981) *Anthropologists at Home in North America: Methods and Issues in the Study of One's Own Society*. Cambridge: Cambridge University Press.

NEWBY, H. (1977) *The Deferential Worker*. London: Allen Lane.

— (1979) *Green and Pleasant Land?* London: Hutchison.

PENNIMAN, T. K. (1965) *A Hundred Years of Anthropology*. London: Duckworth.

RENFREW, C. (1984) *Approaches to Social Archaeology*. Edinburgh: Edinburgh University Press.

STRATHERN, M. (1981) *Kinship at the Core*. Cambridge: Cambridge University Press.

THOMAS, K. (1971) *Religion and the Decline of Magic*. London: Weidenfeld & Nicolson.

URRY, J. (1984) Englishmen, Celts, and Iberians: The Ethnographic Survey of the United Kingdom, 1892–1899. In G. W. Stocking (ed.) *Functionalism Historicized*. Wisconsin: University of Wisconsin Press.

Marilyn Strathern

2 The limits of auto-anthropology

In her account of fieldwork with Travellers in the home counties, Okely records how she 'had to learn another language in the words of my mother tongue' (1984: 5). But this distance did not do away with the Travellers' location in her own social universe. 'Any latent tendency to treat people as objects or distant curios has to be confronted, not left repressed' (1984: 6). Shamsul appeals to Malay anthropologists not to assume that because they are Malay they can bypass the long periods of familiarization in the field that non-Malays have to undergo in studying rural Malay society; he emphasizes the inevitable social distance between scholar and villager. Unless they are prepared to approach their own society in a spirit of honest difference, scholars simply become 'academic mercenaries' (1982: 29). Obviously neither writer means to imply that situations might exist in other places where one did not have to guard against such tendencies. Yet there is more to these two comments than simply the point that moral problems take a particular form when anthropologists turn to 'their own society'. They raise the preliminary question of how one *knows* when one is at home.

For if in adjusting their double vision, as Okely calls it, there is in the end more in common between her and Shamsul than between either of them and their field areas, in what sense can they be said to be working at home? The grounds of familiarity and distance are shifting ones. Home can recede infinitely: would a Traveller studying the Travellers be at home? Or would it have to be a Traveller from this region as opposed to that region? The answer I propose is highly specific, and does not preclude other ways in which one might be 'at home'. But it does point to an aspect of anthropological practice that cannot be ignored. I consider one way, then, of rescuing the concept of home from impossible measurements of degrees of familiarity. The continuum obscures a conceptual break. What one must also know is whether or not investigator/investigated are equally at home, as it were, with the kinds of premises about social life which inform anthropological enquiry. One suspects that while Travellers and Malay villagers are not so at home, in their talk about 'community', 'socialization', or 'class', for example, Elmdoners are.[1] Auto-anthropology, that is anthropology carried out in the social context which produced it, in fact has a limited distribution. The personal credentials of the anthropologist do not tell us whether he/she is at home in this sense. But what he/she in the end writes, does: whether there is cultural continuity between the products of his/her labours and what people in the society being studied produce by way of accounts of themselves.

Starting with two assumptions

Two sets of commonly made assumptions are:[2]

1. That, as ethnographers, anthropologists on familiar terrain will achieve a greater understanding than elsewhere, because they do not have to surmount linguistic and cultural barriers. Greater understanding may appear as immeasurably enriching, or as immeasurably trivializing, but in either case the amount of information to be gained by an insider augments what people know about themselves, or what can be learned about the total society in aggregate.

2. That the systematizing anthropological enterprise will be exposed for the contrivance it is everywhere. It makes the commonplace complex, its systematizations not revealing anything more than everyone knew anyway and amounting to a set of unnecessary mystifications.

Contradictory as these two assumptions are, both stem from what is regarded as a general implication of anthropology at home, greater reflexivity. The assumption is that we become more aware, both of ourselves when turned into objects of study, in thus learning about our own society, and at the same time, of ourselves as doing the study, in becoming sensitive to methods and tools of analysis. The prospect of anthropology at home thus suggests a contribution to the increasing reflexivity which is urged on the subject from numerous directions. Marcus and Cushman, for instance, conclude their analysis of ethnographies as texts with an admonishment to ethnographers to develop a critical sense for the form as well as the content of ethnographic discourse (1982: 65–6); Fabian's (1983) book on the construction of the Other in traditional anthropology explores the premise that the construct is constituted by our knowledge of ourselves (cf. Burridge 1979: 12). The goal is enhanced critical awareness. In the same way as anthropologists attune themselves as registers of alien cultures, they are invited to register the grounds of their own practice (Scholte 1974). Not surprisingly, as Marcus and Cushman indicate, it is difficult to do both at once.

There is a tendency to equate reflexivity with heightened self-consciousness, and thus to regard it like a personal virtue, which this or that sensitive person displays in their writings. It might seem that anthropologists are destined only to increase an ever more exquisite self-consciousness. However, a conceptual reflexivity exists outside the sensitivities of individual practitioners, in the extent to which the anthropological account *qua* anthropological account does or does not render people's conception of themselves back to themselves – a point which applies equally to ethnography and to anthropological analysis. Where it does, in either case one can speak of auto-anthropology. Yet I do not mean rendering back information in the form in which it was given: rather, where the anthropological processing of 'knowledge' draws on concepts which also belong to the society and culture under study.

On the face of it, it looks absurd to make such a claim for (say) an account of an Essex village. The Elmdon project might have begun in a milieu in which it could be assumed that the villagers broadly participated in the world view also held by the anthropologist. Yet what started as continuity ended as disjunction. The ethnographic text was hardly continuous with indigenous narrative form; one was not rendering back to the residents of the village an account immediately contiguous with those they had given, as social history or as biography might be regarded. It is clear that simply being a 'member' of the overarching culture or society in question does not mean that the anthropologist will adopt appropriate local cultural genres. On the contrary he/she may well produce something quite unrecognizable. Commonsense descriptions are set aside. Indigenous reflection is incorporated as part of the data to be explained, and cannot itself be taken as the framing of it, so that there is always a discontinuity between indigenous understandings and the analytical concepts which frame the ethnography itself. These derive from a specific theoretical focus which may make intelligible the anthropologist's behaviour (as an 'academic') but not necessarily what he/she writes. Attempts to make such accounts more accessible rest either on educating the audience anthropologically, or on abandoning the traditional ethnographic genre in favour of a popular one – a history or report. The manner in which anthropologists set aside indigenous framings would seem to make their activities in Essex, then, not so dissimilar from their activities (say) in Melanesia.

This is one source of much recent self-scrutiny of form, that is, the form of anthropological representation itself; hence the experimentation with ethnographic texts, of which Clifford (1983) gives a compelling analysis. At issue is the manner in which ethnographic authority is constructed in reference to the voices of those supplying information, and the part they are given in the resultant texts. Favret-Saada refers to as fantastical the construction of anthropological accounts in which the speaker is denied subjectivity (the informant can never occupy the position of 'I') and the authorial subject (the anthropologist) has no name (1980: 28). The going assumption seems to be that by imaginative effort in the act of representation the ethnographer can play with subject–object relations so as to bring back into his/her texts the distinctive voices of his/her interlocutors. The new genre may display itself as dialogical or polyphonic (Clifford's terms for a construction preserving dialogue and producing discourse rather than text), and taken as standing for shared authorship. I would regard such 'joint products' with suspicion.[3] And I think we must do more than worry about 'voices' and 'speakers', or complicity with informants so-called. Quite critical is not simply the extent to which actors are allowed to speak, the openness with which the original dialogues are reproduced, or the restoration of their subjectivity through narrative device, but what kinds of authors they themselves are. We need to have some sense of the productive activity which lies behind what people say, and thus their own relationship to what has been said. Without knowing how they 'own' their own words, we cannot know what we have done in appropriating them.

This is relevant to the domestic dilemma (knowing more about ourselves as objects and knowing more about ourselves as subjects).[4] The question is the form in which our own productive activity becomes the basis for such relationships as might exist between 'ourselves' as anthropologists and the selves under study. The quality of the social relationship established here is not simply a matter of personal management. It depends on the nature of the society in question. In the same way, anthropological self-knowledge is not simply a function of personal characteristics such as how much is shared with the people being studied (closeness and distance) or degree of sensitivity to one's own scholarly constitution (self-consciousness). Such self-knowledge is also to be located in the social techniques of ethnographic/anthropological production. Gudeman and Penn (1982: 99) refer to this as 'systemic reflexivity'. Fabian's conclusion, 'that our theories of their societies are our praxis – the way in which we produce and reproduce knowledge of the Other for our societies' (1983: 165, emphasis removed), suggests that if we are to be attuned to anything it should be to the nature of the productive activity.

The two assumptions about reflexivity – that it leads to both greater understanding and to unnecessary mystification – are specifically artefacts of auto-anthropology. To demonstrate this, I open up certain differences between the Essex village and a Melanesian one. A mutual context is provided by a criticism which relates directly to productive activity. (This applies especially to 'ethnographies' in so far as they are perceived to be about specific people at specific places and times; but most books which contain ethnography comprise a mixed genre, including attempts at anthropological theory, a state of affair which contributes to the criticism noted here. I intend reference to this mixed genre when I refer to 'ethnographic' or 'anthropological' accounts.) Criticism is made in both places of the relationship which members of the community in question perceive between themselves and the investigator in reference to what the investigator is producing. They suspect that they are being exploited.[5]

Types of exploitation[6]

In the late 1970s the student body of the University of Papua New Guinea became concerned with the issue of exploitation by academics, and singled out anthropologists for attack. They were seen as appropriating information which belonged properly to Melanesians, deploying it for personal gain. No commensurate return could be made to the true owners. On the surface this echoes the distaste with which anthropological accounts on home ground might be greeted: that the anthropologists had used other people's lives and experiences for ends of their own. Not only do they transform experiences into objects of contemplation, they produce analyses informed by terms which apparently belong only to themselves.

Academics may be seen to create an exclusive domain within which their accounts have value. Theoretical models circulate endlessly between practitioners with different analytical intentions, but the origins of these models are attributed to academic discourse itself. Their origins in other lives, other cultures, become overshadowed. Ultimately the use anthropologists make of their data is for ends also of their own making. In this sense anthropology domesticates an exogenous world, making new uses for materials originating under quite different circumstances, and thereby encompassing the different uses which people have for the way they live their lives. Such encompassment is experienced as exploitation when people perceive that others have the power to turn data into materials whose value cannot be shared or yielded back to them in return. Anthropologists are thus seen to convert lived experience into items (units, constructs, concepts) whose usefulness, as elements for their own models, they alone control.[7] Yet when Melanesian students or Elmdon villagers feel they are being used by anthropologists, it is certainly not because they wish they were anthropologists too. They have no desire to enter the domain where the anthropologists' data are valued. So why does it matter to them? One answer lies in the way in which they conceptualize productive action.

Elmdon villagers see the academic as doing something to their private property, which if put to use should be for their own benefit. The academic enterprise has raised the question of its utility. Melanesian students may well espouse private property notions; or they may instead recall indigenous conversion processes typical of male political behaviour – unequal relations arise when one person's 'work' contributes to another person's 'name'. Let me consider not the student, then, whose sensibilities are shaped in part by those of expatriate academics, but the Melanesian villager.

From time to time I have been made to feel that I was exploiting those who assisted my researches in Mt Hagen, in much the same way as all European employers of wage labour were felt to be using people. My relationship with them was going to further my prestige to the exclusion of theirs. In traditional Hagen society prestige is gained through transactions between equals; the gifts they exchange are mutually enhancing. In this sense partners assist one another's reputation. The problem with the itinerant associate is her imminent departure. This constructs the supposition that she will derive prestige from another sphere of interaction, in respect of which previous relationships become reclassified as 'service'. For on departure the fieldworker clearly turns to investing in relationships elsewhere. There is a Hagen term for persons in non-reciprocal service of this kind.

The appropriation of information is not, I think, at issue. Information is normally produced in the context of an exchange in which both parties retain their autonomy. A person knowingly gives or withholds information; under normal circumstances it cannot be extracted. Moreover, information is to be evaluated by its source, and necessarily always has reference to its social point of production; it cannot in this sense be alienated. If one were to think of exploitation at all in the Hagen context, it would be in the way one set of social relations was evaluated in respect of others. Value conversion in this situation, then, results not in one party extracting something from another and using it for ends of his/her own. Rather it consists of one party re-evaluating the relationship between them on the analogy of reducing a partnership to a service.

The reactions (as I construe them) of the Hagen villager as opposed to those of his counterparts (the Elmdon villager/Hagen student), incorporate indigenous models of productive activity, and of the relationship between producer and product. Sahlins (1976) implies that the kinds of dualisms by which 'we' create our exercises – individual and society; symbol and function– inhere in Western bourgeois culture, providing us with both problems and practice, how to understand the cultural productions of other societies and how to embody cultural creativity ourselves in decoding alien systems. There is a coda he fails to add: that this creativity we award ourselves requires that we exploit the creativity of others. In endlessly producing 'products' Western bourgeois culture is constructed as endlessly creative, a model that does not simply involve the permutations of products but the notion that production is also control, including control over the values given to things. What irritates the English villagers is not a wish to gain what the anthropologist has but the way they see the arrogation of authorship. That is, the anthropologist is making himself the author of an account in which their authoring of events, acts, feelings is displaced. Their authorship becomes encompassed as part of the anthropological data.

This I think is the Western sense in which all value-conversions can be seen as potentially exploitative, that is, the value which people acquire for themselves must be at the expense of others. Extraction is envisaged because it is supposed that what lies at the basis of value-conversions is something being done by other agents to the work people do or to the products which embody their agency. The eighteenth-century idea that persons are the natural owners of both themselves and their labour is still with us; this notion of singular ownership/authorship also sets up the conceptual possibility of one author supplanting or displacing another. The anthropologist as Western academic is sensitive to charges of exploitation that derive from such possibilities of encompassment and displacement. One is turning events or situations to ends of one's own, as though extracting 'raw materials' for 'social' use. Not to share with someone is to put oneself into a separate class in relation to such conversions; hence the movement in ethnographic writing towards representing accounts as somehow the product of shared experience. Whoever the Other are, whether at home or abroad, they should be given voice. Yet this model of exploitation as displaced authorship is a particular home-based one.

For the Hagen reactions rest on a quite different political–economic base to people's expectations of one another. The question is not one of extraction, but of who has the power to convert a relationship into personal prestige. Not to share means to devalue an ongoing relationship in respect of relationships elsewhere. If I were thought to be using people in Mt Hagen, it was because my relationships with them were going to further my prestige and not also theirs. Of course people supplied a material dimension where none existed, assuming that one would make vast sums of money in one's own world. Although they were losing little by telling me things, the point is that the profit would be realized in a sphere of activity to which they had no access; a situation, in other words, in which nothing is extracted, yet a relationship exists which one person turns to unilateral advantage. This is akin to what happens between Hagen husbands and wives. Husbands and wives labour together, producing things which the husband then takes off to use in male political exchanges. Indeed, men may refer to women in general as their 'servants'. The analogy is worth pursuing briefly.

There is no doubt that a conversion of value has taken place. In converting pigs from food to be eaten into gifts to be exchanged the husband reclassifies their social origin: the pigs are now seen to be the result of other previous gift-transactions (cf. Josephides 1985). Men thus eclipse their own productive activities, as well as women's. There is a special feature of this value-conversion. It is not the case that converting pigs into gifts reproduces them or reauthors them in terms of production.[8] Men are not claiming the labour belongs to them, and the work does not become disguised as something else because in turn agents are not hierarchized in respect of their ability to turn the less useful products ('raw materials') of one person into more useful ones for another. Gifts do not make useful objects out of useless ones. Whatever work went into the production of the pigs, exchange partners do not appropriate it as 'work' – they acquire the gift as a debt to be repaid (cf. Damon 1980). Moreover, between husband and wife work is evidence of a differentiated commitment to the relationship between them: the wife is no 'owner' who can transfer that ownership, or have it wrested from her control, because there is no one-to-one relationship between her working capacity and the products of her work. When men take off the pigs they are not supplanting women's authorship – or their own for that matter – as producers. For products of labour are conceived as originating from socially heterogeneous sources. One source cannot render the other anonymous. It follows that whatever exploitation exists is not to be grasped through Western notions of single authorship, of a one-to-one relationship between a person and their products.

The intention of this example is to draw attention to the Hagen constitution of 'joint products' when the persons involved – such as husbands and wives – are differentiated by social interest. They sustain their heterogeneity, as do the authors of words. The English concept of a person naturally owning himself, on the other hand, leads to the possibility of appropriating other things for the self. In this view, all knowledge can be turned into self-knowledge: the more one learns about others, the more one learns about oneself. By the same token, in their appropriative acts, selves supplant one another. Above all, if knowledge of others becomes a vehicle for knowledge of the self, then it is turned into the constitution of the self. In respect of those others, authorship has been displaced.

Displaced authorship is not a problem in Hagen. The problem is that of superseded relations. Knowledge is only ever brought into the open as an instrument in the negotiation of relationships; self-knowledge is contained within the inscrutability of people's minds, or evinced in their bodily health. Knowledge of others has a profound effect on the relationship in question, but there is no split between information and the author of it.[9] One author cannot supplant another, a point which Goldman (1983) demonstrates linguistically for the nearby Huli.[10] Accounts may be juxtaposed. But what someone says cannot be recast in a different version by another, for it remains only what he/she said. Such practice, it may be added, does not lead to summary or systematization in an organizational mode. Where does this put the productive activity of the ethnographer? If Hageners are concerned about the amount of money one's books will earn, it is for blatant evidence of superseded or eclipsed social relationships. A mutual activity has become an instrument to exclusive prestige, which is why the magnitude of the gains is important. But there is no way in which the ethnographer can substitute his/her own account for people's own: he/she neither authenticates nor displaces them. From their point of view such accounts are only relevant to the active management ('exploitation') of relations with outsiders, including the ethnographer as outsider.

The conclusion to be drawn is that the kind of author which the ethnographer becomes in his/her writing of texts is not determined by an act of will. What 'our' representations of others will mean must depend in part on what 'their' representations mean to them. And this in turn will depend on whether or not the anthropologist is indeed at home. For it is a question not simply of authorial choice but of cultural and social practice.

Writers and authors

Holy and Stuchlik (1983) conclude their enquiry into anthropological understanding and explanation with the observation: 'When actors' meanings are
replaced in the course of analysis and explanation, the anthropologist is not
explaining social reality as it exists in the only meaningfully possible sense, but
through his explanation creating it' (1983: 121). How that replacement is
accomplished will depend on the status of the indigenous meanings. Do we
know that they function as 'explanations', for instance?[11] It must matter
whether the anthropological framings are exogenous in intention, or whether
one type of explanation is replacing another, indigenous one. In the second
circumstance, the anthropologist has, as it were, substituted his/her authorship of the events under question from that of those who gave them meaning
in the first place (his/her explanation for their explanation). I have suggested
that this might be a significant element in any irritation expressed by Elmdon
villagers: that my version of events supplanted theirs – in not reproducing
their descriptions in their own genre I had, as it were, displaced their authorship of the narrative. It is important to note, of course, that this displacement
could not occur if the ensuing account were not in some way regarded as a
version of their own accounts (e.g. that both 'explained' something). This
view further implies that authors somehow own their words, in the same way
as persons own themselves, and thus have a natural control over their actions
and intentions. The usurpation of natural ownership sets one of the conditions
for exploitation.

Exploitation was raised for the light it might throw on how to construe the
ownership of ethnographic accounts. I used the term 'author' in a metaphorical sense. The single term is not, however, adequate for the differences
in nuance which arise from comparing the producer of ethnographies at home
and abroad. Comprehending the character of the domestic dilemma (see p.
19) is helped considerably by the distinction which Rabinow (1984) brings into
the open between authors and writers.

Rabinow addresses himself to the recent upsurge of self-consciousness in
the creation of ethnographic form. Following self-scrutiny in other disciplines, notably literary criticism, the urgent issue has become just where the
narrator is to be placed, in respect of his text and in respect of his readership.
Rabinow applies to a number of ethnographic productions Barthes' distinction between the writer, on the one hand, who absents himself from the
text, treating language as a transparent tool for the ends of explanation and
instruction, and the author, on the other hand, whose texts embody his
relationship with the world, where language is its own end, supremely self-
reflexive. Rabinow is concerned with the differing intentions which anthropologists display towards ethnographic production, and the ethical significance of form. For the anthropologist is necessarily caught in a triad of
relations, not only with a vernacular readership but with so-called inform-

ants,[12] and cannot speak equally to both as audience (Webster 1982: 108–09). In the difference between being an author and being a writer, the anthropologist–ethnographer holds these sets of relationships discrete.

For Melanesia, at least, it does not make sense to see the ethnographer as supplanting an original account in such a way as to make it a new version for the people concerned. Other people's authorship cannot be displaced.[13] The ethnographer for his/her part is put into the position of laying out the relationship of his/her representations alongside 'theirs'. Here he/she is acting as a *writer*. Writing is used as a vehicle for explanation via comparison, above all the comparison of ideas from different social sources whose origins can be juxtaposed. The analytical job thus includes accounting for people's ideas, which become part of the data, and he/she reveals the relationship between their ideas and those of analytical discourse (actors' models and analytical models, the rationale for Holy and Stuchlik's 1983 enquiry). This explicit theoretical exercise displays the juxtaposition of indigenous and exogenous concepts, a preoccupation of much anthropological writing.

If the ethnographer is also *author*, it is in relation to the readership at home. Presentation through the filtering consciousness of the ethnographer-who-was-present (cf. Kuper 1980: 20; Clifford 1983) is all important. With respect to those at home who will be reading the account of Papua New Guinea, the ethnographer is in total control. On the one hand, his/her readers have no other access to the ideas which are being put forward. Actors' models are rendered through the analytical models. From this is derived the rhetoric of ethnography as translation. On the other hand, its authorship supplants or substitutes for other versions of the same material which the readership at home might also have to hand. It modifies how they think about Papua New Guinea.

Rabinow repeats Barthes' lament, if it is that, that in the self-conscious twentieth century narrators can be neither writers nor authors. Yet the traditional anthropological exercise, in its representation of an exogenous other, allowed these two roles to be separated out, writer and author being oriented to distinct social fields. For the home readership the ethnographer is author, being an authoritative source through which his/her readership have access to the other. Towards those being studied, the ethnographer is writer, creating an explicit relationship between their ideas and his/her framings. In this way the ethnographer traditionally negotiates the 'fundamental contradiction' of 'ethnographic research involving personal, prolonged interaction with the Other' becoming 'a discourse which construes the Other in terms of distance, spatial and temporal' (Fabian 1983: xi). The first allows the experience of immediacy in one set of relations (in the field) to validate authorship apropos another (home readership). The second allows a theoretically constructed distance (fabricated at home) to inform the job of writer *vis-à-vis* the narratives and texts provided by informants (in the field). I have suggested, of course, that this latter position is not simply engineered by the anthropologist but also by the social realities of the other's construction of authorship.

The challenge of anthropology at home is that it sustains a different structure of distinctions. The ethnographer becomes *author* in relation to those being studied. The proposition rests on there being continuity between their cultural constructs and his/hers. For they too analyse and explain their behaviour much as he/she does. At base they are agreed that 'society' or 'culture' can be conceptualized as an object of study. They are familiar with the vocabulary of 'relationships', 'roles', 'community'. What the anthropologist seems to be doing is simply using these ideas in specialist ways.[14] The specialized analysis thus appears to give a further view which encompasses and overrides the original explanations, supplanting them in effect with further versions. Versions can always be challenged, of course. The possibility of authors supplanting one another comes from conceptualizations of productive activity as a process by which useful things are made out of materials thereby relativized as useless. People may object to the value put on what they supply.

If the ethnographer at home remains a *writer* it is not so much for those he/she studies, who may well challenge his/her versions, but for colleagues, the main readership. For the ethnography is always to be compared and brought into relationship with a body of shared knowledge, and the contrivances of method and theory. Now, in reference to other cultures, the contrived nature of anthropological constructs is trivial. The social disjunction between the anthropologist and members of the society under study turns the contrivance into a deliberate bridging. Of course the outsider uses his/her frames of reference, whether it is a definition of 'marriage' or a decision about 'patrilineal descent'. It does not have to be demonstrated that Hageners have arrived at their notions of patriliny by a very different route from the observer. Since it is, after all, a postulate of the enlightenment that objects of study are created by subjective self-awareness, the exotic society is authored through the filter of the observer's consciousness. The contrived appearance of anthropological reportage in its own society, on the other hand, creates writers not authors. It is as writer that the anthropologist must distinguish his study from other professionals in the business of representation (Barnett and Silverman 1979: 17), and make evident the domain that has been captured (Thornton 1983).

But I speak of home in a limited sense here. These contrasts give insight into the initial assumptions which really only applied to auto-anthropology. One was the charge of mystification. For the informants, anthropologists' accounts of the home society may be regarded as partial, obvious, repeating what is known, but also as idiosyncratic and trivial; he/she has merely authored another version. For fellow scholars, on the other hand, the conventional basis of the analytical framework is made transparent; writing is revealed to be a device. The other assumption was in terms of greater understanding. As author the anthropologist may cast people's experiences into a different light in an illuminating way: people will know more about themselves. And in the manner in which, for his/her colleagues, the analysis is given meaning in relation to other analyses, the anthropologist as writer offers reflection on how the bases for those analyses are established. Knowing ourselves better as both objects of study and as the subjects doing the study: the two are fused in the cultural premise that all knowledge is a species of self-knowledge (see n. 4).

Knowledge and self-knowledge

We can now add a second characterization for auto-anthropology. The first was the proposition that this kind of anthropology at home is recognizable by its rendering back, to the culture or society from which it comes, the culture's central constructs, such as 'relationship', 'role', or more particularly the concept of 'culture' itself. This is, so to speak, an outsider's view. The second characterization comes from an insider's view, from the folk model that anthropology contributes to self-knowledge. And this is self-knowledge both for those under study (as author he/she presents a new version for them), and for the anthropologist as scholar (as writer he/she uncovers the premises of scholarship). This must be elucidated by reference to Western cosmology, specifically to ideas about 'the relationship' between individual and society.

Self-knowledge is bottomless. If authors supplant, they can also be supplanted. As authors among authors, auto-anthropologists merely offer 'another view', 'an alternative perspective', or whatever. They add complexity to the understanding of what they are constantly telling themselves is a 'complex' society. To put oneself in the position of an author is to witness the world through different eyes; but what is seen must be provisional by the very act of consciousness in taking someone else's point of view. The charge of triviality speaks to the fact that any number of points of view may be set alongside one another, and measured with one's own seem to offer little which was not already apprehended in other ways. If the viewpoint is not reauthored – absorbed as an enriching process to the ends of self-knowledge – it may be regarded as little improvement. It does not yield anything not already known, even if it is known in other ways.

The effectiveness of authors' versions is supposedly registered in the impact they have on individual consciousnesses. Where it is self-knowledge about ourselves that 'we' are after, society may be perceived as a singular person. 'It' comes to know more and more about 'itself'. But knowledge can also be regarded as collectively constructed, the product of many minds working together, and laying out the relationships between them. A discipline does not merely give a point of view, but also organizes itself in relation to other disciplines; as writers, anthropologists place themselves in respect of the theoretical premises of others.[15] From the inside, this may feel like contrivance; from the outside, scholars talking exclusively to one another.

Anthropologists at home are thus also fulfilling the conditions of auto-anthropology when they produce as writers. They turn findings into artefacts of a particular kind, of which the most notable is the concept of 'culture' or 'society' itself. Understanding comes to be contingent on the elucidation of 'society', say, as a social system, or set of interrelated parts, or whatever. Thus the investigation of x or y is justified in terms of its contribution to the general understanding of English/European/Western society. At the least, there is refuge in the postulate that self-knowledge is possible. The individual (particularly the individual mind) as a microcosm of society is the effective register of self-knowledge, and the improvement of individual knowledge is taken to contribute to collective knowledge. The very idea of society is significant here – that as a 'society', 'we' can improve knowledge of 'ourselves' (i.e. of 'our society').

Anthropology first developed among a people who thought of themselves as forming 'a society'. They were conscious both of their distance from and proximity to others. This self-description is based on a quasi-ethnic model (the world is made up of numerous societies all dealing with similar problems in different ways), which sets the scene for the traditional monograph, bringing an exotic place to a home audience. The contrivance of the anthropological ideas, the hypothetical nature of the constructs ('convention' in Wagner's phrasing), is transparent in the mere disjunction of cultural content (cf. Marcus and Cushman 1982: 48). The contrivance itself is regarded as a necessary means of access to the unfamiliar. The monograph thus emerges as the implicit comparison of two cultures or societies – ours and theirs. This leads to a routine reflexivity, the constant discovery that analytical concepts are context-dependent.

When the anthropologist turns to home, contrivance, I have suggested, must take a different place. The auto-anthropologist cannot use language simply as a device for comparing (say) two cultures or societies: he/she is talking, more or less, about his/her own. He/she locates him/herself as a professional within that culture over all (an acceptable genre) but must show the way the culture contrives. What comes over is an account of contrivance. Thus people's commonsense understandings of the roles they play and their place in society are shown themselves to be contrived. Their interrelationships are displayed through a form of knowledge exhibited as the interconnection of units within a system (Barnett and Silverman 1979). Now 'models', 'structures', 'systems' are apprehended not simply as objectifications (Asad 1973: 17) but as a mode of organizing data (Anderson and Sharrock 1982).[16] In so far, of course, as anthropologists take for granted how they know (as a matter of overview, functional interrelation, organization, shared experience), they evince their own society's or culture's knowledge of itself. Yet the notion that events can be summarized and systematized, individuals organized, social rules and cultural maps elucidated (cf. Salmond 1982) begs the question, to whom is the knowledge directed. For as a cultural construct self-knowledge is not to be confused with self-expression. Knowledge has an instrumental element; at a minimum it is 'for' the self.[17] The self (individually or collectively) thus benefits from its knowledge. In this context, to become conscious of convention and contrivance is to produce knowledge of anthropologists as contrivers: first, as participating in a social life which rests on contrivance; and second, as active contrivers in constructing knowledge about that social life.

Auto-anthropology has its own advantages and pitfalls, then, but one might reasonably ask whether the same circumstances do not arise whenever an anthropologist turns to study 'home'. Are not the conditions for auto-anthropology met when, say, a Hagener trained as an anthropologist embarks on a study of Hagen? Neither of the conditions can, in fact, be satisfied. The indigenous anthropologist[18] in this kind of situation is not contributing to self-knowledge in any straightforward sense. He/she is not in a position to reauthor events, and thus set his/her version alongside other proprietary narratives; nor is he/she as a writer utilizing the conceptual resources of that society as the foundations of description.

Consider again Malinowski's claims to 'create' the Trobrianders.[19] He meant that he alone would bring them to life for his readership, that he would be their author in that sense; at the same time, in juxtaposing the world as seen through Trobriand eyes with European prejudice about primitive society, he had also to be writer: to make his narrative transparent enough to be an authentic description of the Trobriands which required technical elucidation. As author, he was displacing no Trobriand accounts as far as they were concerned, because he could not possibly have been an author in respect of knowledge of local social interest. Nor did his organization of material, his functionalist models and principles of social organization, participate in Trobriand modes of self-knowledge. Their self-scrutiny was managed through different techniques. When, many years later, Kasaipwalova (1975) planned for Trobriand 'cultural development', it was through hopes of founding an art school based on the inspirational balance between meaning and form whose elucidation till then had been in the hands of master prow-board- and house-carvers.

It would be absurd, however, to imply that Malinowski's relationship with the Trobrianders was contentless. It did matter what he wrote, in so far as he mediated between themselves and the colonial world in the information conveyed. This is the significance of subsequent accusations that he got things wrong, or gave an unrealistic view of Trobriand society to the outside world. The point to stress is very simple. Anthropological accounts of exogenous societies such as the Trobriands can never be self-knowledge in the way that a parallel account of the social world of Elmdoners (say) would be. It does not matter where the anthropologist comes from: it cannot be self-knowledge in a reflexive sense because it does not draw on the specific techniques by which people know themselves.

Conclusion: where home is matters

Shamsul was right when he said that a Malay anthropologist should deliberately familiarize himself with Malay society. We cannot conclude that non-Western anthropologists will stand in the same relationship to their own society or culture as a Western anthropologist does to his/hers. This is a projection of a specific (Western) modelling that supposes societies are a series of homologues, that if other societies throw up anthropologists then these would all be anthropologists at home, in an analogous relationship to one another as far as their relations with the home society were concerned.

Many of our constructs conspire in that modelling. 'Culture', for instance, is construed as a repository of information, explicit in the techniques of ethnomethodologists whose entry into another culture is through acquiring the tools of 'knowing how' to operate within its categories. The goal is to uncover ground rules, templates, codes, structures as information-bearing devices. The concept of culture thus demarcates the distinctiveness of the kind of information needed to be a member of a particular group, enclave, institution. To elucidate the culture of this or that congeries of persons is to elucidate such information. In this view all cultures, like all societies, are homologues of one another. They all do the same job, informing the members of each society what they should do and how they should do it. All societies thus 'have' culture, and the 'how to' rules and practices by which people conduct their lives afford an unwitting reservoir of information for the outsider. It is because we thus think that all societies have cultures, we can play one off against another, engage in comparison, and ultimately use one's own culture as a foil for understanding others (cf. Kuper 1980: 18). This gives rise to that further source of routine reflexivity, that one learns more about one's own culture while studying others, as one learns more about any culture by placing it alongside any other. Moreover, any social distinction, among sets, groups, clusters of people, will know itself through internal cultural practice, and thus be open to anthropological scrutiny. Here there is an infinite regression, as many 'cultures' as there are systems of self-knowledge. For the supposition that all societies 'have' cultures means that, in reference to these other cultures, the anthropologist can turn their self-knowledge into information for him/herself about them. This model of cultures as systems of self-knowledge suggests that auto-anthropology could be done everywhere. My argument is to the contrary, of course. It is all very well for Giddens to state blandly that 'all social actors . . . are social theorists' (1984: 335), but the phrase is an empty one if techniques of theorizing have little common ground. I have laid stress on the production and writing of ethnographic texts in order to stress the specificity of techniques, as far as 'knowledge' is concerned.

As writers, auto-anthropologists participate in the varieties of self-knowledge which are gained through systematic enquiry and scrutiny. It is thus part of a genre of knowing: that knowledge is organization. This genre of knowing is not necessarily analogous to self-knowledge gained through divination, myth, the gathering of ritual congregations, or the infliction of injury. The question is not simply one of consciousness. People set up a variety of avenues to self-knowledge in a conscious manner. They may test their own system, so to speak, through the interpretation of events, health and sickness, and so on, and implement ('probe') their interpretations in social action. It is a short step for Wagner (1975) to argue that in their encounters with Western cultures, the reverse anthropology contrived by Melanesians should take the form of cargo cults, as an active engagement in a new social field. Outsiders tend to explain cargo cults as greater self-knowledge on the Melanesians' part – they were making cognitive sense of a new situation, using old tools for new problems. Jarvie (1984: 126–27) still argues from this position, and it is intriguing to note that homologously the only positive role he awards anthropology itself is self-knowledge. Those Melanesians who embarked on cargo cults of course told us otherwise (and cf. Harrison 1985); they insisted that their break with the past was radical, that they had accomplished ways of knowing and created relationships previously inconceivable.[20]

On occasion it is misleading to take too far the methodological premise that all societies 'have' cultures. A notion of 'culture' does not form part of the techniques of knowledge all peoples have of themselves, any more than is true of the concept of 'society'.[21] If elucidating culture or society is not part of the way in which they organize their experiences, then it cannot hold the same place in anthropological accounts of them as it does for the auto-anthropologist. Were techniques of self-knowledge to constitute a universal class, then we could argue the case for acknowledging anthropology at home wherever anthropologists turned to their own societies. But we should not mystify ourselves here. It is anthropologists themselves who constitute a universal class, they who share precepts and concerns and who as writers manage data in specific ways.[22] Such 'self-knowledge' in turn can only be expressed in circular form: the auto-anthropologist comes from a culture/society that 'has' a concept of culture/society. Whether anthropologists are at home *qua* anthropologists, is not to be decided by whether they call themselves Malay, belong to the Travellers or have been born in Essex; it is decided by the relationship between their techniques of organizing knowledge and how people organize knowledge about themselves.[23]

The students who carried out the Elmdon study were really too coy, though none of us had any problems with imagining that Elmdoners would concur with our stated interest in 'history'. Pressed to the point, I think they would also have agreed that society is a proper object of study. I wish now we had pressed the point – it would have helped us to feel more at home.

Acknowledgement

I am grateful to Paul Rabinow for permission to quote from his paper in press (1984), and for his interest in the topic. Anthony Cohen was an original source of inspiration, Timothy Ingold of several comments and criticism from which I have benefited.

Notes

1 Elmdon is a village in Essex, the subject of a 'survey' by social anthropology students from Cambridge in the 1960s/early 1970s. Wright (1984) gives an interesting account of her official brief for a study of decision-making in rural areas: it was packed full of assumptions about 'communities' and 'communication' which had to be unravelled in terms of both bureaucratic and local theory. Everyone was participating in promoting the idea of community as an explanatory concept in the description of rural society. I might add that the idea that 'rural communities' in Britain are somehow peripheral ones effectively blocks our understanding of the way their self-acknowledged differences draw on common British ideas *about* difference. One thinks of Ennew's work among Hebrideans who turned to the bookshelf for answers (for a summary see Condry 1983), or the essays in Cohen (1982).

2 The examination was stimulated by Anthony Cohen's observation (personal communication) that we imagine anthropology at home either takes too much for granted or else mystifies everything. The first assumption is stated clearly by Bradley and Lowe (1984: 8); apropos the second, Giddens (1984: 334) proposes that sociology might be construed as a critique of lay knowledge.

3 Elsewhere (Strathern 1985) I offer a brief critique of the postulate of jointly authored products. Rabinow (1977: 153; 1983: 204) emphasizes their hybrid nature; Crapanzano (1979: xv) cautions against dialogical interchange being taken as 'the cultural reality' of the other.

4 It should be clear that I am simply taking such a subject–object dichotomy as one culturally appropriate ('positivist') formula for the contemplation of our own activities; I go part of the way towards elucidating its contrived nature (see Webster 1982). This makes my account ironic (aware of its own context), especially in the passages on self-knowledge developed below.

5 The issue of exploitation is germane for the wider equation Asad notes (1973: 16–17) between unequal power relations and anthropological understanding as 'overwhelmingly objectified in European languages'. I acknowledge the criticism made (by Raymond Firth and Lydia Sciama) when this paper was delivered, that I appear to rely on an 'economic' metaphor. Apart from the fact that 'exploitation' was a term used by the Papua New Guinea students to whom I refer, it is intended as a comment on the anthropological aspiration to enlarge the 'moral community', in Hymes' words (1974: 53 - 'building a world culture that is a moral community'). What I expound in a property idiom apropos anthropological products could equally well be put in terms of subjective relations: the extent to which the investigator properly regards others as versions of him or herself.

6 There is some evidence – mainly from men, not women – that I was 'using' the people I knew in Hagen. Many were quite cynical about what my relationship with them would do for me as opposed to themselves. That I myself put a different construction on that relationship meant I was always a little upset, or at least

surprised, by such reactions. This was a felt ('real') disjunction. In the Elmdon case, on the other hand, my account here is largely fiction. That is, I have almost no evidence that Elmdon villagers really did think I was using them in any way. I just thought they would think that. Most of the evidence is to the contrary – in so far as people knew about the book, it was in terms of mild interest. However, I sustain the fiction because my projection of such reactions on to Elmdoners – my version of what I imagine they must be thinking – profoundly shaped my attitude towards writing the ethnography and my own feelings about the village. That they might feel exploited is a social fact in the context of what I thought I was doing as far as they were concerned. This paper, then, adopts two approaches to ethnographic verity, treating the Hagen 'facts' and the Elmdon 'facts' in different ways, corresponding to the distinction pursued below between being a writer (apropos Hagen) and being an author (apropos Elmdon) in respect of one's subjects of study.

7 Yet, in seeing that enterprise as transformative, anthropologists also have to preserve the discrete origins of the subjects under study. These subjects cannot be collapsed into replicas of the observers. It is important that their exogenous status is retained, for in making differences intelligible, anthropological 'work' is seen to have been done. Some of the following remarks are taken from Strathern (1984).

8 Apropos the production of pigs, neither the woman's nor the man's labour encompasses the labour of the other partner; as an embodiment of labour the pig in question cannot stand for one and not the other: it constitutes the product of the relationship. The one partner does not convert or transform the work of the other into use for her or his own self, but consumes the products of a specific other. Things produced for the use of others are thus not subordinated to some overriding purpose which redefines the ends for which they are conceived. But when Westerners imagine that everything can be turned to use, what emerges are hierarchies of use, fashioned by agents who turn the artefacts of others into useful things for their own ends. In this latter model, both the provisioning of raw materials and the productive transformation is 'work', so that one can be measured against the other, not as separate domains but as stages in a process. One 'uses' the work of another in one's 'own' work.

9 Compare Favret-Saada's (1980: 26) complaint that traditional ethnography accomplishes a split between the stating subject (the author of the account) and the statements (the text). Such facility in splitting is a culturally appropriate approach to a world conceived as beyond the subject.

10 Goldman demonstrates that this is both a matter of syntax (one cannot appropriate another's words through indirect speech; they are reported as direct speech) and the structure of discourse, which in the disputes he examines proceeds by example and counter-example (there are no summations). He relates these linguistic features in turn to the management of Huli talk oriented to agreement though consensus rather than judgement.

11 As Cohen (1978) suggests, this is like the introspection of Whalsay islanders who find themselves in the position of having to give a cultural accounting of their past. This seems to me an appropriate extrapolation, whereas for instance Jarvie's (1984) account of cargo cult activity as 'explanation' does not. Here Southwold's (1983) critique of the notion 'belief' affords a parallel comment. In spite of its propositional form, a credo which manifests a state of body and spirit is not to be confused with the credo of a detached consciousness which imagines truth in the specific form of an intellectual proposition. 'Belief' in the first sense cannot be taken as a variety of 'belief' in the second sense.

12 Favret-Saada attempts to generalize this triad as at once a social and a syntactical proposition: 'only a human being who names himself "I" can refer to another human being as "he"; and he can only do so by addressing a "you" ' (1980: 27). It

should be clear in what follows that I do not regard the triad as universally determined by such subject–object relations (cf. Fabian 1983: 85–6). If one *must* go to the syntax of representations (as an ethnography is a representation) then one should recall the syntactical possibilities of the New Guinea constructions already referred to (see n. 10). The juxtaposition of 'reported' speeches allows a simultaneity of single authorship (the speaking agent) and dual authorship (what another said remains what 'he'/'you' said); similarly, the Hagen dual pronoun can pair distinct social agents on an alliance rather than an incorporative model (cf. Strathern and Lancy 1981), and is not to be understood simply as an inclusive 'we'. The dual in effect elides 'he' and 'I' (Favret-Saada 1980: 28).

13 As far as domestic consumption is concerned. I am not dealing here with versions which might be useful in transactions with the 'outside world'. In cases where people might go to the anthropological account for a record of what was done 'in the past', I think the account would be regarded as a transparent rendering of what significant social others said (even if their identity is no longer recoverable). I intend a technical observation here about ownership and production.

14 Although in order not to burden the account with too much abstraction I have presented the case as though it were a matter of what people understand, the argument does not require evidence that people share a common vocabulary with the anthropologist. The point is that they and he/she belong to the culture which, so to speak, produced ideas such as that of 'society', or of 'culture' itself.

15 Disciplines may thus be seen to respond to particular social interests. Here is not 'ourselves' as a mass whose self-knowledge will be augmented, but ourselves as divided and split between numerous different interests, including academics as an interest group.

16 The metaphor of 'observation' (Fabian 1983: 106 ff.) displaces the construction of 'organization'. We imagine our organizing metaphor in the visual one (cognitive maps etc.), but that particular self-reflection hides the role of organization itself in our images. Sight is a world-wide metaphor for knowledge; it is the '*systemic* reach' into other cultures which is 'unique to the European or Western intellectual tradition' (Burridge 1979: 9). One would need to specify the kind of systematics, however. For one account of non-Western systematizations of knowledge, see Salmond's work on Maori oratory with its claim to be non-universalistic (1982: 83; 1983).

17 Haraway (1983: 333), observing that 'projects aiming at self-knowledge' are 'basic to the history of Western thought', raises a question against assuming too much about the identity of the selves so referenced.

18 For anthropology students from the University of Papua New Guinea, investigations at 'home' may well constitute a form of personal self-knowledge, but their project is not auto-anthropology. It is likely to have much more the character of Malinowski's, of deliberate mediation between different worlds, with different interests to hold in mind.

19 The claims are made in various forms throughout Malinowski's writings. They have remained a topic of anthropological contemplation, cf. Leach's (1957) early exposition; Sahlins (1976); Kuper (1980); Clifford (1983).

20 Southwold's comments on Buddhism (that it is not 'concerned to reflect and endorse social life as it is, but rather to transform it', 1983: 20) mean that one cannot interpret such religious practices as reflexive sociology. It also follows that one cannot make naïve assumptions about the reflexive status of 'representations' (1983: 78, 86).

21 As anthropologists 'we' treat 'other' cultures as though they had a culture as we do, and other societies as though they modelled themselves as societies. The idea is the

essential frame for the organization of data – to reveal the 'society' and 'culture' supposedly latent in people's conceptualizations. It also follows that if we were actually to consider the operational analogues of 'culture' one might have to confront very different techniques of knowledge – for instance the concept of 'cargo', as Wagner argues. In respect of Western society, however, what the Western anthropologist reveals is different: he/she offers a 'holistic' or 'systemic' perspective, the interconnections between parts. That is, people's own organization of knowledge, their explanations, are capped with a superorganized account. Here the difference is one of degree rather than of kind (cf. p. 17: the more ⱪ organized our knowledge is, the greater the 'understanding' possible).

22 Shamsul makes an analogous point in terms of the responsibilities anthropologists (and sociologists) have for the training of others in their disciplines (1982: 29).

23 And thus where 'the process of inquiry has been accepted as part of the ambient pluralist author' (Barnes 1979: 186).

References

ANDERSON, R. J. and SHARROCK, W. W. (1982) Sociological Work: Some Procedures Sociologists Use for Organizing Phenomena. *Social Analysis* **11**: 79–93.

ASAD, T. (1973) Introduction. *Anthropology and the Colonial Encounter*. London: Ithaca Press.

BARNES, J. (1979) *Who Should Know What? Social Science, Privacy and Ethics*. Harmondsworth: Penguin.

BARNETT, S. and SILVERMAN, M. G. (1979) *Ideology and Everyday Life. Anthropology, Neomarxist Thought, and the Problem of Ideology and the Social Whole*. Ann Arbor, Mich.: University of Michigan Press.

BRADLEY, T. and LOWE, P. (1984) Introduction. *Locality and Rurality: Economy and Society in Rural Regions*. Norwich: Geo Books.

BURRIDGE, K. (1979) *Someone, No One. An Essay on Individuality*. Princeton, N.J.: Princeton University Press.

CLIFFORD, J. (1983) On Ethnographic Authority. *Representations* **1**: 118–46.

COHEN, A. P. (1978) Oil and the Cultural Account: Reflections on a Shetland Community. *Scottish Journal of Sociology* **3**: 129–41.

— (1982) *Belonging: Identity and Social Organization in British Rural Cultures*. Manchester: Manchester University Press.

CONDRY, E. (1983) *Scottish Ethnography*. Edinburgh: Association for Scottish Ethnography, Monograph 1.

CRAPANZANO, V. (1979) Preface to *Do Kamo* (translated by M. Leenhardt). Chicago: University of Chicago Press.

DAMON, F. (1980) The Kula and Generalized Exchange: Considering Some Unconsidered Aspects of *The Elementary Structures of Kinship*. *Man* (NS) **15**: 267–92.

FABIAN, J. (1983) *Time and the Other. How Anthropology Makes Its Object*. New York: Columbia University Press.

FAVRET-SAADA, J. (1980) *Deadly Words. Witchcraft in the Bocage*. Cambridge: Cambridge University Press.

GIDDENS, A. (1984) *The Constitution of Society. Outline of the Theory of Structuration*. Cambridge: Polity Press.

GOLDMAN, L. (1983) *Talk Never Dies. The Language of Huli Disputes*. London: Tavistock Publications.

GUDEMAN, S. and PENN, M. (1982) Models, Meaning and Reflexivity. In D. Parkin (ed.) *Semantic Anthropology*. ASA Monographs 22. London: Academic Press.

HARAWAY, D. (1983) Reply to Arditti and Minden (Correspondence). *Signs, Journal of Women in Culture and Society* 9: 332–33.

HARRISON, S. (1985) Ritual Hierarchy and Secular Equality in a Sepik River Village. *American Ethnologist* 12: 413–26.

HOLY, L. and STUCHLIK, M. (1983) *Actions, Norms and Representations. Foundations of Anthropological Inquiry*. Cambridge: Cambridge University Press.

HYMES, D. (1974) The Use of Anthropology: Critical, Political, Personal. In D. Hymes (ed.) *Reinventing Anthropology*. New York: Vintage Books.

JARVIE, I. C. (1984) *Rationality and Relativism. In Search of a Philosophy and History of Anthropology*. London: Routledge & Kegan Paul.

JOSEPHIDES, L. (1985) *The Production of Inequality. Gender and Exchange Among the Kewa*. London: Tavistock Publications.

KASAIPWALOVA, J. (1975) *Sopi: The Adaptation of a Traditional Aesthetic Concept for the Creation of a Modern Arts School on Kiriwina*. Port Moresby: Institute of Papua New Guinea Studies, Discussion Paper 5.

KUPER, A. (1980) The Man in the Study and the Man in the Field: Ethnography, Theory and Comparison in Social Anthropology. *European Journal of Sociology* 21: 14–39.

LEACH, E. (1957) The Epistemological Background to Malinowski's Empiricism. In R. Firth (ed.) *Man and Culture*. London: Routledge & Kegan Paul.

MARCUS, G. E. and CUSHMAN, D. (1982) Ethnographies as Texts. *Annual Review of Anthropology* 11: 25–69.

OKELY, J. (1984) Fieldwork in the Home Counties. *RAIN* 61: 4–6.

RABINOW, P. (1977) *Reflections on Fieldwork in Morocco*. Berkeley, Calif.: University of California Press.

— (1983) 'Facts are a Word of God': An Essay Review. In G. W. Stocking (ed.) *Observers Observed: History of Anthropology*, Vol. 1. Wisconsin: University of Wisconsin Press.

— (1984) Discourse and Power: On the Limits of Ethnographic Texts. Paper read at conference *The Making of Ethnographic Texts*, Santa Fe. To be published in *Dialectical Anthropology*.

SAHLINS, M. (1976) *Culture and Practical Reason*. Chicago: Chicago University Press.

SALMOND, A. (1982) Theoretical Landscapes. On a Cross-Cultural Conception of Knowledge. In D. Parkin (ed.) *Semantic Anthropology*. ASA Monographs 22. London: Academic Press.

— (1983) The Study of Traditional Maori Society: The State of the Art. *Journal of the Polynesian Society* 92: 309–31.

SCHOLTE, R. (1974) Toward a Reflexive and Critical Anthropology. In D. Hymes (ed.) *Reinventing Anthropology*. New York: Vintage Books.

SHAMSUL, A. (1982) The Superiority of Indigenous Scholars? Some Facts and Fallacies with Special Reference to Malay Anthropologists and Sociologists in Fieldwork. *Manusia dan masyarakat (Man and Society)* 3: 24–33.

SOUTHWOLD, M. (1983) *Buddhism in Life. The Anthropological Study of Religion and the Sinhalese Practice of Buddhism*. Manchester: Manchester University Press.

STRATHERN, A. and LANCY, D. (1981) Making Twos: Pairing as an Alternative to the Taxonomic Mode of Representation. *American Anthropologist* 83: 773–95.

STRATHERN, M. (1984) Localism Displaced: A 'Vanishing Village' in Rural England. *Ethnos* 49: 43–60.

— (1985) Dislodging a World View: Challenge and Counter-Challenge in the Relationship between Feminism and Anthropology. *Australian Feminist Studies* 1: 1–25.

THORNTON, R. (1983) Narrative Ethnography in Africa, 1850–1920: The Creation and Capture of an Appropriate Domain for Anthropology. *Man* (NS) **18**: 502–20.

WAGNER, R. (1975) *The Invention of Culture*. Englewood Cliffs, N.J.: Prentice-Hall.

WEBSTER, S. (1982) Dialogue and Fiction in Ethnography. *Dialectical Anthropology* **7**: 91–114.

WRIGHT, S. (1984) Rural Communities and Decision Makers. *RAIN* **63**: 9–13.

Edwin Ardener

---

3 'Remote areas':
some theoretical considerations

I hope that this title will be pleasantly misleading. I have gone behind the theme of this conference, to the idea of places, or peoples, or locations, that anthropologists have considered to be 'fit' for their study. For, if there is anything controversial about the idea of the social anthropologist working at home, or relatively near home, it is because some may fear that the very nature of the subject may be thereby transformed out of all recognition. There is clearly something in the idea that distance lends enhancement, if not enchantment, to the anthropological vision. Yet the work in Europe, for example, has clearly yielded results of great general interest. This paper therefore starts from a deliberately obscure and ill-defined term: 'remote'. I choose it from the natural language, and show that in an anthropological sense it can be 'unpacked' in rather striking ways. This paper is related to my basic theoretical papers on the nature of the social space (Ardener 1975, 1978). I shall refer to the new concept of 'event-density' or 'event-richness', which (since the space is analysable at all levels in essentially the same way) is the event-homologue of the phenomenon of 'semantic density' described in the concluding parts of my recent paper on social anthropology and reality (Ardener 1982). 'Semantic density' is a statistical feature, at the point where definition and measurement intersect and collapse together. We have a number of difficult paths leading away from us, so let us start.[1]

The problem of identity

It will be no surprise that interest in 'minorities', 'embedded groups', 'plural societies', and the like, has led to problems of definition. The term 'ethnicity' was a useful step on the road, which produced its own difficulties. The resort to 'identity', as a term, was an attempt to restore the self-definitional element that seemed to be inherent in the idea of 'ethnicity', but which was shared by entities other than ethnicities as normally conceived – many kinds of entities have identities. As far as 'minorities' are concerned, majorities are just as important for our comprehension of this problem. We know (at least since Ferguson in 1767) that the definition of entities by mutual (binary) opposition is part of the point.[2] There is always the danger, however, that we may run the risk of so relativizing the distinction that we forget the original problem. The excellent volume called *Belonging* (Cohen 1982) has a title from a fuzzy part of the English lexicon which leaves all options open.

Let me remind you of the statement, that 'among the many things that society *is* or *is like*, it *is* or *is like* identity' (Ardener and Ardener 1965). The social is, in virtue of its categorizing and classifying structures, a space that 'identifies'. It is a chief source of any concept that we may severally have of identity. That there is a multiplicity of identities that coexist together from any single perspective is not strictly speaking a problem theoretically. It is one of the proofs – and one of the costs – of the apparent paradox of the continuity between the space and individuals that constitute it. They are defined by the space and are nevertheless the defining consciousnesses of the space.

We hear now a great deal about 'reflexivity'. Before that word loses its concreteness, let us remember that (to state it oversimply) our heads are full of categories generated by the social, which we project back upon the social. Perhaps, in the 'normal course of events' (as we put it), the 'native actor' does not perceive this interaction, for the social space is not for him or her an 'object', except intermittently. For the non-native social anthropologist the act of interacting with an alien social space, even relatively successfully, forms the basis of that 'daily experience of *mis*understanding'[3] (at not only the ethnographic level but the theoretical level) which is the undoubted source of our greater readiness to see the space as object (of study), and thus, like Durkheim, to see 'social facts as things'. To treat the social space as object is almost literally child's play, when it is located in unfamiliar scenes and is already, in any case, predefined as 'other' in relation to our own world. 'Reflexivity' has become a popular, as opposed to a specialist, term in social anthropology as those conditions have changed. The task has not changed, however, save in that the individual/social interaction must be more minutely scrutinized. The currency of the term arises from an increase in theoretical awareness. It will no doubt acquire soft-centred connotations and be abandoned as the situation which produced it becomes commonplace. Nevertheless, it should not be confused with 'subjectivity'.

There was a time when the relativity of cultural categories was raised to a philosophical bogey as 'relativism'. Anthropology then was discovering a mismatch between the categories of the observer and those generated by the purported object – other people. When the differences are more subtle, the gap is narrower between these two; the mismatch is virtually simultaneous. Since mismatch *is* our experience of relativity, then the reduction of 'transmission time' (between the observer and the purported object) and the narrowing of the mismatch (between the categories of the observer and the other), demonstrates that the process that we first called relativization is *not* a form of anti-objectivity, but (as its application to 'familiar' experience more clearly shows) is on the contrary our only mode of objectivization. This is quite an important theoretical proof of what has for social anthropologists been intuitively sensed, and it will be illustrated in the treatment that follows.[4]

Remoteness: some phenomenology

After these essential preliminaries, I start here from another English term: 'remote'. For the moment it has no theoretical taint (sadly we may change that situation). I wish, by using it, to recapture the feature that started the personal interest of many anthropologists in their traditional areas of study. Elsewhere, I have pointed out that, for Europe, 'remote areas' of the globe have had a different conceptual geography, and have been perceived to exist on a different time-scale from the 'central' areas (Ardener 1975, 1985). But we are not now opening up a familiar 'centre/periphery' discussion – if only for the reason that most such discussion depends on an acceptance of known centres with known peripheries. On the contrary, the age of discovery showed us that the 'remote' was actually compounded of 'imaginary' as well as 'real' places; yet they were all of equal conceptual reality or unreality before the differences were revealed. 'Brazil', 'California', 'India', 'Africa', 'Libya', 'Ethiopia' – all were to one extent or other imagined (names ransacked from various sources), yet all were located eventually in limited and specific places.[5] Occasionally we are conscious of a loss. Almost the most imaginary of all: the Antipodes (once the outlet of the Celtic Other World, and a home of King Arthur), and Australia (Terra Australis), are now almost the most mundane of all.[6] On the other hand, and conversely, pockets of imaginary places have remained still unrealized within the European centre. When the far Antarctic was made real, Brittany and the Gaels were still 'unrealized', still 'removed' from the canons of Western realities, or indeed *remote* (Latin *removeo*). In the West we are 'space specialists': we easily realize our conceptual spaces as physical spaces – for that is, in many respects, the European theme. 'Remote' areas are, for us, conventionally physically removed, but this obscures the conceptual phenomena associated with 'remoteness', which are real enough for biological anthropologists (for example) to perceive commuter-ridden villages of Otmoor (5–10 miles from Oxford) as 'remote'.

Let me begin from a näive point of view, with a little personal anthropology. The fact has frequently been noted that the discipline of social anthropology itself belongs to a part of the 'academic vocabulary' that is concerned with marginality, regarded from a Western perspective. In that sense, anywhere an anthropologist chooses to go is likely to show the quality I have just called 'remoteness'. There are, however, interesting nuances. I went first to the Ibo of Southern-Eastern Nigeria. It had, however, been expected that I would go to the Plateau area of Central-Northern Nigeria. I had read all the available literature on the many peoples of that zone at the International African Institute in Waterloo Place, guided by the quizzical attentions of Miss Barbara Pym, the then unpublished novelist, who was then embarking on her own peculiar fieldwork.[7] In the event, the Nigerian government vetoed the worker who was going to the Ibo, and I went there instead. I did not personally like the change, for various reasons, and strangely the Ibo never came to seem 'remote' to me. The Plateau certainly *had* seemed so. It was not that the Ibo were lacking in conventionally exotic features. In fact, no people were more 'anthropological' or 'ethnographical' in other ways than the Ibo, but they never fitted the qualities I now examine in retrospect as 'remote'. Of course, once there, parts of Ibo country began themselves to acquire the purely topographical characteristics of 'remoteness' – places more than walking distance, then more than cycling distance, then places in the north and north-west of the area. Nevertheless, I now see that the Ibo were, in the particular sense I am trying to unpack, essentially definers of remoteness in *others*, although with normally unperceived pockets of internal remoteness – in a way, rather like England itself. Indeed, taken as a whole, Southern Nigeria has that quality, compared with certain other African countries. For the moment I am merely trying to pinpoint the quality; what I mean may become clearer when one opposes Nigeria to the Cameroons, which are, in contrast, commonly experienced as 'remote' – not only by me, but by almost everyone who visits the country, and it retains this quality even when after ten or twenty years you are an 'expert' in the area. The more expert, the lonelier you seem to become. To know the Cameroons well is to feel that you are outliving your contemporaries. The Cameroons does not become less 'remote': you become more and more remote yourself. Perhaps this condition is, at a higher level of opposition, one that is characteristic of all anthropologists – as against (say) sociologists. I am feeling towards the statement that although there are always 'real' centres, and 'real' peripheries which move relative to each other, there is an added feature of a more puzzling kind.

There are certainly some topographical elements that are relevant. Mountains conventionally add to the 'remoteness' experience, but so very frequently do plains, forests, and rivers – so much so that the inhabitants of 'unremote' places sometimes say that they do not have 'real' mountains, plains, forests, or rivers – only something else, hills (say), woods, or streams. Contrariwise, some areas (like Brittany) call their hills 'mountains'. The Scots, resisting the 'remote' vocabulary, perhaps, call their mountains 'hills'. The actual geography is not the overriding feature – it is obviously necessary that 'remoteness' has a position in topographical space, but it is defined within a *topological* space whose features are expressed in a cultural vocabulary. The Bakweri of Cameroon cannot really be said to be objectively remote from the coastal belt of that country. Their more elevated settlements overlook an area of superficial commercial modernization and the sea. Yet they live up the Cameroon Mountain, and the higher seems to be the remoter in this elastic semantic realm.

With the Cameroons we are getting close to the problem I want to discuss. For example, the feature I describe of 'remoteness' (this term you see now is a label for something which is only gradually casting its shadow in language during my exposition) persists when it has lost its geographical correlates – that is, when the 'remote' area has been reached, and when it should now be merely present. Thus people would visit the Cameroons, and (as it were) stagger in to see us as if they had surmounted vast odds; as if the Cameroons had a protective barrier. Yet, from the inside outwards, there was an almost exaggerated contrary sense of the *absence* of any barrier to the world – a peculiar sense of excessive vulnerability, of ease of entry. With every improvement of communication over the decades, the more speedily did people appear to pour in uninvited; and yet the more they seemed to be on the last stages of an expedition to some Everest that terminated in the middle of your floor. That is a law of 'remote' areas – the basic paradox, for that is how you know you are in one. The West still maintains ideals of such places. 'Shangri La' is an image used by French visitors to the former British Cameroons, and by United Nations visitors to both Cameroons. You know you are 'remote' by the intense quality of the gaze of visitors, by a certain steely determination, by a slightly frenetic air, as if their clocks and yours move at different rates. Perhaps that is why the native of such an area sometimes feels strangely invisible – the visitors seem to blunder past, even through him. I think that to formulate this point you have to have stayed for very long successive periods in various spaces, in order to separate out this quality, which I take to be a real one and connected to the experience of time. It is, of course, a conceptual experience. The one-way invisible barrier is a singularity in the social space, which I have mapped already in formal terms in the Munro Lecture (Ardener 1975).

Yet, as I have mentioned, remoteness does not appear to protect the 'remote areas'. In the Cameroons we penetrated more and more parts which, on the ordinary level of the relativity of conventional geographical remoteness, were remote even in the Cameroons. There were areas so 'remote' anthropologically that there was nothing written on them. Yet, when reached, they seemed totally exposed to the outer world: they were continually in contact with it. Why were they not equally known to 'the world'? Remote areas turn out to be like gangster hide-outs – full of activity, and of half-recognized faces. As the years went by, we had the choice of the blankest part of the Cameroon map: the Fungom area of the Bamenda Plateau, and within that area the Chiefdom of Esu. A thatched house was built on a hill, round which the village-capital nestled. The paradox of living in that blank area summed up the experience of remoteness very well, some of which I shall touch on soon. For the moment I will note that an uncompleted dirt road led to a log over a stream, and a path that wound up that hobbit-like hill. From its top any distant Land-Rover could be heard approaching for miles, its cloud of dust being visible for further miles, until its minuscule occupants alighted and began their ominous ascent, gathering children and helpers as they came.

To the strange arrivals the village was either a scene of 'traditional hospitality of a simple highland folk' or the location of incomprehensible reticences. The very act of having arrived was its own justification. Years later, the new arrivals were a unit of gendarmerie, for this was the remote area of all remote areas for the new Francophone government and, like all areas of this peculiar type, not only perceived to be Shangri La but also the home of purported smugglers and spies. How shall the inhabitants of a 'remote area' evaluate the arbitrary love-hate of its visitors? Are alternating periods of 'unspoiledness' and violence their inevitable fate? After the destructions of one generation of strangers how is it that they are asked to play the role of ideal society to the next, before being unthinkingly redeveloped or underdeveloped out of existence by the next? The history of 'remoteness' in Cameroon merges historically into the universal history of political states; my discussion is to show its minimal reflection in 'states of mind'.

The cognoscenti will recognize by now that Western Scotland is an area in which canonical levels of 'remoteness' are to be found. Indeed some may suspect that this has been an elaborate way of introducing the really basic economic and political factors. Such important matters as the Highland Clearances, for example, cannot surely derive from mere conceptualizations? That would be a false opposition, although the improver of the Duchess of Sutherland's estates, the well-known James Loch, was fired with high levels of what looks suspiciously like conceptualization: late-eighteenth-century ideas of betterment, much more powerful than malice. And what conceptualizations fired the undoubted and more easily handled villains of the piece like the factor, Patrick Sellar?[8] Those old ladies carried out of their houses so that the thatch could be burned: beware of being a conceptualization in another person's mind!

The great contribution of Malcolm Chapman's book, *The Gaelic Vision in Scottish Culture* (1978), was to approach this point from its literary expression. A Gael once asked in a poem: '*Cò sgrìobh mi?*' ('Who wrote me?'). When the anthropologist Chapman with the freshness of inexperience innocently replied, 'Oh, didn't you know?: it was Macpherson, Arnold, Renan, the Edinburgh intellectuals . . .', all hell broke loose. Professor Derick Thomson, in his incarnation as Ruaraidh MacThomais, poet, had himself often asked the same question, but he did not like *that* answer.[9] The reasons are understandable as we shall see, for Chapman, in showing how the very definition of Celticity and Gaeldom was inescapably tainted at source, and how the imposition of it had led to a 'symbolic expropriation' of the

Gaelic identity, seemed to ignore the experienced reality of being a Gael. Nevertheless, for the first time, the paradox of Gaeldom was brought out from under the comfortingly drifting layers of binary oppositions: development/underdevelopment, traditional/modern, centre/periphery, that had covered it for years like the soft patter of autumn leaves.

A similar experience occurred for Maryon McDonald (1982) among the Bretons.[10] In her case she showed brilliantly how the Breton militant language movement coexisted uneasily with the native speakers who were cast as ideal types by their kaftan-wearing admirers. This time it was the militants who filled the newspapers with their violent reactions. I am personally sure the work of Chapman and McDonald will stand as genuine advances. The Gaels and the Bretons have a proper point, however. They want to know, 'Who then are we, *really*?' They behave as if they were indeed privileged enough to require to know something that no one can ever know. It is, however, an important feature of the 'remote' social spaces – indeed, as I argue, it is of the peculiar structure of such spaces – that the question imposes itself; and so far it is true that we have given the appearance of tackling only one half of the problem. On one side 'remote areas' are indeed parts of an imaginary world. I had kept for some years an image to print as a dedication to this phase of our studies, and I gave it to Malcolm Chapman to use on his fly-leaf; it is from Lewis Carroll's *Through the Looking-Glass*:

> ' "He's dreaming now," said Tweedledee: "and what do you think he's dreaming about? . . . Why, about *you*! And if he left off dreaming about you, where do you suppose you'd be?" "Where I am now, of course," said Alice.
>
> "Not you!" Tweedledee retorted contemptuously. "You'd be nowhere. Why, you're only a sort of thing in his dream!"
>
> "If that there King was to wake," added Tweedledum, "You'd go out – bang! – just like a candle!" '

The expropriation of an image of another is a puzzling thing. I have mentioned the novelist Barbara Pym. Now that she is dead, a strange simulacrum of her is taking shape, which is analogous in its processes to that effect caused by visitors to a remote area. Experts on Barbara Pym now begin to appear who know more about her than she knew herself, or than any single friend knew, while those of us inserted into her novels become symbolized figures, merely narrative elements.[11] There never was, in any purely physical location, that Barbara Pym – it is all 'true' perhaps, but it never existed. The new Pym is a series of storage points in a fuzzy network of information, whose general distribution signals the existence of the ex-Pym, the late Pym, the Pym that passed away. And who has selected those points, and in what space are they located? Similarly, the Gaels, the Cameroonians, and others, have had the privileged experience of being made, as collectivities, part of a similar process. They have become, like Pym, at worst a 'text', at best 'art'. The 'remote' social spaces thus merely exhibit, in an exaggerated form, a feature which affects all human beings to some extent. Yet we assert that we are still 'there', in some experienced way, behind the textualization – at least while we are still alive. The social space consists of human persons, so it is right that the Gaels and others should assert: 'However we are perceived or constructed in the worlds of others, nevertheless there *are* real Gaels.'

It is not necessary, therefore, with this readership, to say that the Western Islanders do not see themselves as resembling that artistic or textual remoteness. They are quite ordinary – as ordinary as anybody can be who has the regular experience of wild-eyed romantics tottering through his door. The social space is a material one. A lifetime of being treated as a princess turns you into an ordinary – princess; a lifetime as an untouchable makes you just an unexceptional – untouchable. A lifetime of being in a remote area, turns you into an ordinary . . .? What?

To answer the question we must consider some paradoxes.

1. *Remote areas are full of strangers*. I know people who hardly experience the idea of 'a stranger'. No suburbanite sees the unknown mass of neighbours as 'strangers'. The city-dweller does not inhabit a world of strangers. To make a city-dweller perceive a stranger he must be marked by such criteria that total rejection is likely to be his reaction. As a result incoming New Zealanders can *really* believe they are Londoners.[12] Try to get away with that, however, in the Hebrides. There every social inter- action has its marking preliminaries ('*Cò às a tha thu?*' 'Where are you from?', or the like). People in remote areas have a wide definition of 'strangers', so that, whatever the real numbers of the latter, there will always appear to be a lot of them. This conceptualization interacts, however, with the undoubted tendency for perceived strangers actually to congregate in remote areas. We must be careful in formulating this point. First of all, the stranger remains 'marked' longer, perhaps for ever, so that the residue of strangeness accumulates. We can see already the difficulty of talking of 'real' highlanders, when biographies are well remembered. But even this is not enough, for the kinds of strangers that congregate in remote areas are quite peculiar and all over Europe one can list them: painters, jewellery-makers, vegetarians, cultists, hunters, prospectors, bird-watchers, and *innovators* as we shall see. Some of these categories have been present at all times under different historical guises, including those of monks and invaders.[13]

2. *Remote areas are full of innovators*. Anyone in a remote area feels free to innovate. There is always a new pier being planned, and always some novelty marking or marring the scene. For the Western Islanders there is always the new Highlands and Islands Development Board scheme. The next boom is always on the way: kelp, sheep, deer, sheep again, oil,

fishmeal. There is always a new quarry for new road materials. We are always seeing the end of some old order. Meanwhile, beyond the new pier is the old pier, and behind the old pier the even older pier. The Cameroons have had an endless sequence of innovations since 1884, or even since 1858: yet the innovations seem to have a short life.[14] The paradox is that there is always change and intervention in remote areas, while in timeless Leeds stagnation seems to rule.

3. *Remote areas are full of ruins of the past*. The corollary of the above is that the remains of failed innovations, and of dead economic periods, scatter the landscape. There is another paradox here: that remote areas cry out for development, but they are the continuous victims of visions of development. The Cameroons has presented a steady sequence of innovation and ruin. The Highlands and Islands Development Board has been in existence long enough for its history already to be marked by the monuments of its own failed projects: Breasclete on the Isle of Lewis, Ardveenish on Barra, bidding fair to join the even earlier projects of Lord Leverhulme – before the HIDB period itself passes away as another golden age of innovation, into the past.[15] Remote areas offer images of unbridled pessimism or utopian optimism, of change and decay, in their memorials. The Highlands are, as a whole, a great monument at one level to a Malthusian experiment on a disastrous scale that filled most of the nineteenth century. Within that total landscape with ruins (and few human figures) nest many smaller landscapes with their own lesser ruins.

4. *Remote areas are full of rubbish*. This is a minor corollary of the last. Remote areas are the home of rubbish, because rubbish is not a category there. What appears remarkable is that people elsewhere expect to tidy up the formless universe. Such an aspiration belongs to the worlds that *define* remote areas. These defining worlds do not, of course, perceive their own refuse tips, their own black holes, full of rubbish. In the Hebrides German tourists feel free to criticize your rubbish.[16]

5. *Remote areas are in constant contact with the world*. We must interpret this carefully. Remote areas are obsessed with communications: the one road; the one ferry; the tarring of the road; the improvement of the boat; the airstrip on reclaimed ground or even on the sandy beach. The world always beckons –the Johnsonian road to England, or the coast, or wherever it is, an attraction to the young, for it leads from your very door to everywhere. It is quite different in this respect from a city street. The road to Cathay does not flow from No. 7 Bloomsbury Mansions. The assiduity with which television is watched in remote areas has a particular quality. A programme on the Mafia is squirrelled away as part of the endless phantasmagoria of life that begins at Oban or Kelvinside. Are we making the contradictory statement that, after all, *remote areas are not remote*? If it

seems like that, it is a result of our earlier perception that remote areas, from the inside, feel open and unprotected – the one-way barrier.

6. *Strangers and entrepreneurs* or *remote areas are full of pots*. 'Lianish' is on the very end of the road from the island centre, one of the longest continuous journeys: there are fifteen houses, two bed-and-breakfast ladies, an English potter/cowman/temporary postman, and one child under eleven. The postbus runs until 4 p.m. Only an incomer will work the 'unsociable' evening round. The Englishman takes seriously his 'social service' function, does the drunks' trip to town, and gets home late in the evening. The real postman will be watching the television. A typical incomer, many Gaels will think, without animus. Incomers suffer frequently from remote-area anxiety: the arrival of another new incomer is a sign that the fastness has been penetrated – we may call it the Crusoe effect.

7. *The incomer as entrepreneur*, which we have been gradually approaching, is a cliché of the Hebrides (the phenomenon is widespread, however). On one island the best private bus is run by an in-married incomer – a woman. The place it stops for tea is at the 'croft' of a man from Bolton, Lancashire, who admirably carries on traditional crofting activities, such as weaving. Almost all the hotels are run or managed by incomers. The Lewis Pakistanis may not all speak the fluent Gaelic that legend says, but the legend marks their assimilation to the averageness of strangeness that characterizes incomers. No amount of Gaelic would turn them into Gaels, but their existence is used to contrast with those incomers who have learnt no Gaelic at all. It is easy to document the entrepreneurs that are recent incomers. But when one looks at the 'island-born' entrepreneurs, there emerge the names of old tacksmen's families, of introduced mainland shepherds, and persons of odd biography – internal incomers, former incomers, products of mixed incomer-island marriages.

One may easily concede that bed-and-breakfast ladies will be an exception, that they are from a random selection of hospitable families. Islands differ markedly and on the Long Island it is a matter of report that the Isle of Skye has taken to the hospitality trade to a remarkable extent. In the Outer Hebrides the time, trouble, and expense of catering for guests can hardly be worth the £10 or £12 return that is characteristically charged. Once more the bed-and-breakfast entrepreneur is likely to be upwardly mobile. A surprising number are not Gaelic-speaking. Indeed, the ubiquitous Scandinavian linguist is directed to lists issued by the *Gaelhols* enterprise. Gaels in the general trade are frequently families in which the husband is already the holder of another job.

8. *In remote areas the same set do everything*. Connected to the last point is the interesting observation (which is an actually voiced complaint) that the

same people take all the new jobs. Although this seems at first sight strange, the phenomenon is not restricted to the Hebrides. Development money tends to channel through the same entrepreneurs, however tiny their activities by world standards. A kind of micro-economic pluralism is endemic, as a pen-picture will illustrate.

9. *Under Milk Wood of a remote island.*[17] Down to the ferry every evening go the teenagers, earnest with purpose; the grocer fills the cars with petrol (he is in charge of both food and fuel); the taxi-driver hires out the cars, to drive to his two rentable holiday homes; the dustman drives up with the travelling library; the retired English officer's daughter bakes the cakes, and ranges Sloanely to serve them to the airport passengers; the Commander bakes wholemeal bread (for incomers – Gaels prefer Mother's Pride sliced); the retired teacher grows vegetables to be sold in his sister's hostelry (she whose husband in Edinburgh writes for *Acarsaid*, the national journal, edited by the Revd Archie Hill alias Gillesbuig Mac an Dùin, professional Gael), while the sister's son discusses introducing 'speed boats between the islands' with Donald G., who bought an HIDB craft centre costing the EEC £200,000, for only £40,000, when two managers (incomers) each left to open their own shops; the latter, bearded, twice the size of an ordinary islander, spends much time on the plane to Glasgow and Corfu; seeing below Mr Mackenzie running his ferries, in turn with taking pay to skipper a subsidized ferry in competition with himself; the postman mows the lawns of his, the Caolas, guesthouse at Creagnaculist; Mrs McNeil inscribes her name on the list of Gaelhols for language learners; in the loch the Dean of Wyanunk Theological, Ohio, paints the wood of his restored castle with creosote; the Dutch wife of an Australian professor opens her guesthouse and craftshop; A. F., former serviceman and performer in *Man of Arran*, tells oft-told tales to an anthropologist; his charming daughter has 300 Christmas cards from Americans from whom she half-knowingly extracts the admiration due to the identity-constructing Gael . . .

So we come to the nub.

By now something in the paradox of remote areas can be seen to be systematic. It will be evident that I have used the terms 'remote' and 'remote area' as mere semantic grains upon which to grow a theoretical crystal. I wished to propose an 'empty formative' that would generate the interaction between the anthropologist and his field, the definer and the defined, the classifier and the classified, the imagined and the realized. The condition might have been given any code name, or a letter, or a number, and not illustrated by local colour. Nevertheless, the 'remoteness' paradoxes are well known (although not necessarily in all aspects everywhere the same), and so 'remoteness' may now finish its life in this paper as a technical term. I will therefore provide a theoretical conclusion, inevitably somewhat condensed.

Remote areas are event-rich, or event-dense

In the social space, not everything that happens is an event. Much of what passes has for the participants an automaton-like quality. Events are defined within the space by a certain quality which, to avoid a special terminology, we may for the moment call 'significance'. The nature of the event-matrix may be modelled synchronically (Ardener 1978), or diachronically (1975). Essentially, specifying something in the space introduces a singularity into it, which 'twists off' the specified. The latter is bounded one way – from the perspective of the specifier.

The phenomena outlined above may be expressed in another form, by saying that the information content is high. That is: randomization, the ultimate condition of active systems, is continually resisted. These areas delicately teeter on the edge of perpetual innovation. This feature is both internal and external. Thus 'remoteness' is a specification, and a perception, from elsewhere, from an outside standpoint; but from inside the people have their own perceptions – if you like, a counterspecification of the dominant, or defining space, working in the opposite direction. Thus in the Cameroons the Bakweri were defined by general repute, in their multi-ethnic area, as apathetic (Ardener 1956; Ardener, Ardener, and Warmington 1960), while the silent villagers saw themselves as involved in a life-and-death struggle with zombies and their masters, which gave deep significance to the slightest act (Ardener 1970). All the materialities of dominance, economic and conceptual, were present in their traumatic history. These spiritual events are, however, of the utmost seriousness, as serious as the Diwygiad in Wales, or the Disruption in the Kirk which led to the sense of continuous spiritual battle that marks the characteristic religious life of the Presbyterian Hebrides. Their materialities do not lack some possible analogies with those that summoned up the zombies: expropriation, depopulation, landlordism, and definition as dwindling, dying, and out of time.

The double specification of remote areas, or double-markedness, produces that note of eccentricity and overdefinition of individuality, if you like an overdetermination – or to exaggerate slightly, a structure of strangers. In the large stable systems of dominant central areas, in contrast, there are equally large regularities, with more automatisms, in which only in periodic 'prophetic situations' do major singularities occur (Ardener 1975). They are event-poor. It is evident that the event quality is not a direct function of numbers or population for, in contrast, it is remote areas as we have defined them that are 'event-rich'.

Event-richness is like a small-scale, simmering, continuously generated set of singularities, which are not just the artefact of observer bias (as we have seen, observers commonly perceive only a puzzling blankness) – but due to some materiality, that I interpret to be related to the enhanced defining power of individuals. Event-richness is the result of the weakening of, or probably the continuous threat to, the maintenance of a self-generated set of overriding social definitions (including those that control people's own physical world), thus rendering possible the 'disenchainment' of individuals, and that over-determination of individuality, to which I referred. The peculiar driving force of abortive innovation is precisely due to this, and the sense of vulnerability to intrusion experienced in such areas is genuine. The structural time is quite different, and in so far as a 'remote' area is (as it always is) part of a much wider definitional space (shall we say the dominant State) it will be perceived, itself, *in toto*, as a singularity in that space.

If that is so, then event-richness can occur within any social space. That is the meaning of our earlier paradox, that we can travel to internal remotenesses that have not yet been actualized, or which still form singularities in our otherwise more informationally random social space. It will be recalled that all individuals are potentially singularities in a social space through their (only intermittently exercised) power of self-definition. Since remote areas are singularities in the total or wider space, all singularities there are reinforced. As more and more internal remotenesses are defined out of our changing societies, it will be no surprise that social anthropologists, addicts of the event-rich, will be disappearing into them.

I am afraid that many will think this terminology unnecessarily arcane. They will not have far to seek in the literature for more conventional terms. For them I will, however, phrase it another way. The lesson of 'remote' areas is that this is a condition not related to periphery, but to the fact that certain peripheries are by definition not properly linked to the dominant zone. They are perceptions from the dominant zone, not part of its codified experience. Not all purely geographical peripheries are in this condition, and it is not restricted to peripheries.

Finally, I do not need to stress here that while human beings have theoretically unlimited classifying power, not all classifications have equal experiential density. The feature of a 'remote area' (in our technical sense of a singularity of a particular type) is that those so defined are intermittently conscious of the defining processes of others that might absorb them. That is why they are very crucibles of the creation of identity, why they are of great theoretical interest, and why social anthropologist 'at home' may be very far away indeed.

Notes

1 This is a paper of some degree of abstraction. It is not an account of the Western Isles, but it should not, despite the terminology, be other than obvious to Gaels. It takes a great deal of explanation, they will be aware, to state the facts to those outwith.

2 Adam Ferguson wrote, in *An Essay in the History of Civil Society* (1767: 31): 'The titles of *fellow citizen* and *countryman* unopposed to those of *alien* and *foreigner*, to

which they refer, would fall into disuse, and lose their meaning.' This had a great influence on Evans-Pritchard (see Pocock 1961: 78; Ardener 1971: lix). Despite this, an ESRC correspondent referred to it as a recent and untried theory.
3 Ardener 1971: xvii. Also: 'Even the most exemplary technical approach to language would not in fact have solved the basic problem of communication. The anthropological "experience" derives from the apprehension of a critical lack of fit of (at least) two entire world-views, one to the other.'
4 There is endless useless confusion between relativity and relativization on the one hand, and a chimera called (usually by non-anthropologists) 'cultural relativism' on the other. Like many contemporaries (cf. Gellner 1983; Edwards 1985) I am not a 'cultural relativist'. The very act of the comparison of cultures implies the existence of appropriate canons of comparison. By those canons judgements can be made. The relativity of social worlds is a mere fact, beyond all judgements: they are constructed differently, not equally. It is, of course, inappropriate to charge a culture with inferiority because it has few hue terms, or does not separate arm from hand terminologically. Judgements may, however, be made about the 'adequacy' of a terminological system. It is sufficient evidence to support this assertion to point out that judgements of inadequacy are daily made, even *within* a culture. Thus doctors devised anatomical terms, and artists construct colour charts. It is no great step further to assert, if we want to: 'cultures are extremely unequal in their cognitive power' (Gellner 1968: 401). The sentence remains, of course, a sentence in our own language.
5 'Brazil' was a red dye-wood; later an imaginary Atlantic island was so named in maps; even after it was localized in South America, a non-existent 'Brazil Rock' remained on British Admiralty charts until the second half of the nineteenth century. California was taken from a story of 1510, published in Madrid; it was near the Indies and the terrestrial paradise. India: variously placed, particularly in Indonesia and the Antilles. Libya: once Africa. Africa: once Tunisia. Ethiopia: once any African land occupied by people with 'burnt faces'.
6 See Loomis (1956: 61–76) for the Arthurian Antipodes, and once more the terrestrial paradise.
7 Barbara Pym included known anthropologists and African linguists in several of her novels, in particular *Less than Angels* (1955), or as composite characters ('Everard Bone' and the like).
8 The Highland Clearances were already under way at the time of Samuel Johnson's visit to the inner isles in 1776. The sagacious doctor greatly blamed the landlords for encouraging emigrations. In some sense they are still going on. The period for which the term is notorious, some time between 1790 and 1860, was marked as such precisely because of its *ideological* nature. The Duchess of Sutherland's commissioner, James Loch, wrote: 'It was one of the vast changes which the progress of the times demand and will have, and I shall feel ever grateful that I have had so much to do with (these) measures' (cited Richards 1982: 185). At ground level the Morayshire agricultural entrepreneur, Patrick Sellar, with his colleague William Young, provided a practical sense of purpose to the implementation of the fashionable ideas after 1809. 'It was during these removals' (in Strathnaver) 'that Patrick Sellar was alleged to have set fire to houses and barns, and caused the deaths of several people, including a nonagenarian woman called Chisholm. He was brought to trial and acquitted in 1816' (Richards 1982: 312).
    Derick Thomson writes, in his well-known poem, 'Srath Nabhair':

'Agus sud a'bhliadhna cuideachd
a shlaod iad a' chailleach do'n sitig,
a shealltain cho eòlach 's a bha iad air an Fhìrinn,

oir bha nid aig eunlaith an adhair
(agus cròthan aig na caoraich)
ged nach robh àit aice-se anns an cuireadh i a ceann fòidhpe.'

In his own translation: 'And that too was the year/ they hauled the old woman out onto the dung-heap,/ to demonstrate how knowledgeable they were in scripture,/ for the birds of the air had nests/ (and the sheep had folds)/ though she had no place in which to lay down her head' (Macaulay 1976: 153).

9 The line is from Iain Mac a' Ghobhain:

'Cò sgrìobh mi? Cò tha dèanamh bàrdachd
shanas-reice de mo chnàmhan?
Togaidh mi mo dhòrn gorm riutha:
'Gàidheal calma le a chànan.'

'Who wrote me? Who is making a poetry/of advertisements from my bones?/ I will raise my blue fist to them:/ "The stout Highlander with his language" ' (Macaulay 1976: 179).

Derick Thomson writes:

'Cha do dh'aithnich mi 'm brèid Beurla,
an lìomh Gallda bha dol air an fhiodh,
cha do leugh mi na facail air a' phràis,
cha do thuig mi gu robh mo chinneadh a' dol bàs.'

'I did not recognize the English braid,/ The Lowland varnish being applied to the wood,/ I did not read the words on the brass,/ I did not understand that my race was dying' (Macaulay 1976: 157).

The Glasgow and Edinburgh reviewers of Chapman's book were unnecessarily outraged, but see the careful consideration, in two long articles by James Shaw Grant, in the *Stornoway Gazette* (1978), and the appreciative review by Parman in *Man*.

10 The tendency for publicists to react ambiguously to those using the threatened language in a non-private way is comprehensible.

11 See Holt and Pym (1984), and its reviews.

12 It is not thought odd that the London regional television programme should have the Scots presenter interviewing local representatives with northern accents. The suddenness of city explosions, when they occur, suggests that there are some pockets of remoteness within these blank spaces!

13 Adomnan's *Life of St Columba* is a medieval classic of remote area studies.

14 The Baptist settlement of 1858 had an 'improving' philosophy; the German annexation of 1884 led to the establishment of plantations.

15 HIDB friends will not be offended; they read worse every day in the press. Ardveenish may yet take off. Lord Leverhulme's ambitions for Lewis and Harris were a benign form of paternalism.

16 Round a crofthouse in Lewis were the following items, according to the writer Derek Cooper (one of the most sensitive reporters of the Hebrides): '5 cwt van (*circa* 1950s); Ford tractor minus one wheel; fragment of pre-Great War reaper; upright piano; 37 blue plastic fishboxes; 7 green lemonade crates; 2 chimney pots; a sizeable pyramid of sand; a pile of cement blocks; 7 lobster creels; assorted timber; 2 bales of barbed wire (rusted); broken garden seat; Hercules bicycle frame; piece of unidentifiable machinery (loom?); a sofa' (Cooper 1985: 192).

17 This is a carefully fictionalized picture, and several islands are combined. Tamara Kohn has pointed out that Hebrideans nevertheless are used to pulling apart composite pictures and painstakingly reassembling them. In any case, there are no prizes!

References

ARDENER, E. (1956) *Coastal Bantu of the Cameroons*. London: International African Institute.
— (1970) Witchcraft, Economics and the Continuity of Belief. In M. Douglas (ed.) *Witchcraft Confessions and Accusations*. ASA Monographs 9. London: Tavistock Publications.
— (1971) Introductory Essay. In E. Ardener (ed.) *Social Anthropology and Language*. ASA Monographs 10, ix–cii. London: Tavistock Publications.
— (1975) The Voice of Prophecy: Further Problems in the Analysis of Events. The Munro Lecture, Edinburgh. Publication forthcoming.
(1978/1980) Some Outstanding Problems in the Analysis of Events. In E. Schwimmer (ed.) (1978) *Yearbook of Symbolic Anthropology* I: 103–21. London: Hurst. Reprinted in M. Foster and S. Brandes (eds) (1980) *Symbol as Sense*. New York: Academic Press.
— (1982) Social Anthropology, Language, and Reality. In D. Parkin (ed.) *Semantic Anthropology*. ASA Monographs 22, 47–70. London: Academic Press.
— (1985) Social Anthropology and the Decline of Modernism. In J. Overing (ed.) *Reason and Morality*. ASA Monographs 24, 47–70. London: Tavistock Publications.
ARDENER, E. and ARDENER, S. (1965) A Directory Study of Social Anthropologists. *British Journal of Sociology* (16) 4: 295–313.
ARDENER, E., ARDENER, S., and WARMINGTON, W. A. (1960) *Plantation and Village in the Cameroons*. London: Oxford University Press.
CHAPMAN, M. (1978) *The Gaelic Vision in Scottish Culture*. London: Croom Helm.
COHEN, A. (ed.) (1982) *Belonging*. Manchester: Manchester University Press.
COOPER, D. (1985) *The Road to Mingulay. A View of the Western Isles*. London: Routledge & Kegan Paul.
EDWARDS, J. (1985) *Language, Society and Identity*. London: Blackwell/Deutsch.
FERGUSON, A. (1767) *An Essay in the History of Civil Society*. London.
GELLNER, E. (1968) The New Idealism: Cause and Meaning in the Social Sciences. In I. Lakatos and A. Musgrave (eds) *Problems in the Philosophy of Science*. Amsterdam: North Holland.
— (1983) *Nations and Nationalism*. Oxford: Blackwell.
HOLT, H. and PYM, H. (1984) *A Very Private Eye. The Diaries, Letters and Notebooks of Barbara Pym*. London: Macmillan.
JOHNSON, S. and BOSWELL, J. (1775/1785) *Journey to the Western Islands and A Tour to the Hebrides* (edited by R. W. Chapman, 1930, and subsequent editions). Oxford: Oxford University Press.
LOOMIS, R. S. (1956) *Wales and the Arthurian Legend*. Cardiff: University of Wales Press.
MACAULAY, D. (ed.) (1976) *Nua-Bhàrdachd Ghàidhlig (Modern Scottish Gaelic Poems)*. Edinburgh: Southside.
MCDONALD, M. E. (1982) Social Aspects of Language and Education in Brittany. Oxford: unpublished thesis.

PARKIN, D. (ed.) (1982) *Semantic Anthropology*. ASA Monographs 22. London: Academic Press.

POCOCK, D. (1961) *Social Anthropology*. London: Sheed & Ward.

RICHARDS, E. (1982) *A History of the Highland Clearances. Agrarian Transformation and the Evictions 1746–1886*. London: Croom Helm.

Judith Okely

4 Fieldwork up the M1:
policy and political aspects[1]

In Britain, academics are moving into an era when social science, like the arts and humanities, as academic and intellectual production for its own sake, may regrettably receive diminishing financial support. In a post-colonial age, after the entry of Britain into the EEC and the weakening of trade links with the Commonwealth, there is even less rationale for what may masquerade as useful research in areas beyond a British 'home'. And home is an increasingly narrow territory in a post-colonial era. One panic response to this change was demonstrated at the 1983 ASA conference where it seemed that some anthropologists were ready to abandon any pretensions to intellectual research for its own sake and sell themselves and their protegés as merchant bankers and social engineers (Okely 1983a, 1983b). Little or no consideration was given to the political and academic implications of doing research to order.

There are indeed cases where social scientists might find lucrative pickings in servicing the state or multinationals. There are also other less clear-cut policy-oriented research projects where intellectual and possibly ethical/political compromise might not be inevitable. Policy-oriented research, either directly commissioned by government bodies or sponsored indirectly because it is vaguely considered useful, may in fact offer opportunities for advancing the subject, and for representing the interests of vulnerable groups in a practical way. For this to be so, greater awareness of the mechanics, constraints, and potential of policy-oriented research is necessary. Sustained contact between the researchers and the academy may yet salvage intellectual integrity and expand the anthropological field of knowledge. The academy in turn will be confronted by questions of political commitment which in the past may have been too easily swept aside.

Policy-oriented research of a kind has already been conducted by social scientists outside their own country. Those engaged in development studies, economists especially, have thrived on foreign consultancies. Some of the classical anthropological monographs, despite their authors' denials, were indirectly the result of the colonial administration's identification of 'problem' groups and areas (e.g. Evans-Pritchard's research on the Nuer). Access to the specific society depended in part on the administrators' belief that any information about the colonized might be useful to those in power. This context affected the focus of the research, in some cases encouraging the anthropologist to avoid comment on the interrelationship between the colonizer and colonized (Okely 1975). In other instances the anthropologists were directly commissioned to produce reports.

As British research funding becomes more insular, Eurocentric, and indeed ethnocentric, British social scientists may find themselves obliged to work only this side of Dover. A shift in research area among British anthropologists from Africa, Asia, and other parts of the globe towards Europe has already been noted (Rivière 1983). This may be a consequence both of funding limitations and of visa restrictions by new independent regimes. A similar swing towards anthropological research 'at home' has been occurring in the US (Messerschmidt 1981). Development studies have all but disappeared from the ESRC agenda. Although life does not end at Calais, it certainly ceases beyond the EEC, if we recall an MP's objection a couple of years ago to the then SSRC (now the ESRC) financing of a study of rural Poland. Publicly funded research which is policy oriented and deemed relevant to Britain seems to be the blueprint for the immediate future (Bell 1984). The notion of 'relevance' is quite different from that used by the student movements in the late 1960s when they, not governments, asked for 'relevance' in academia. For the students, relevance implied revolutionary change and a critique of the state rather than its enhancement.

In this paper I present as a case-study my experience in Britain of one policy-oriented research project in the early 1970s, when such research by anthropologists in Britain was considered peripheral in academia. My project was initiated within a research centre which, although nominally independent, was established by a Labour government in the 1960s. Half of the centre's finance came from the Department of the Environment and half from the Ford Foundation. The Centre was directed explicitly towards policy issues in planning, housing, traffic, poverty, and welfare benefits in Britain. The permanent research staff consisted mainly of economists, mathematicians, social administrators, and geographers. Professors of poverty flew in from the United States to conduct comparative research. The controversial quantitative study, *The Symmetrical Family* (1975) by the sociologists Young and Willmott received its major funding from the centre. The centre's director was a former professor of social administration. When the Conservatives were elected in 1970, a special meeting was arranged with the new minister of the DoE, Peter Walker, who appeared to favour the centre's continuing. However by 1980 it was closed as a 'quango' by a subsequent minister, Michael Heseltine.

In the early 1970s I was the only anthropologist employed at the centre, and on a fixed contract for a study of Gypsies and government policy in England (Adams *et al.* 1975). A historian and an educationalist were later recruited for part of the time. The project was financed by an independent charity and initiated by a civil servant seconded from the DoE. Although independent and indeed initiated with neither the Ministry's knowledge nor consent, the research was influenced by civil service practice and defined as policy oriented.

The context of this research cannot, of course, be replicated in the 1980s. In those days the centre's facilities of unlimited secretarial, photocopying, and clerical assistance cannot be presumed in university departments or elsewhere today. In the relative affluence of the 1960s and early 1970s, considerable research was encouraged both inside and outside Whitehall to back up legislative reforms. By the late 1970s, for reasons of economy, short-term contract research outside Whitehall was encouraged in preference to internal research by permanent staff. Some opportunities in policy research may therefore have increased for non-governmental researchers and academics. Social anthropologists have not, on the whole, obtained these contracts, although a few have been recruited as research officers, for instance, in university departments of planning and social administration. Here I also draw on my discussions with other anthropologists who have been engaged in policy-oriented research in this country.[2]

In policy-oriented research as generally practised in Britain, the topic tends to be set by those in political power, who define what knowledge is required and what should remain invisible. This is a very different tradition from the academy where research topics may be generated from current intellectual problems within the discipline and from the grass roots, in the case of Ph.D. students. Despite a tradition of knowledge for knowledge's sake, both scientists and social scientists have presented many examples of 'useful' research which would not have emerged if a narrow utilitarian topic had been defined at the outset.

The priorities of policy-oriented research are likely to be short-term expediency and may even have become irrelevant by the time the research is completed. The research topic risks being narrowly focused and bounded. Paradoxically, the caricature critique of anthropology that it ignores history and the wider structure is far more applicable to policy-oriented research which presumes short-term variables. The investigation of long-term historical processes, so often demanded of anthropology today, is not on the policy agenda. In addition, the strength of social anthropology's holistic tradition, if only at the micro level, is fractured in this kind of research. The interrelationship between beliefs and socio-economic structures is dismissed as too complex for immediate analysis. Instead, policy-oriented research may have to presume the macro structure as given, while emphasis may be placed on a dislocated theme and on the individual or household as isolate. Usually, the individuals are not known to each other, another contrast with traditional anthropological research where the so-called informants are known to each other and constantly intermingle.

This focus on the individual (or in some cases the household) as isolate is a legacy of positivism which in turn provides a neat methodological fit with the immediate demands of political decision-makers concerned with the predictable behaviour of an amorphous electoral majority. Political demands for the crudest representativeness or typicality can be supplied by empirical positivism which seeks trends, or dare I say laws, in terms of statistical majorities or averages. Apparently subject to electoral pressures, policy-makers will seek samples gathered randomly from vast and varied geographical regions within their constituency. Thus the interests of sub-groups, unless deemed 'problematic' (e.g. ethnic minorities) are lost in generalizations. Emphasis is placed on quantitative data in contrast to qualitative data which may be raided for 'anecdotes' and seen as mere soft flesh for the hard bone structure. People's attitudes and beliefs are reduced to the level of opinion polls.

Market research firms, the specialists in opinion polls, respond to and in turn dictate the format of policy-oriented research. They may, indeed, be in a position to exploit a certain naïvety and incompetence in the academic. The director of one market research firm informed me in an interview that contract research from academics was easy money since their demands were so simplistic, whereas contracts with small businessmen tended to be loss-makers because they sought to squeeze out as much information as possible.

Some of the techniques adopted as 'scientific' by empirical positivists have been abandoned, not only by physical scientists but also by the campaign managers of some political parties. The efficacy of certain qualitative methods has been recognized, even in the short term. For example, in the 1983 general election, the Conservative party geared its campaign to the daily reactions of the floating voter in marginal seats, mainly in southern England. These potential supporters were the subject of in-depth qualitative interviews several times a week. Feedback from these data was used within days to adjust the emphasis in campaign issues. Alternative attempts to investigate and respond to the interests of voters in safe Labour seats or in a nation-wide numerical majority of voters were recognized as strategically unproductive. Similarly, commercial research is also exploring the efficacy and straight financial rewards of qualitative material.

Despite these developments, it seems that the techniques of qualitative research, so finely developed by social anthropologists, have not penetrated the bureaucratic perspectives of policy-oriented research, either in government institutions or in the upper echelons of research bodies. Instead, the latter appear to feel pressures to police themselves in accord with scientistic criteria and an imagined public utility. Research proposals reflect the expectations of positivism with impeccable but often bogus hypotheses.

The sociologists Ditton and Williams who have specialized in topics such as deviancy, which are among the few accepted within sociology as best studied by qualitative methods, have described the elaborate smokescreen necessary in research applications where credence is given to formal techniques which are in practice unworkable (1981). Rather than owning up to this on completion of the research, the beneficiaries present their findings under another smokescreen, as close as possible to the initial proposal lest they jeopardize future applications. Consequently the grant-givers' prejudices remain unchallenged.

Social anthropologists will not, of course, have to justify their methods to their peers, or when applying to study the exotic abroad. Policy-makers and positivists cannot exert the same type of controls, indeed they may be both astonished and grateful that anthropologists are prepared to travel and risk hardship up the jungle. But when moving into areas more familiar to home-based policy-makers and into topics previously considered the preserve of other social scientists, anthropologists face problems of credibility. Social anthropology in the Third World also faces criticism, being alone mistakenly conflated with colonialism while sociology and economics are seen as 'scientific' and without a colonial past. There is also a preference among social scientists who themselves come from an urban élite to conduct a survey study of home-based urban topics rather than to attempt participant observation in rural areas where they might have to face isolation and discomfort. This is despite the fact that the vast majority of the world's population live in rural areas.

Social anthropologists doing research in Britain, but independent of anthropology departments, may be called upon to prove the viability of qualitative methods even before embarking upon fieldwork. In a number of research projects a great deal of valuable time has been wasted on crash courses in anthropological methods and theories for the research directors. Eventually the confidence of the young researchers is undermined. No such demands are made of those who propose quantitative techniques because they are a basic tenet of the British empiricist cosmology. This pressure on anthropologists to abandon their training will be exacerbated as long as they are compelled to work under the direction of other disciplines, e.g. those of university departments of planning and social administration which have extensive experience of contract research. The pressure may also increase now that anthropology is lost in multidisciplinary research committees of the ESRC. This is an unfortunate outcome of the abolition of the social anthropology committee when the SSRC was reorganized.

Beyond the positivistic inertia and the search for typicality in an amorphous majority, there may be another explanation for the continuing preference for quantitative methods. Such methods favour 'umbrella men' in a rigid research hierarchy with a division of labour between data-gatherers and armchair analysts who retain control of the material. The subordinates will have only a partial view of the results and may not understand the implications of the questions. They cannot innovate and stray from the format. The armchair analysts write up the material and publish it under their own names. Conventionally the data-gatherers, usually female, are nameless, although a new benevolence is indicated in the preface of Young and Willmott's later study, *The Symmetrical Family* (1975: xi) where nearly a page is devoted to the names of those who administered the questionnaires (forty-nine women and three men) in what remains an asymmetrical research tradition.

By contrast, the methodological traditions of social anthropology do not favour a similar hierarchy. The participant observer will have the clearest access to and comprehension of the material. It cannot be read through like a checklist with neat boxes and columns. Field-notes can best be made sense of by the same participant observer. In my own case, my research centre was so unfamiliar with the implications of qualitative anthropological research that it was stated that ideally a different person should write up the material from my field-notes in order to avoid 'bias'. But when the thirty daily pages of field-notes over twelve months began to appear in the central office, the idea was abandoned! The separation between fieldworker and final author would have been possible if I had merely administered questionnaires. Given these structural differences between the two types of research, anthropologists employed as research assistants for non-anthropologists may succumb to pressures to become mechanical data-collectors so long as their employers need to produce publications and reports under their own and not their assistants' names.

A case-study

Throughout the 1960s the Gypsies or Travellers had increasingly been identified by local and national government as a political 'problem'. Elsewhere I have documented how this was largely as a result of 1960 legislation which encouraged local authorities to drive Gypsies off land which hitherto they had used legally (Okely 1983a: 105–24). The 1965 census was published as an expanded HMSO report (1967) after controversy within Whitehall, some of whose senior representatives would have preferred only limited information to be made available to the public. Both this report and that chaired by Plowden on primary school teaching presented the Gypsies as a deprived group rather than as an ethnic one with little desire for assimilation into the dominant sedentary society. Thus any potential state policy presumed that the eventual aim would be one of assimilation.

The deprivation approach, combined with the report's exposure of the Gypsies' lack of legal stopping-places and harassment by the police and local authorities, was used to argue for an additional section to Eric Lubbock's 1968 Caravan Sites Act. Ostensibly a private member's bill, the Labour government secretly provided free drafting in exchange for Lubbock's acceptance of the Gypsy section. No political party past or present could afford to be associated directly with seemingly pro-Gypsy legislation. The Act made it a duty for local authorities to provide sites, but only for a limited number and in exchange for ruthless powers to move all remaining Gypsies out of their area. The Act was mistakenly heralded as a victory for the Travelling people. Some anxiety was felt among Gypsy supporters within the civil service, there being a feeling that whereas the local authorities were amply represented through their well-organized lobbies, no one really knew what the Travellers wanted. Hence the imaginative move to instigate research independent of Whitehall but which would inform and influence policy-makers.

The controversy over research into the wishes of an ethnic minority spread to unexpected quarters. A younger core of the centre's permanent research staff who regarded themselves as on the left threatened a revolt. 'They're only a minority,' protested a radical geographer. 'That's our money,' declared a brilliant mathematician. They attempted to veto the research. Here again, like the positivists, the emphasis was on the needs of an amorphous liberal or utilitarian majority. The would-be radicals were not concerned with the more sophisticated political question as to whether research among minorities might be intrusive and exploitative.

More worrying was the reaction of a senior civil servant in the DoE who sent a letter to the board of governors of the 'independent' research centre reminding them of the source of half their funding and protesting at the research project, insisting that all research on Gypsies should be done within Whitehall. The familiar argument was reiterated that the needs of the majority (e.g. the problems of house dwellers, not those of nomadic caravan dwellers) should be top priority. This type of response within Whitehall towards research into a controversial minority showed little change whether under a Labour or Conservative government. It was never envisaged, as some have stated (Acton 1983), that research would be useful for controlling the minority. Rather, it was feared that the research might stimulate demands for sympathetic reforms and thus increase the government's problems. This is a very different standpoint from that articulated by some representatives of minorities who may also resist research, but because they (rightly in some cases), equate it with espionage. In all instances, there are parallels with the problems faced by anthropologists seeking permission to do fieldwork abroad. Contrary to some expectations, anthropology at home, without the need for visas, in no way ensures free access. Moreover, political controversy cannot be encapsulated in the period of fieldwork when conducted in the anthropologist's country of residence; it has to be lived with before, during, and after fieldwork.

Perhaps the indifference or hostility towards Gypsies from both ends of the political spectrum is explained by the fact that since they were 'only a minority', research into their plight was not seen as informative for any grand theory or politics for the amorphous majority. It seemed that the Gypsy project was only supported in the upper echelons of the research centre because it was sincerely believed that a policy of assimilation into the majority society was the inevitable outcome. When, for instance, towards the end of the project I produced evidence of the Gypsies' viable and continuing economic niche when geographically mobile, thus undermining a 'deprivation' theory, an unexpected response was, 'so the communists were right in destroying the Gypsies' waggons and horses and outlawing travelling in Eastern Europe!'.

Gouldner has described how in the US in the late 1960s and early 1970s there were ample opportunities for 'well-heeled' researchers who collaborated with federal agencies. Such a 'sociology of young men with friends in Washington' (Gouldner 1973: 49) found some echoes on a lesser scale in the major policy programmes in Britain and in my research centre. There is a familiar ring in Gouldner's description of American social science funding agencies:

'whose cosmopolitan sympathies are not personally and deeply engaged by a daily encounter with urban suffering: and whose fears are not deeply aroused by a close dependence upon the deteriorating urban community . . . they approach the task of modern urban reform with a thin-lipped, business like rationality.'

(Gouldner 1973: 48)

The view of Regent's Park from the centre's Nash Terrace offices which my colleagues and I enjoyed was very seductive. In the quest for scientific objectivity and typicality through random samples, it would have been simpler to submit to my employers' determination that I organize questionnaires for social workers and others to interview Gypsies nation-wide. Under that format I could have got by with an occasional day trip to Gypsy camps near the metropolis for a few hours of what sociologists call 'p.o.', instead of living in a caravan for over twelve months in the shadow of motorways. The often overwhelming pressure to deploy quantitative survey methods arose from my employers' sincere belief that these would be the only means of influencing government policy-makers. At the outset the declared ideal was to be a report 'with a statistical table on every page'. Fortunately, after five months these plans were abandoned, partly because the Gypsies proved brilliant at deflecting questions (Okely 1983a: 38–48).

Here my experience is relevant to future novice anthropologists working in intellectual isolation with policy researchers and other disciplines. The successful outcome to the struggle over methodology was thanks to the moral and intellectual support which I received during intermittent visits to the Institute of Social Anthropology at Oxford, where I was simultaneously registered for a higher degree. Without this I might have succumbed to the prevailing orthodoxy. There would have been no investigation of the total context – the

Travellers' economy, pollution beliefs, political and kinship organization, all of which are crucial in discussing policy. They are not just knowledge for knowledge's sake. In so far as a publication based on a conventional survey would have revealed anything, it would have been a further record of the imaginative and deliberately confusing answers which Gypsies give to naïve outsiders. The majority of Travellers would probably have said that they wanted to give up travelling, move into houses, send their children to school, and take up 'regular' wage labour employment. If policy-makers had acted upon this they would have been bewildered by the Travellers' resistance to a mass assimilation programme.

There are similar examples of conflicting results arising from different types of research in the study of Third World societies (Leach 1967). Tambiah, in a devastating critique of development programmes and theories, asserts that many anthropologists are in a position to insert a corrective to prevailing paradigms 'precisely because we have pitched our tents on the peripheries of societies, both territorially in distant provinces and socially among the common people at the bottom of the hierarchy' (1983: 10).

Tambiah also documents the preference for quantitative techniques among planning experts and implementers of development programmes who saw anthropology:

'Not as the queen of the social sciences but as the mother of low status servants and handmaids fitted for the labour intensive job of pitching their tents in the outbacks and wilderness. Anthropologists were to collect information which "could then be processed and converted to variables like 'the cultural factor' or 'the psychic components of income and consumption' in macro models". . . . Because of the anthropologist's search for an authentic knowledge of the other, which required a relatively long period of residence in the field as participant and witness, she or he readily consented to employment as a field consultant while other professionals landed the contracts with AID and the IMF, and cooked up the designs and the budgets, seasoned with surveys, censuses and cost-benefit equations.'

(Tambiah 1983: 4)

Eventually field research on Gypsies vindicated the method of intensive participant observation. Questions about viable samples and adequate numbers never surfaced when the report was publicized. In fact I accumulated accurate, in-depth quantitative material for seventy-three families. My three colleagues, employed on other aspects and for shorter periods, produced information for a further fifty families. There were some quantitative tables, but more important was the systematic field material which *explained* the figures and gave the total context. Detailed case-studies and direct quotes authenticated the arguments and conclusions. Such concrete information cannot easily be discredited in the way that experts play with others' statistics. The Travellers' continuing commitment to an independent identity, their viable economic niche, their social reproduction through marriage alliances and an alternative education, and their rejection of house dwelling and wage labour demolished the deprivation model and any assimilationist policies. From then on, any government planning mass assimilation could no longer claim it was in accord with the Travellers' wishes.

Despite Whitehall's earlier attempts to stop the research, government officials finally made use of it. Indeed, by the time the research emerged, repeated questions in parliament exposed the government's paucity of knowledge of the Travellers' conditions. A new Labour government therefore employed an official, John Cripps, in 1976 to investigate. His report is in many sections a paraphrase of our book and in the preface he acknowledges this debt (1976). Our observations coincided with those from Gypsy representatives, and the government finally recognized the Gypsies' right to continue their way of life as Travellers. Thus a major shift in policy was effected in principle and our research team were pleased to have been implicated.

This use by policy advisers of the independent research was only, however, via a circuitous route. The research was not immediately read by the key officials in Whitehall, so that the earlier pressures to mould the format to their liking would have been, as I had suspected, to waste an opportunity to do solid work of both political and intellectual import. Some time after the centre's report was published, a senior civil servant in the Gypsy unit at the DoE telephoned to ask, 'Are you sure they were the *real* Gypsies you studied?' The research director pointed out that the second chapter of the book was devoted entirely to dispelling the myth of the 'real' Gypsy. A copy of our conclusions was sent to the relevant officials of every local authority in England and Wales who were then invited to attend a mass meeting in Caxton Hall. The research team shared a platform with Gypsy representatives and other interested parties. The book was liberally displayed around the hall. In the end, only two copies were sold, one fortunately to a literate Gypsy. The research has continued to filter through to students, teachers, support groups, literate Gypsies, social workers, and other local authority employees. In the long run the research has been used by some local authorities who have sought alternative policies to harassment (e.g. the former Greater London Council). Its wider anthropological content has been its strength. As predicted, it remains largely unread by racist councillors and journalists who have vested interests in stereotypes and myths (see Davie 1985).

It would be naïve to suggest that policy research by academics will automatically influence the decision-makers in line with the policy recommendations. The research may not be read in ways which the authors intended. It depends on the political circumstances and interests of those in power. Politicians will not be converted to tolerance of an ethnic minority if they have a vested interest in assimilation. A Durham local official grinned mischievously as he described to me how he deliberately quoted some bits of our conclusion and omitted others, thus emphasizing our mild acceptance of some permanent residential sites while concealing our pleas for temporary transit camping-sites. The 1979 and 1983 Conservative governments have speeded up the granting of special powers against Gypsies, but have ceased to prompt local authorities into making any camping provisions. Thus the use that is made of policy research is subject to the vagaries of those in power.

There was one area where the argument for intensive, qualitative methods was not fully won, and that concerned the attitudes and experience of the local authorities and house dwellers towards Gypsies. The historian recruited to the team wrote a chapter on the history of policy and confrontations in one area, but no systematic participant observation study was completed of officials and rate-payers. Instead, questionnaire interviews were conducted with a representative from every local authority which had provided an official site in England and Wales. In order to gain access and disguise our real motives, it was suggested that questions be included on the site facilities, followed by questions on attitudes. Gradually the details on water closets, taps, huts, and rents developed their own momentum and the attitudinal questions lost significance. The chapter on attitudes spoke more of plumbing than of politics and processes (Adams and Dean 1975). The interviewers found that the officials were ready to reveal a great deal more through asides, once the formal interview was completed, but this information was lost, partly because the questionnaires were delegated and because the information could not be followed up. No information on house dwellers' relationships with Gypsies was adequately studied. Here again, a qualitative study would have been valuable. I suspect that participant observation was ultimately seen as the only viable methodology for a non-literate stigmatized minority, whereas questionnaires were still clung to as best for members of the literate, 'rational', dominant society. Thus the struggle over methodology for anthropology at home still needs to be won. It speaks also of the relations between the dominant society and a minority.

In addition to the theoretical and methodological problems associated with arguing with others the case for anthropology in policy-related research, there may also be institutional constraints quite unfamiliar to those accustomed to research practice in universities. The ensuing discussion may look rather like undigested field-notes. I did not set out to study anthropologically the differences in work practice found in bureaucracies and universities. My perspective was from the latter and, with a personal commitment to anthropological research, it is difficult to present the bureaucratic practice as neutral subject matter. However, the bureaucrat's own commitment cannot be explained as mere conspiratorial pettiness.

On this project, it was surprising and painful to learn that 'academic' was a pejorative word meaning 'useless, obscurantist, idoysncratic' and in a binary opposition to the word 'policy'. No library research could be conducted without permission and even then only occasional visits were allowed. This attitude was consistent with the restricted perspective believed necessary for such policy research and where a broad context for its questions is seen as mere diversion. Occasional day visits to a university anthropology department for background reading, seminars and discussions with lecturers and postgraduates had to be taken out of my three weeks' annual leave. This problem was neatly resolved when each weekend in the field was calculated as owed leave. When not engaged in fieldwork, the formula remained a nine-to-five office routine in a room with others engaged in quite different activities. Two telephones rang at intervals in the communal office, housing experts held discussions with visiting fellows, and job interviews took place while the other researchers sat in a corner attempting to write. After a brief period with the place to myself, I was joined by a lonely American professor completing his book on urban traffic. He was either at his typewriter, which sounded like a light machine-gun, or interrogating me about 'swinging London'. Attempts to be allowed to write in peace and isolation at home or in a library were seen as near truancy. Such working conditions for the civil service may explain the difficulties involved in preparing reports.

There is a fundamental difference between university-based work and that linked with bureaucracies. In a university, undergraduates from the age of eighteen are given separate study rooms, are expected to work in silence in communal libraries and to organize their own routine. In bureaucracies, only the senior staff towards the end of their careers can expect to have an individual room, and work is clearly demarcated in time and space. On the Gypsy project, both before and after fieldwork, time spent in the office was often wasted, but our bodily presence in the correct location was perceived as sufficient justification for a salary. I would find myself looking forward to the evenings when I could get down to *real* work. The conflict between university and bureaucratic research, artificially dichotomized as academic versus policy, is not easily resolved. Even separate office space for the researcher does not guarantee intellectual freedom. Another anthropologist employed as a research officer described how her employer, a planning professor, also demanded a nine-to-five presence in her personal office and would check up on her activities every twenty minutes, making any consistent train of thought impossible. His previous experience was as a government planner with the task of 'managing' sixty planning staff. Professors of social administration with experience of training social workers may also supervise researchers according to 'good' management rather than intellectual criteria. This form of supervision associated with office work contrasts dramatically with that between Ph.D. students and supervisors who, in the arts and social sciences, meet once a week at most.

Policy-oriented research conducted in a civil service/bureaucratic ambience may entail diminished control over the authors' final product and a bias in favour of those with political power. During the Gypsy project, draft chapters on the history of two local authorities' policies were sent to the local officials for comments. Not surprisingly, they objected to any criticism of their policies and practices. One colleague had to consent to sections of his chapter being eliminated by the 'independent' research centre. In my case, an opposing interpretation written by the local official was inserted into the conclusion of my chapter making nonsense of the preceding evidence, and confusing the reader into thinking that the conclusion was written by the same author. No parallel consultation and intervention was ever considered necessary for representatives of the Gypsies.

Unlike the priorities in universities, named publications are not crucial in the career advancement of bureaucrats, who often seek anonymity for self-protection. These conflicting priorities may be acted out in policy research. Despite a written assurance from the governor of the research centre as to copyright, individual authorship of all the chapters in our final publication was erased at the proof stage. Attempts to obtain a footnote acknowledging authorship of my chapters failed. The work of the different research officers disappeared under 'et al.'. (Adams et al. 1975.) My chapters continue to be credited to others (Cripps 1976; Forrester 1985) and I have been thought to be co-author of chapters with which I disagree. In the 1980s, anthropologists employed on policy projects have experienced similar difficulties and have been reluctant to press their case, for fear of jeopardizing references for future employment. Recently, for example, an anthropologist research officer saw her final report truncated and reassembled under her employer's name.

There may be similar problems at home or abroad concerning control over the raw material of confidential field-notes. In the final publication, the anthropologist will have meticulously concealed people's intimate revelations and identities, whereas field-notes remain necessarily unexpurgated, and pseudonyms are impracticable. The fieldworker has an overarching obligation to restrict the readership of field-notes, especially when he or she has been the confidant of the vulnerable and underprivileged. Tambiah makes a parallel statement concerning the anthropologists' loyalty in the Third World. The development anthropologist has to 'serve and interpret for his Western donor and patron' and negotiate with the 'ruling élites and intelligentsia who have their own interests and even misconceptions' and he must 'serve, fortify and protect his third master, who though not immaculate in their conceptions, shall always claim his primary loyalty, namely the ordinary people, both beneficiaries and victims of the outsiders' (Tambiah 1983: 14).

When our project ceased at the London research centre we were informed that all our field-notes and files belonged to the centre and that if we wanted to consult them we would have to do so on the premises. This was probably just the cautious response of a civil servant. But the centre was in no way affected by any Official Secrets Act. Notwithstanding, I retained a copy of my notes for doctoral work, for which I had in any case received government funds via the then SSRC. More serious than the problem of personal access to one's own field-notes was the risk that these same notes might be used for other purposes and to the Gypsies' detriment. In the late 1970s, when the independent centre was closed, it was decided that all research material would be automatically allocated to the Department of the Environment. This would have meant a betrayal, with perhaps terrible consequences, for the Gypsy families who had confided in us. Named individuals in files could have been located immediately in clearly identified areas. Presuming that my former director and I were of the same opinion, I arranged for the removal of all the material, since we had once discussed sending it under a thirty-year restriction to a university whose library had a special collection of Gypsy studies.

The new research centre off Trafalgar Square now had an atmosphere of the last days of Saigon. I traced our precious notes and files, scattered and mildewed in a basement, formerly a morgue, and with the help of companions, loaded them into a van. Triumphantly I informed my colleagues only to learn that someone had arranged for our material to be sent straight to the 'Gypsy section' of the DoE. I found myself negotiating with a person who now identified entirely with Whitehall interests and who believed that the material belonged to the DoE, although the project's finance had come from an independent charity under the centre's umbrella. By contrast, I saw it as a moral and political duty to retain every copy of my own notes, despite orders to deliver them to the Ministry. Today the detailed confidences of Gypsies encountered by my colleagues are in the hands of the 'appropriate' government department.

Fortunately, the Gypsies are likely to be protected by the civil servants' indifference to any material dating back even two years; the files will just gather dust. A Scottish official concerned with Travellers has ingenuously attempted to allay my fears by affirming the liberal, good intentions of civil servants who would use information only to the Travellers' benefit. However, there are dangerous precedents of which any anthropologist must be aware. The Nazi government in Germany made use of 'well-meaning' anthropologists' genealogies and other material on Gypsies to facilitate arrests and genocide. In turn, post-war German anthropologists continued working secretly on the family files accumulated by the Nazis, until in the 1980s Gypsies staged a protest at the research institution. These facts about Germany have been well publicized among Gypsy representatives in Britain. Anthropology could be in bad odour at home as well as abroad, if it was thought that anthropologists were supplying confidential data to a government department.

Having outlined the difficulties of inserting an anthropological approach into policy research, which in Britain has long been associated with bureaucracy, I may have distracted the reader from the intellectual as well as the political potential in policy research. My intention in this paper is to encourage anthropologists in this venture. It becomes a challenge to demonstrate the profound contribution which social anthropology can make to fundamental issues at home, as well as abroad. But that contribution risks being lost through the tunnel vision of the patrons of policy research. Take, for example, the Gypsies' pollution beliefs, which would be seen as a worthwhile topic within British social anthropology. These beliefs demonstrated, at the symbolic and perhaps unconscious level, the Gypsies' continuing desire for ethnic autonomy and a rejection of assimilation (Okely 1983a). However, analysis could only be pursued after the completion of the policy project mainly because, at the research centre, this area of research was seen as mere scholastic indulgence. The same feelings were indicated towards the historical treasure trove of *The Journal of Gypsy Lore Society*. The more obviously 'relevant' aspects, like the Gypsies' economy, were also best understood by intensive anthropological research.

Ultimately, the requirement in policy research to answer specific questions offers a stimulating dialectic between these and the broader, less focused ethnography. An examination of the state's policies brings the anthropologist precisely into areas which the discipline has been criticized for neglecting, namely the relationship between the micro-community and the wider system. The anthropologist is also drawn into investigating not only the so-called 'problem group', but also the powerful who may have created the problem. Laura Nader argues the case for 'studying up':

'If we look at the literature based on fieldwork in the United States, we find a relatively abundant literature on the poor, the ethnic groups, the disadvantaged; there is comparatively little field research on the middle class and very little first hand work on the upper classes.'

(Nader 1974: 289)

When embarking on the Gypsy policy project, I was encouraged to read a vast number of local government reports on Gypsies, ostensibly in order to find out about the latter. When I had finished I had instead gained significant insights into non-Gypsy classifications of Gypsies and attitudes which guided the dominant society's policies.

Policy research may give the anthropologist access to a range of officials as well as to their documents. Local government officials were desperate to confide in me about their experiences of negotiating with house dwellers and Gypsies about camp sites. I was seen as a surrogate official, and the non-Gypsies assumed that we shared the same world view (Okely 1984). Already, some anthropologists have been looking at planners and planning as major field material rather than as unproblematic factual sources (Wright 1984). The potential anthropologist employee on a policy project may protest that his/her brief is too restricted to allow much intellectual breadth. It is a considerable reassurance to discover that, once the argument for extended participant observation is won, no matter how limited the questions and focus demanded by the contractors, intensive fieldwork in the end produces the necessary wider ethnography. This material, like that from any standard field-trip, can be mined long after the contract is over. The problems today for the research workers are finding the incentives, maintaining contact with the academy, and acquiring time and financial resources for writing up. These are the major difficulties, but the intellectual, methodological, and technical obstacles outlined earlier can be overcome.

The anthropologist researching at home cannot get on to a plane after fieldwork and disappear into the academy. The people studied remain around; both they and others have a different kind of interest in the resulting publications. There may be repercussions in detailed note-taking which anthropologists returning from fieldwork abroad never face. Professional ethics may be closely scrutinized both inside and outside the academy. It is acceptable for an anthropologist to describe the life of headhunters in Borneo or to discuss overseas practices of infanticide. It is a different matter to confess to having been drawn into a shoplifting spree in the home counties or to having been a character witness at the Old Bailey for a Gypsy charged with attempted murder and possession of firearms. Anthropologists abroad may exchange mutual exoticisms with detachment, but presented with parallel practices at home, they respond as citizens.

These aspects pale before decisions of a political nature, with which the anthropologist is regularly confronted. Awareness as to possible collaboration with the ruling authority is as relevant at home as it was abroad in colonial times. There may be occasions when there seems to be no conflict in policy research between the interests of the patrons, and those of the client anthropologist and the people studied. Vulnerable minorities in land disputes have commissioned the services of anthropologists. But generally, policy research contracts are offered by those with superior financial resources and political power. In all cases, the anthropologist cannot simply retreat into academic neutrality.

Policy-oriented research should be distinguished from action research. The former may be directed towards the interests of a governing élite, whereas action research is concerned with the interests of the governed and may be geared to produce change at grass-roots level instead of from above (see Huizer 1979). This can be a creative challenge for the research skills of the anthropologist.

Although the Gypsy project was defined as policy oriented, my colleagues and I were determined that it would be of use to the minority. Indeed, the research was initiated with that intention. Since only a tiny number of Gypsies are literate, we were not faced with the question of the extent to which we were writing for them. Some social scientists working with literate groups try to resolve this dilemma by writing two books – one for academic peers, and another for a popular readership and the people concerned. In the case of non-literate Gypsies, there was the embarrassment of garbled, false versions of my publication being reported to them. My later book was given a media hype in the *Daily Mirror, Daily Telegraph*, and on national and local radio stations. The findings were exoticized and distorted. Thus we are faced with the loss of control over the reading and presentation of our writing, especially when it is published in the country of the people concerned. But, at the same time, publicity may bring the work to a wider 'relevant' readership. Sometimes a popularizing style adopted by the anthropologist has satisfying results. My most rewarding review came from a Gypsy who read my article in *New Society* (Okely 1983b) and wrote a letter to the magazine describing it as 'well written' and asking for more like it. Another Gypsy hearing me at a meeting with police officials said, 'You put into words what we want to say'. Such comments are a moral and political vindication for long-term research by an outsider.

At home, the anthropologist will jostle with alternative experts and political representatives. In the case of the Gypsies, there are a number of individuals who have filled the power vacuum between Whitehall and the decentralized nomadic group. Some have no Gypsy descent. One, a public school son of an East Anglian estate agent, has appeared on television in Gypsy kerchief talking of 'my people'. I have been damagingly described in a journal of race studies as a government agent and criticized for not distributing machine guns to Gypsies – as if they needed an outsider to advise on strategy. The anthropologist working at home is not cosily cocooned from questions of commitment.

While being ready to lampoon the Gorgio (non-Gypsy) groupies (who are of the same class and ethnic origins as myself) for their delusions of grandeur, there is a real dilemma concerning any public exposure by the anthropologist of emerging 'leaders' of Gypsy origin. Some Gypsy representatives can be compared to the colonial chiefs invented and salaried by the British abroad in exchange for controlling 'their' people in a system of indirect rule. They have no grass-root following, but power and salaries from Whitehall (see Davie 1985). In some instances, they may be effective as a pro-Gypsy lobby, but in others they may do a great deal of harm in collaborating and compromising with the state to the detriment of the group. In this vacuum, the anthropologist may present an alternative perspective as intermediary, but cannot presume to be a representative, let alone a fictive member of the group.

To conclude: the anthropological academy has to consider in depth the implications of its bland hopes for policy research contracts commissioned by government and bureaucratic institutions. Policy research as practised in Britain confronts the anthropologist with a range of questions only partially discussed in the academy. The anthropologist has often to argue the case for participant observation, qualitative methods, and a holistic approach at every stage of research. The subject matter risks being focused according to the interests of the powerful, if not censored at the outset. Questions of allegiance to the people studied are not debated in a personal, moral vacuum. Neutral professional ethics may broaden into profounder questions of political commitment. There may be conflicting obligations when the people studied may include both representatives of the government and the governed. And there are grave dangers that the material will be misappropriated, rewritten, or misquoted. Nevertheless, there are exciting possibilities in such research. Once given the theoretical and methodological freedom, the anthropologist may be obliged to explore crucial questions of the links between the state and local processes, thus stretching the discipline beyond its traditional boundaries. There can be moral and political rewards in seeing informed and effective policies put into practice, and the anthropologist is given the opportunity to use academic skills to the advantage of people who are often unrepresented.

Notes

1 For reasons of space I have had to exclude the last section of this paper delivered at the ASA conference which discussed personal aspects, to be developed in a future publication.
2 They may prefer to remain anonymous.

References

ACTON, T. (1983) Review in *Ethnic and Racial Studies*. Oxford.
ADAMS, B. and DEAN, C. (1975) Local Authority Site Provision: Policies, Practices and Attitudes. Chapter 9 in Adams *et al.* (1975).
ADAMS, B., OKELY, J., MORGAN, D., and SMITH, D. (1975) *Gypsies and Government Policy in England*. London: Heinemann.
BELL, C. (1984) The SSRC: Restructured and Defended. In C. Bell and H. Roberts (eds) *Social Researching*. London: Routledge & Kegan Paul.
CRIPPS, J. (1976) *Accommodation for Gypsies*. London: DoE and HMSO.
DAVIE, M. (1985) Notebook. *The Observer*, p. 18, 3 February, and correspondence 10 and 17 February.
DITTON, J. and WILLIAMS, R. (1981) *The Fundable Versus the Doable*. Glasgow: University of Glasgow Press.
FORRESTER, B. (1985) *The Travellers' Handbook*. London: Interchange.
GOULDNER, A. (1973) *For Sociology*. Harmondsworth: Penguin.
HMSO (1967) *Gypsies and other Travellers*. London: HMSO.
HUIZER, G. (1979) Research through Action: Some Practical Experiences with Peasant Organization. In G. Huizer and B. Mannheim (eds) *The Politics of Anthropology*. The Hague: Mouton.
LEACH, E. (1967) An Anthropologist's Reflections on a Social Survey. In D. Jongmans and P. Gutkind (eds) *Anthropologists in the Field*. Assen: Van Gorcum.
MESSERSCHMIDT, D. (1981) *Anthropologists at Home in North America*. Cambridge: Cambridge University Press.
NADER, L. (1974) Up the Anthropologists – Perspectives Gained from Studying Up. In D. Hymes (ed.) *Reinventing Anthropology*. New York: Vintage Books.

OKELY, J. (1975) The Self and Scientism. *Journal of the Anthropology Society*, Oxford **6**(3): 171–88.

— (1983a) *The Traveller-Gypsies*. Cambridge: Cambridge University Press.

— (1983b) Why Gypsies Hate Cats and Love Horses. *New Society*, February.

— (1983c) A View from the Terraces. *RAIN* **58**: 12.

— (1984) Fieldwork in the Home Counties. *RAIN* **61**: 4–6.

RIVIÈRE, P. (1983) The Future of Anthropology. Paper given to ASA Conference, Cambridge.

TAMBIAH, S. (1983) An Anthropologist's Manifesto for the Eighties. Paper given to ASA Conference, Cambridge.

WRIGHT, S. (1984) Rural Communities and Decision Makers. *RAIN* **63**: 9–13.

YOUNG, M. and WILLMOTT, P. (1975) *The Symmetrical Family*. Harmondsworth: Pelican.

Orvar Löfgren

---

5 Deconstructing Swedishness:
culture and class in modern Sweden

ૐ

Between national character and the little community

The old saying 'Anthropology begins at home' was until quite recently more of an unwelcome economic and practical necessity than a moral virtue among social anthropologists.

In that other branch of anthropology, among the European ethnologists, the situation has been a different one. With great simplification one can argue that nineteenth-century Western nations with colonies tended to develop an anthropological study of primitive societies, while the ethnographical interest in countries with few or no colonies was first directed towards 'the primitives within', the rapidly disintegrating, traditional peasant culture.

This was the case in the Scandinavian countries as well as in most of Central Europe, where folklorists and ethnologists salvaged the past and helped to construct the myth of a traditional and national peasant culture (cf. Löfgren 1980: 189 ff).

During the last few decades European ethnologists have developed the study of contemporary Western societies as well as continuing to work on the historical anthropology of pre-industrial Europe. This shift was greatly influenced by theoretical perspectives from general anthropology. When I started out as a European ethnologist in the early 1960s there was an influx of British structural-functionalist and later interactionist ideas. The study of contemporary Sweden took the form of fieldwork in rural areas and marginal communities. The search for the little community, 'the organic whole', took most of us out to the Swedish periphery rather than to the core. (My own Ph.D. thesis dealt with a fishing community, not an atypical choice, as the idea was to steer away from anything that smelled of sociology and find as 'anthropological' a setting as possible.)

The influence of the British tradition of community studies was very marked. There was the idea that somehow a picture of Swedish society and culture could be created by adding community study after community study, creating a typology-cum-continuum of the kind represented by Ronald Frankenberg's classic book on communities in Britain (Frankenberg 1966).

Early in the 1970s the influence of mainly American interactionism and 'the new ethnography' increased. The focus was moved from communities to subcultures, from the study of social structure to cultural scenes and Goffmanian total institutions. These were the years when American cultural anthropologists rediscovered the USA and started to work in more or less exotic ethnographic settings, from dope joints and cocktail bars to retirement homes. Again the focus was often on the cultural periphery rather than on mainstream society (cf. the bibliography in Spindler and Spindler 1983). Later in the 1970s there was a gradual drift away from micro-level analysis under the influence of historical materialism and structuralism. Marxist perspectives reintroduced a historical interest but at first also a disinterest in cultural analysis. In the 1980s we find among Swedish European ethnologists a somewhat eclectic blending of different perspectives, as for example in attempts to combine Marxist and symbolist approaches in a new interest in the study of the production and reproduction of cultural systems.

There is hardly anything surprising about this academic scenario, which can be found in many other anthropological settings. The reason for this short outline is to set the theoretical scene for a research project on culture and class in nineteenth- and twentieth-century Sweden, which has been carried out by ten of us at the Department of European Ethnology, University of Lund.[1] When the project was started in 1979 most of us had been socialized in the community study tradition, later developing interests in various forms of symbolic anthropology and culturalist Marxist perspectives. We wanted to find a different approach to the study of Swedish society and culture, based upon an idea of approaching the totality rather than the local variations, focusing on mainstream cultural formations. The problem was that the study of something like Swedish culture was more or less defined as an impossible or an unsuitable task for an ethnologist. Back in the 1930s European ethnologists had been busy generalizing about national character, popular mentalities, folk psychology, etc. Some of these interests took the road towards *Blut und Boden* in Nazi Germany, others were abandoned because of their speculative nature. Later attempts by cultural anthropologists schooled in the Culture and Personality tradition also acted as a deterrent. The pictures given of, for example, Japanese and German culture were very much reflections of an American middle-class culture. The insensibility to class differences and the ahistorical approach certainly gave this whole field of study of national cultures a bad reputation in the 1960s and 1970s. Cultural generalizations were definitely *out* (cf. the discussion in Bock 1980).

Another problem was the realization that we lacked the tools to problematize contemporary everyday culture. Our home-blindness was marked and the often trivial observations of many contemporary sociological studies of

Swedish society underlined this dilemma. While students of more exotic settings have devised techniques for getting *into* a new culture, European ethnologists have struggled with the problem of getting *out*, of distancing themselves from their far-too-familiar surroundings.

An historical anthropology of the present

For us the historical perspective became such a tool. Instead of starting in the 1970s we decided to move a century back, to analyse the cultural roots of the present: for example, how could a middle-class world view of today or working-class images of society be studied as cultural products, constructed over time? We decided to focus on the period of the last hundred years or so, when Sweden was transformed from an agrarian to an industrial, and then to an urban, society. This development was later, and thus more compressed, than in many other European settings. At first we had somewhat vague ideas about how to tackle this rather grandiose task. One thing was certain, our aim was not to write social or cultural history. Our starting-point was a theoretical interest in cultural dynamics and the problems of how culture is produced, reproduced, and changed in society over time. First of all we wanted to look at the relations between class formation and culture building.

We did not want, however, to fall into the same trap as some historians and sociologists who had tried to study class cultures as separate and isolated entities. The main advantage of working together as a team was that the culture building of, for example, the emerging working class could be studied in relation to the same process in middle- and upper-class settings during the period. The focus was thus on the *relations* between culturally distinct groups and subcultures, and the dialectic processes whereby different classes and strata develop their identity and culture in both dependence on and opposition to other social units: how social hierarchies are transformed into cultural ones (or perhaps even vice versa), how relations of cultural domination, subordination, and resistance are developed, how, for example, social conflicts can be expressed in terms of cultural battles.

The vagueness of these questions was intentional as our aim was to combine some materialist and symbolist approaches, and we wanted to avoid the theoretical metaphor of base/superstructure which we found somewhat limiting in this type of cultural analysis.

We were interested in the extent to which class boundaries and cultural boundaries tended to overlap or were blurred by other factors such as gender, urban/rural polarities, regional and occupational subcultures as well as generational differences.

This focus on cultural differentiation was also a reaction against popular ideas of a national Swedish culture. Was that a meaningful analytical concept and on what levels did such a form of collective consciousness exist? How had it been constructed over time and by what processes had it become a shared experience and identity? We felt the need first to deconstruct Swedishness before reconstructing it. Again this brought forward the question of cultural heterogenization or homogenization. Was the Sweden of 1980 a more homogeneous society than that of 1880? Or had old forms of cultural differentiation been transformed into new ones?

The problem here was also one of choosing a level to study. Many observers of modern Swedish society had stressed its homogeneity. Economic differences were less marked than in most other European countries and the language of class seemed rather muted. Similarities in consumption patterns and life-styles were striking, at least on a superficial level. The problem here, of course, is one of relations between form and meaning. Shared forms of cultural expression may hide differences in the level of meaning. This problem is also evident in judging the extent of cultural change and continuity in society. Cultural forms can be carried through history, giving an impression of stability while being charged with new and different meanings and used in various ways by different groups. In the same way the rapid replacement of commodities, cultural fashions, and attitudes may hide a continuity on a deeper level. Old problems, old principles are dressed up in new forms.

These issues were also important for challenging some established views about modernization and change, which saw Swedish culture travelling the road from tradition to modernity, from distinct subcultures to shared mass culture. We wanted to approach the problem of social and cultural change in a less unilinear fashion.

Research strategies

So much for theoretical perspectives. Our next problem was choosing the actual fields of empirical research. We lacked the resources for a broad coverage of the period c. 1880–1980 and had to develop a choice of strategic case-studies, which aimed first of all to illustrate the theoretical problems formulated. Again, our task was not one of writing the history of an epoch but of developing an understanding of the cultural organization of a complex society in a historical perspective. Our approach was anthropological rather than 'historical' or 'sociological' in the sense that our level of generalization did not primarily concern the distribution of cultural forms over time; we wanted to generalize about the cultural processes which produced variations in form. This meant that the atypical case had an analytical value as well as the search for frequencies. We also wanted to experiment with rather varied approaches at the empirical level, mixing quite different types of sources, units of study, forms of comparison, etc.

The scope of our studies has varied from life-histories and community studies to explorations of cultural systems on a nation-wide scale. Generally we have tried to compare ideological and normative definitions of the good and proper life with everyday praxis, as for example in patterns of socialization, interaction across class boundaries, the organization of work, home life, and leisure. Furthermore, we have singled out specific fields for more intensive studies: cultural domains, key symbols, social arenas, critical events, and social groups, which we thought would be crucial to our analysis. The list of such case-studies contains explorations of middle-class table manners, working-class drinking-rituals, village fights, ideas of interior decoration, work ethics, animal symbolism, notions of pollution and taboo, different types of moral panic, and vulgar holiday postcards, as well as definitions of good housekeeping.

Behind this mixed collection of studies lies a heuristic approach. We have aimed at a certain amount of anarchy in order not to let the ethnographic quest follow too narrowly defined paths. The important point is that the integrating principles behind this empirical bricolage are organized by a theoretical framework, focusing on the dialectics between class formation and culture building.

From counter-culture to national culture?

The first part of the research project took as one of its points of departure the popular stereotypes of Swedishness, common to both outside observers and natives. These stereotypes portray the typical Swede as a nature-loving and conflict-avoiding person, obsessed with self-discipline, orderliness, punctuality, and the importance of living a rational life. You don't have to know much about Swedish society to realize that most of these ideas are middle-class virtues. Tracing the problem of the extent to which a middle-class life-style had become the mainstream Swedish culture in public discourse as well as in private life, we decided to look at the formation of a middle-class world view and everyday experience over the last hundred years.

The first book from the project was an attempt to analyse the culture building of the Victorian bourgeoisie during the period c. 1880–1910, a period when we can talk of a middle-class culture being established as the dominant life-style in Swedish society (see Frykman and Löfgren 1979). In order to make this culture, from which we have inherited so many basic notions and ideas, more visible we used our ethnological knowledge of nineteenth-century peasant life as an analytical contrast to the ways and views of the Oscarians (as these late Victorians were called in Sweden). We compared the very different attitudes towards time and time-keeping, as well as the uses and perceptions of nature. We compared gender constructs and patterns of child socialization in the two settings, and looked at the new polarization between work and leisure, between public and private life, together with the new ideology of home and family life. Finally, we studied notions of dirt, pollution, and orderliness, discussing the emergence of a new ideology of health and cleanliness, as well as changing perceptions of sexuality and bodily functions.

The next step was to select another era of middle-class life. We chose to concentrate on the inter-war years, when political initiative in Sweden was taken over by the working-class movement and the foundations of the new welfare state were laid. The idea was to contrast the culture building of a later generation with that of the Oscarians at the end of the nineteenth century, and to study how the drastic social and economic changes had affected both the middle-class world-view and everyday culture (see the studies in Frykman and Löfgren 1985).

Currently, some of us are working on the post-war years, the period of growing affluence and ideas of an egalitarian consumer society, but we have also felt the need to go back in history to tackle the problems of the birth of a bourgeois culture in late-eighteenth- and early-nineteenth-century Sweden.

By choosing strategic periods we have tried to illustrate how different historical situations have affected the process of culture building. Leaving aside for a while the important question of internal divisions in the bourgeoisie (which later defined itself as the middle class), I would like to present a somewhat simplified picture of this transformation.

At the beginning of the nineteenth century the emerging bourgeois culture could best be defined as a kind of counter-culture, challenging the dominant, aristocratic élite. To understand the cultural profile of the bourgeoisie in this early era we have to remember that its quest for power was a battle waged on two fronts. The new class had to define itself not only *vis-à-vis* the old gentry but also *vis-à-vis* the common people. This structure of cultural warfare is mirrored both in the use of key identity symbols, in techniques of symbolic inversion, and in other forms of self-presentation and boundary maintenance. The bourgeoisie defined itself as a class which was fit to lead because of its many virtues: its self-discipline, moderation, rationality, its firm beliefs in progress and science. The old élite culture was pictured as degenerate, irresponsible when it came to handling both private and public spending, immoral in its manners, and *shallow* in its social life. Against the traditional courtly etiquette with its empty rituals, the bourgeoisie emphasized a new intimacy and a familistic life-style. The importance of *home* became a powerful symbol along with the stress on emotional involvement between spouses, parents and children, as well as between friends.

The grey mass of the peasants did not represent a degenerate culture, but rather a lack of culture and civilization, living too close to nature, without being able to exercise restraint, moderation, and long-term planning.

By the end of the nineteenth century the bourgeoisie no longer represented an antagonistic subculture, having rather taken over the role of the dominant culture. In part this was the result of a social and cultural merger with the old élite, but also of shifts in the political and economic structure of Swedish society.[2] Now the main enemy was the emerging working class rather than the disintegrating peasantry, and the decades around 1900 are a period of massive missionary activity and attempts to enculturate the masses.

The new, victorious culture defined itself in evolutionary terms. The Oscarians saw themselves as representing higher forms of cultural development and sophistication than other social classes. They represented not *a* culture but *Culture*, defined as a National Culture, a form of life and thought which other groups in society should use as a model. It is during this period that the Oscarians were busy creating a cultural charter, constructing ancestor myths, genealogies, a national history, and a cultural heritage. This also had to do with the sharpened class conflicts of the period. For the new élite it seemed as if the nation was about to be torn apart. There was a search for symbolic expressions of national solidarity. The love of a common peasant heritage and a common Swedish landscape should bind the nation together and appeal to interests and emotions above class strife and political struggle. This was the period of the erection of national monuments, the building of folk museums, celebrations of national jubilees, flag-waving, and the writing of national songs. It is, however, important to see this process not only as a nostalgic construction of a peaceful past, but also a utopian vision of a future, harmonious society.

The importance of being modern

When we move from this period at the turn of the century into the 1930s the situation is radically different. The middle-class generation of the inter-war years in some ways defined themselves as rebels against their parent culture. They could mock the stern, authoritarian upbringing in Oscarian families, the obsession with rituals of avoidance, the many taboos on sexuality, and the stuffy interiors of their childhood homes. They talked of themselves as the *modern* class, or rather as representatives of a new kind of classlessness. If the Oscarians had defined their culture as the National Culture, the next generation defined theirs rather in terms of human nature. The middle-class way of life came to represent *normality*.

These changes were partly an adjustment to the very successful political mobilization of the Swedish working class during this period. The old élite redefined itself as a middle class rather than as a more flamboyant upper class. Upper-class manners were often presented as something of the past. This new ideology of classlessness can be contrasted with an everyday obsession with rituals of social distinction and boundary markers. On one level class differences did not exist, on another level they permeated even the most trivial details of everyday life. During this period the language of class became much more indirect and metaphorical. Problems of hierarchy, power, and class conflict were relocated to new cultural arenas, as in discussions of the disintegrating home, the youth problem, the dangers of consumerism, questions of rational living, matters of mental and physical hygiene, and so forth (cf. the discussions in Frykman 1981; Frykman n.d.; Löfgren 1984).

This tendency became even more marked during the post-war years, in the 1950s and 1960s. With growing social mobility and a new affluence among the working class, an intensified middle-class debate emerged on the question of whether ordinary people were ready for greater freedom (more money, longer holidays, etc.), and if they had acquired the cultural competence which was necessary for a life of high quality. Did they demonstrate enough taste, moderation, and long-term planning in their patterns of consumption? In the age of consumerism, taste and tastelessness became a new cultural arena of muted class conflict (cf. Löfgren 1985b: 98 ff.).

From a middle-class perspective the fears of a social and economic levelling, the disintegration of traditional forms of social control and deference, as well as a radical redistribution of power in society were not bogus fears, but were experienced as real enough. In the same way middle-class reformers and intellectuals often saw it as their task to spread progress, enlightenment, and science to the masses. They were seldom conscious of the class bias and the moral overtones in their preaching.

The point I have tried to make is that changes in middle-class self-images are also mirrored in representations of the social other. I have summarized the process through which middle-class culture building moved from the position of counter-culture to dominant culture and then to national culture, and finally became invisible as ideas about human nature. In the same manner the images of 'the lower classes' changed from one of a total lack of culture among the common people, to an evolutionary view of the working class representing a lower form of culture, to ideas about working-class life representing a deviance from (middle-class) normality. Later on, in the post-war years, we have many complaints about working-class rigidity and traditionalism. Now the problem is not that people lack culture, but that they have too much of it, they are stuck in a traditional, ritualistic life-style which makes them suspicious of new, modern ideas, be it questions of industrial management, interior decoration, baby-feeding, sex-roles, or leisure patterns. They have not grasped the importance of being modern, of being culturally flexible and open to new opportunities.

In these changing images of the social other we can observe a shift from moral arguments to scientific ones. Working-class habits were not condemned because they were bad habits or culturally unsuitable, but rather because they were 'not *good* for you'.

There are internal divisions and subcultural variations in the social entity labelled middle class, which make this transformation more complex. These are conflicts between *town and gown*, between commercial and industrial groups as contrasted to the intellectuals and the professionals, who in Sweden were often civil servants. 'We middle-class people' could mean different things in different settings and situations.

Working-class culture

In some ways this internal division was even more marked in Swedish working-class settings. Middle-class experiences and ideas were integrated on a national level through many channels of communication and scenes of interaction. The construction of a public sphere and a public discourse was very much a task for the middle class. It was their world that was reflected in the ideas presented in most newspapers, on the radio, or in public policies. In school, at the doctor's, or in other public institutions a middle-class person could feel at home. In short, there was often a good fit between personal experiences and public discourse in middle-class life.

When a Swedish working class emerged in the nineteenth century it had to build its culture within a societal framework organized by another class. It had to create its own social institutions and take care of its own welfare, and most of these tasks had to be accomplished on a local level, in very different material conditions.

In our attempts to study working-class culture building we had to develop a strategy differing from the study of middle-class culture. First of all, there was a lack of historical sources. The Oscarian bourgeoisie had documented their own lives in endless streams of autobiographies, collections of letters, and other types of written evidence. Few such sources were left from working-class settings of the same period. In the search for material, interview became a crucial technique. Second, there was the danger of looking at working-class life through middle-class cultural lenses; much of the historical material on the conditions and everyday life of the former had been organized and presented in the categories and frameworks of the latter. Third, there was the problem which is evident in much labour history: the tendency to focus on well-organized and well-documented working-class groups, and to look at formal institutions (trade union activities, associations, etc.) rather than informal everyday life. In some presentations the male, skilled worker, the heroic pioneer and trade union activist overshadows other working-class groups.

Instead of studying *the* working-class culture, we decided to start by contrasting some very different, local forms of culture building. We compared the social experiences of workers gathering in a newly built factory around the turn of the century in a rural setting with life in a working-class city. We looked at the kind of experiences gained in domestic service, in a lumberjack camp, or as a farm labourer in contrast to the life of a factory hand. Up to the 1930s domestic help, lumberjacks, and agricultural workers formed the vast majority of the Swedish working class, but they were also the least visible groups historically. Again, we were interested to see how gender and urban–rural polarities made class boundaries more complex. From these comparisons we would then move on to discussions of the kind of experiences which would tend to create a more general working-class consciousness during different periods.

In many ways working-class culture had to be constructed under a middle-class dominance of public life and institutions. I have talked earlier of the many conscious and unconscious attempts to discipline and educate workers in many cultural arenas, from shop-floor management to family life and leisure activities. If you study this process from a middle-class perspective, there is a risk of exaggerating the effectiveness of this moral rearmament. The same attempts at cultural dominance take on a different character when you observe them from below.

While middle-class persons could to a large extent integrate their everyday experiences with external messages about the good and proper life, working-class life contained more cultural contradictions and inconsistencies. The messages from school or the mass media often did not correspond to daily experiences. People were told that class did not exist but, at the same time, they lived in a world where class differences were constantly communicated and reproduced. They were taught codes of behaviour which did not correspond to those which existed at home. The structural conditions of middle-class and working-class culture building tended to differ.

A closer look at the forms of cultural resistance to middle-class ideology, advice, and instruction reveals a whole range of guerrilla techniques, which are typical of a culture fighting from a position of social inferiority. From the missionaries of middle-class normality we meet many complaints of the lack of appreciation found among common people. There is a constant wall of suspicion, of sulking or sudden deafness, and a lack of cultural flexibility and openness. Rarely did the missionaries realize that this could be explained as attempts at self-protection from the constant barrage of advice and admonitions, a way of creating a breathing-space. One effective way of counteracting rational arguments is to act irrationally, or to say yes and then go back and do the opposite. In such a situation acting dumb or moving slowly can be an effective form of resistance.

Situations of cultural confrontation may produce two faces of working-class culture: one of sluggish and uncommunicative behaviour towards representatives of the dominant culture, which is in strong contrast to the talkative and quick-witted behaviour inside their own group. Working-class wit and humour, the flourishing folklore of jokes, stories, sayings, and nicknames, was an effective cultural weapon. A snigger or laugh behind the back of the schoolmaster, the pompous clerk, or the supervisor could disarm a cultural advantage. It is no coincidence that the trickster figure has a key role in working-class folklore. One could also fight the dominant culture with its own weapons by exaggerating or parodying its authority and self-righteousness. You could shock a middle-class visitor by behaving in an even more vulgar, coarse, and uncouth way.

Another effect of these cultural confrontations was the construction of an alternative symbolic capital. Middle-class virtues can be defined as vices or mannerisms in working-class settings; the cult of masculinity and anti-intellectualism are examples of this. Sometimes it could become a double-edged weapon as it set groups of workers against each other, for example in conflicts between young and old, strong and weak. The same tendency is evident in the pride of endurance and hardiness, which was common among lumberjacks and agricultural workers. To complain about bad working conditions could be seen as demonstrating weakness.

In the fight for creating self-respect in a society where you were often told that you belonged to a second-rate culture or did not live up to desirable standards of conduct, the idea of working-class respectability became important. It would be wrong to view this phenomenon in terms of *embourgeoisement* or a copying of middle-class standards. I have looked at this problem in a study of working-class childhood and youth in an urban setting during the inter-war years, from which the following examples are taken (see Frykman and Löfgren 1985).

Playing on home ground or away?

In the childhood memories from this small, working-class town there are many more *we*'s than in middle-class reminiscences from the same period. Above all the notion of *neighbourhood* stands out very much in the social landscape: it is 'our street' more often than 'our home'. Another important difference lies in notions of work. While work was a distant world from which fathers returned in the evening in most middle-class childhoods, work was an economic necessity and a constant companion for working-class children. In middle-class homes 'work' could be a moral lesson, rarely a necessity. You prepared yourself for the distant future of work and career by being a good and diligent child. For working-class kids work represented both prison and freedom. You had to spend a lot of time after school, at weekends, and in the summer, helping parents or taking odd jobs. In the 1930s urban households still lived in a kind of hunting-and-gathering economy. Periods of unemployment as well as low wages meant that all kinds of extra sources of income had to be developed. People grew potatoes in the garden and visited the nearby countryside to buy or exchange farm products cheaply, while kids collected coal and firewood down at the harbour, and so on. Work took up much of children's free time, but also gave a certain amount of freedom, teaching them to earn their own money and to fend for themselves, in contrast to the more sheltered middle-class childhood.

Many children experienced class differences strongly at school. There were all kinds of subtle class symbols which communicated social position – who had to wear clogs, who could afford leather shoes, what kind of sandwiches did you bring for lunch? Children soon learned that social background mattered for the teachers, who tended to be much more lenient and understanding towards children from 'better homes'.

Class differences were also expressed in a rich vocabulary of 'us and them'.

There was an element of irony in the labels for middle-class people and behaviour. They were called *the nobs, the cream, those who set themselves apart* or *think they are a bit better*.

In defining your own position in society there was also a line to draw below your station in life. The idea of working-class respectability was expressed in many cultural domains and social situations, and must be seen partly as a defence mechanism and a fight for self-esteem.

The urban setting I am describing was populated by families who had moved in from the countryside around the turn of this century. They faced a life of very narrow economic margins and had to make a constant effort to keep the family afloat. In this life they were perpetually reminded that their behaviour did not measure up to the standards of the official, dominant culture. Ideas about being an honest and respectable working man or woman can be seen both as a defence against an intruding middle-class moralism and as a boundary marker against those 'who had lost control of their own lives', those unfortunates 'who lived at the mercy of the welfare people', those 'who could no longer fend for themselves' and thus had to subordinate themselves to the rules and admonitions of the official institutions. This constant fear of losing one's footing in society was based upon the knowledge that one's position was very precarious. Unemployment, sickness, a man who started to drink, or children who get themselves into trouble could wreck the family.

Thus rather distinct boundaries were established between those husbands who took a drink on Saturdays and those who squandered their meagre earnings in pubs every evening..There was the distinction between those who dressed up for Sundays and those who did not care, the distinction between women who could keep a good home and those who lived in chaos. These ideas about respectability should be seen as a cultural defence rather than as embourgeoisement. Working-class families fought a two-front battle, against both middle class and lumpenproletariat, and in this process of culture building firm rituals and rules of social life were created. Sex roles, drinking-patterns, forms of socializing were often quite rigidly defined, which led middle-class intellectuals and progressive reformers to sigh about working-class traditionalism and lack of flexibility.

There is a strong *defensive* element in this culture building. In the 1930s the Swedish working class was very much on the offensive, politically, forcing the middle class to keep a low profile or develop a strategy of compromise and understanding. Paradoxically this resulted in a much stronger *cultural* offensive on behalf of the middle class. In the making of the new welfare state everybody should become a good responsible citizen. The individual was integrated into a wider, national community through new forms of interaction with the state and its many institutions. New forms of mass media invaded the home at the same time. Much of this communication came to be dominated by middle-class definitions of normality, as I have stressed earlier. The Social Democrats, who came to power in 1932, were so busy building a new, modern society, that they rarely had time to think about where the cultural definitions of this modern living were taken from. In some ways the cultural competence of ordinary people was lifted into the waiting arms of a new collective of experts, who saw themselves representing the life of the future and who were busy carrying out a scientific reorganization of everyday life. It was no longer certain that mother knew best.

Arenas of cultural confrontation

This cultural offensive meant that many working-class people felt more under surveillance than before, but also that the different classes came to interact more often in situations where middle-class rules were the norm. This feeling of being under constant observation is expressed in memories of youth and leisure during the 1930s. It was during the teenage period that working-class kids more frequently ventured into the public territories of the town. They soon learned about the ways class boundaries were drawn.

Public streets, parks, department stores, dance halls, and restaurants were often policed by the middle-class, represented by the snobbish waiter, the haughty shop assistant, the stern lady in the public library, or the strolling schoolteacher. Under their watchful eye people often felt out of place and awkward. Experiences like these created a need for working-class home ground, for territories and institutions where they could decide the rules of behaviour for themselves. The 'People's Halls' and 'People's Parks' which sprang up in the first decades of the twentieth century gave the working class the institutional arenas they needed. A painter who played in a dance band in such places remembers how sensitive one was to middle-class intruders:

> 'We called ourselves *The Light of the Stars*, but we didn't know what it meant. And I sung in English and German without knowing a single word, but I sung it the way it was written on the music sheets and nobody understood.
>
> Once during the summer we noted the white caps worn by high school graduates in the audience and then I stopped singing. But otherwise I sung "vorgon vells" just the way it said and everybody thought we were a damned good band who could play in English.'

The appearance of a couple of students was enough for an element of social insecurity to enter. Such situations underlined the importance of having cultural territories of one's own.

These examples give a glimpse of how a cultural hegemony can be experienced from below, but if we change the perspective, the same situation or cultural scene may take on a different look. In our research we have continually tried to compare social viewpoints in order to find out how different versions of reality are constructed.

It is, for example, striking that the same public places where working-class youth could feel uneasy and out of place could be felt by middle-class children to be dominated by a threatening working class. In *their* childhood memories the street could be a jungle, populated by a strange tribe which behaved and talked in ways they were not used to. Their whole appearance was often seen as menacing and aggressive. Middle-class schoolchildren made sure to avoid certain neighbourhoods and run quickly past some corners.

One way of studying the processes of cultural confrontation and negotiation is by looking at such arenas of social interaction. Another research strategy consists of selecting crucial *cultural domains*, in which class differences and conflicts are expressed in more or less symbolic forms. Let me give a few examples of such metaphorical fields from different periods and settings.

In several studies Jonas Frykman has focused on the concepts of health and hygiene, and the various discourses surrounding them. The word 'hygiene' acquired the status of a key concept, especially in the middle-class world-view of the inter-war years, when many social and moral problems were redefined as problems of hygiene, with new constructs such as school hygiene, mental hygiene, work hygiene, sexual hygiene, race hygiene, etc. In this process the occupational subculture of the medical profession had a key role. The men in white slowly took over the definition of good behaviour from the traditional authority of black-coated clergymen and judges (see Frykman 1981 and Frykman and Löfgren 1985).

A rich field of social metaphors is found in the uses of animal symbolism among the Oscarian middle class. Magazines, school readers, and nursery storybooks are crammed with animals of highly varying moral standards. There are civilized and refined species, like the songbirds, as well as more proletarian and animalistic beasts. In their compassion for our friends in nature the middle class also asserted its moral superiority over the less animal-loving lower classes, who were often accused of indifference and a lack of sensitivity towards animals (see Löfgren 1985a).

Another symbolic battlefield concerns ideas about the *good home* and the threatened home. This powerful image has been used by different groups at different periods for different purposes. By asking why the home (or the family) is portrayed as a threatened institution, and who is supposed to be threatening it and who feels threatened – in changing historical situations – it is possible to learn something about social conflicts and cultural anxieties. The debates on the future of the home usually contain statements about the past, ideas about the good old days or the bad old days, which also mirror contemporary concerns (cf. the discussion in Löfgren 1984 and Åström 1985). A similar metaphorical analysis can be carried out for other favourite topics during the last century, such as 'the youth problem' (see Frykman n.d.) and the shallowness of modern life-styles.

Many of these discourses are based on premises of degeneration or cultural devolution. The Oscarians lamented the passing of the old sturdy peasant life and its many virtues. Later middle-class generations could talk nostalgically about the stable and sound family life of the Oscarians. Middle-class radicals of the post-war generation could mourn the good, old, traditional working-class culture, a heroic era of true class consciousness, solidarity, and fighting spirit. The past is constantly reorganized for the present.

A different approach in the study of cultural confrontation and negotiation concerns special social groups, whose position in society exposes them to conflicting messages. For us the study of *class travellers*, socially mobile persons, has been especially rewarding. Their life-stories illustrate the problems of leaving one class culture for another, and the process of learning and unlearning codes of behaviour. Often they express the experience of being alienated from the cultural settings of their youth, while never being fully integrated into their new cultural surroundings. Other case-studies deal with occupational groups which are situated on the margins of one class or social stratum, as for example shop assistants, whose cultural orientation has been divided between middle-class ambitions and working-class identity. Women in domestic help mirror similar social experiences. They have working-class backgrounds but spend their first adult years in the backstage world of middle-class homes, later to return to a working-class marriage. Some of them integrate new middle-class standards into their behaviour, others return with firm convictions about 'the shallow pretensions' and double standards they have witnessed in the fastidiousness of middle-class domestic life.

The Swedish experience

In my presentation of a research project as yet unfinished I have discussed some approaches to the study of one's own culture. I have argued the need for a historical perspective but also for a research strategy which differs from that of social historians or historical sociologists. Our anthropological contribution to an understanding of how Swedish society and culture have developed over the last century focuses on the ways culture is produced and reproduced in a complex, stratified society undergoing rapid changes. We still lack many of the analytical tools for this task, but let me point to some of the important themes in our study.

For us the term 'culture building' has been a central one, because it stresses the need to study culture in terms of process and praxis. We have been interested in the ways in which individual social experiences are processed and integrated with existing ideas and patterns of thought, or how they stand in conflict with earlier experiences or with those of other people. How is a collective consciousness established and maintained over time? The term culture building focuses on the constant reworking of culture, on processes of learning and unlearning, on the ways contradictions and inconsistencies are handled. The concept must not, however, lead to images of a conscious strategy in which blueprints are drawn up and construction platforms nailed together. People seldom view themselves as culture builders in their everyday task of integrating new experiences or giving new meanings to old knowledge. The structure and direction of this task is more easily seen in retrospect by the outsider, the researcher, than by the participants themselves.

We are not primarily interested in this process as an individual project; the focus is on the formation of shared cultural systems, but we would argue for an emphasis on agency rather than structure in this type of analysis. Another problem concerns the relations between ideas and actions. Our perspective is materialist in the sense that we maintain that ideologies and cultural notions must be consistent with material experiences in order to be taken in and to survive. The material basis of culture building is the simple fact that different groups of people live under different conditions which produce different experiences. On the other hand, it is important to see that new ideas about society, dreams, and utopias contain a potential for change, a cultural force which may transcend existing material conditions and social frameworks: the new emerges out of the given.

It is in this process that 'objective' and 'subjective' forces are interwoven. I am aware of the fact that I have used both the concepts of culture and class in a rather undisciplined manner, sliding between emic and etic perspectives as well as using them as active and passive categories. I find that the old controversy between objectivism and subjectivism in class analysis has to some extent blocked a better understanding of the dialectics between material experiences and class identity, and between cross-class interests and class-based conflicts.[3] These problems are central to our future work.

A part of the anthropological perspective consists of a painstaking ethnography of the trivialities of everyday life. While historians and sociologists have often focused on the level of ideology in their study of cultural change, we find it important to study how ideas are anchored in the routines and rituals of daily activities. How are cultural messages embedded in the material world we create, and how is it that they are often communicated in a much more effective way through non-verbal rather than verbal forms of interaction? This type of silent socialization is found in the sharing of a meal, in the structure of work, in the physical arrangements of the home or the welfare agency, and so on.

I am stressing this level of study because it is important to remember that an understanding of the workings of a society at large, like modern Sweden, its power structures and webs of dependencies, does not necessarily call for a 'macro-level' study. The metaphorical polarities of micro and macro may often obscure the fact that society is not organized on these two levels, and that the analysis does not have to start 'up there', working its way down. To take seemingly trivial everyday phenomena as starting-points and look at their wider implications and connections seems to me a fruitful anthropological approach which may produce surprising insights.

Another aspect of the anthropological perspective is the interest in studying culture at different levels. How do new ideas slowly become invisible or unconscious parts of everyday life? How can cultural contradictions between normative ideals and actual praxis be mediated, reconciled, or contained? Such questions raise problems of cultural integration and transformation, but they can also allow for an acknowledgement that the entities we as researchers term cultures can be rather messy systems, especially in this type of society.

It is evident that an 'anthropology at home' such as ours faces the problem of adjusting anthropological tools which have been developed in less complex societies (or at least settings with a different type of complexity). The problem is not solved by an import of concepts from micro-sociology or social psychology, which often tend to dissolve cultural patterns into situations and individual strategies, a world of all scenes but no plot, to quote Richard Sennett (1977). Until our understanding of the organization of cultural complexity is further developed we will probably have to live with a very mixed bag of concepts like cultural dissonance, compartmentalization, situational selection, and cultural repertoires.

These observations may be rather trivial, but the reason for making them is that I want to point out that an anthropological approach produces other types of knowledge than, for example, the analyses of historians and sociologists. An anthropology at home always faces this question of what the specific anthropological contribution consists of in a field where many social sciences meet.

Our task has been to study the Swedish cultural experience in a historical perspective, and especially the dialectic between cultural systems and social formations. We have stressed the importance of looking at the relations between class cultures, focusing on the social and cultural organization of dominance, subordination, and resistance. In my presentation I have given a rather simplified version of this cultural warfare, concentrating on relations between middle-class and working-class culture building. The social landscape of modern Sweden is, of course, more complex than that. My aim has been to illustrate some of the ways in which cultures are confronted in a complex society, how cultural differences are produced, maintained, or dissolved. Here we are dealing with processes of persuasion, negotiation and compromise, rather than examples of embourgeoisement or subjugation. In a process of cultural confrontation both parties are changing, as Raymond Williams has stressed (1977).

Confrontations also look quite different from the viewpoint of the dominant and the subordinate culture. This underlines the need for a constant change of social perspective in order to understand the interaction. Subtle forms of cultural persuasion may be created, only to be counteracted by even subtler forms of resistance. The really important battlegrounds may be hidden in the most surprising arenas and domains, which calls for a rather flexible research strategy. In this interdisciplinary field of research much more work has been done on the processes of cultural indoctrination and dominance than on resistance.[4]

My presentation of the project has focused on the culture building of the middle class. One of the reasons for this lies in the fact that this field of study represents a special challenge for anthropologists, which in a way can be seen as the *real* home-coming. Although intellectuals love to see themselves as outside (or above) class, there is no escaping the fact that a spell in Academia will leave its middle-class imprint on anybody. Any study of middle-class life-styles and world-view will turn the anthropologist into a key informant. The problem is, of course, that much of our anthropological discourse is rooted in a middle-class vision of reality: a way of perceiving, classifying, and organizing the world. Many of our analytical tools have been produced or redefined in this intellectual setting, for example polarities like nature/culture, public/private, individual/collective. There are many strategies for curing this type of home-blindness; I have argued mainly for a historical-comparative perspective.

But what about the Swedishness of the cultural transformation we have studied? There is no final answer to that question yet, but in comparison to, for example, the German, French, or British experience during the last century, there are striking differences. The late and very rapid formation of a Swedish urban working class meant, for example, that the rural background was an important part of the building of their culture. It is also important that middle-class intellectuals and professionals have so often been servants of the state and seen their role as a neutral or mediating one. The extremely strong and effective mobilization of the Swedish labour movement in the 1920s and 1930s also led to a development of cultural compromise rather than direct confrontation. In the making of the new welfare state both middle-class and working-class self-images were changed. Compared to, for example, the French or the British middle class of the same period, the Swedes have kept a very low profile in some ways.[5] In any case, the dominant Swedish culture of the 1980s cannot be seen as a mere reflection of middle-class thoughts and values. Maybe there is a case for the stereotype that Swedes are wary of direct confrontation and love to compromise. The answer to that and many other questions will have to wait for further research.

Notes

1 Although this presentation of the project is coloured by my own research interest, I have a great debt to the rest of the research collective: Gunnar Alsmark, Jonas Frykman, Ella Johansson, Mats Lindqvist, Karin Salomonsson, Margareta Stigsdotter, Magnus Wikdahl, Lynn Åkesson, and Lissie Åström.
2 The nineteenth-century bourgeois perception of the aristocracy contained elements not only of distancing and polarization but also of (secret) admiration, imitation, and co-option.

92　Orvar Löfgren

3　Cf. the constructive discussion of these problems in Thompson (1978), Newby *et al.*
(1978: 276 ff.), Bourdieu (1984: 101 ff.) and Furbank (1985).
4　This is perhaps most evident in French cultural theory, from the writings on the
history of mentalities to the perspectives of social scientists like Michel Foucault
and Pierre Bourdieu. An interest in the strategies and forms of cultural resistance is
more often found among British social historians and the cultural sociologists of the
Birmingham school (cf. Clarke, Critcher, and Johnson 1980).
5　Cf. Peter Gay's discussion of the European and North American middle classes
during the nineteenth century (1984) and Raphael Samuel's The Middle Class
between the Wars (1983), Zeldin (1973) and Weber (1976) on France, and
Marwick's comparison of class images in Britain, France, and the USA (1980).

References

ÅSTRÖM, L. (1985) Husmodern möter folkhemmet. In J. Frykman and O. Löfgren (eds)
Modärna tider. Vision och vardag i folkhemmet. Malmö: Liber.

BOCK, P. (1980) *Continuities in Psychological Anthropology. A Historical Introduction*.
San Francisco: W. H. Freeman.

BOURDIEU, P. (1984) *Distinction. A Social Critique of the Judgement of Taste*. London:
Routledge & Kegan Paul.

CLARKE, J., CRITCHER, C., and JOHNSON, R. (eds) (1980) *Working Class Cultures. Studies
in History and Theory*. London: Hutchinson.

FRANKENBERG, R. (1966) *Communities in Britain. Social Life in Town and Country*.
Harmondsworth: Penguin.

FRYKMAN, J. (1981) Pure and Rational. The Hygienic Vision: A Study of Cultural
Transformation in the 1930s. *Ethnologia Scandinavica* **81**: 36–62.

— (n.d.) *Who Cares? Generation Conflicts as a Moral Problem*. Paper presented at the
HSFR Conference on Generation Conflicts in History and Anthropology, 4–6
February 1985.

FRYKMAN, J. and LÖFGREN, O. (1979) *Den kultiverade människan*. Lund. Revised edition
in translation in press, *Culture Builders: An Historical Anthropology of Middle Class
Culture*. New Brunswick, NJ: Rutgers.

— (eds) (1985) *Modärna tider. Vision och vardag i folkhemmet*. Malmö: Liber.

FURBANK, R. N. (1985) *Unholy Pleasure. Or the Idea of Social Class*. Oxford: Oxford
University Press.

GAY, P. (1984) *The Bourgeois Experience. Victoria to Freud. Vol. I: Education of the
Senses*. Oxford: Oxford University Press.

LÖFGREN, O. (1980) Historical Perspectives on Scandinavian Peasantries. *Annual
Review of Anthropology* **9**: 187–314.

— (1981) On the Anatomy of Culture. *Ethnologia Europea* **XII** (1): 26–46.

— (1984) The Sweetness of Home. Class, Culture and Family Life in Sweden.
Ethnologia Europea **XIV**: 44–64.

— (1985a) Our Friends in Nature: Class and Animal Symbolism. *Ethnos* **1985** (3/4):
184–213.

— (1985b) Wish You Were Here! Holiday Images and Picture Postcards. *Ethnologia
Scandinavica* **1985**: 90–107.

MARWICK, A. (1980) *Class: Image and Reality in Britain, France and the USA since 1930*.
London: Oxford University Press.

NEWBY, H., BELL, C., ROSE, D., and SAUNDERS, P. (1978) *Property, Paternalism and
Power. Class and Control in Rural England*. London: Hutchinson.

SAMUEL, R. (1983) The Middle Class between the Wars. *New Socialist* **1983** (1–2).

SENNETT, R. (1977) *The Fall of Public Man*. New York: Alfred A. Knopf.
SPINDLER, G. D. and SPINDLER, L. (1983) Anthropologists View American Culture. *Annual Review of Anthropology* **12**: 49–78.
THOMPSON, E. P. (1978) Eighteenth-century English Society: Class Struggle without Class. *Social History* **III** (2): 133–65.
WEBER, E. (1976) *Peasants into Frenchmen: The Modernization of Rural France*. Stanford, Calif.: Stanford University Press.
WILLIAMS, R. (1977) *Marxism and Literature*. Oxford: Oxford University Press.
ZELDIN, T. (1973) *France 1848–1945, Vol. I Ambition, Love and Politics*. Oxford: Oxford University Press.

Kirsten Hastrup

6 Fieldwork among friends:
ethnographic exchange within the Northern civilization

The present paper is an attempt to explore the epistemological implications of doing fieldwork among a people who, one way or another, belong to the same cultural area as the anthropologist. In this case the cultural area is the Northern civilization, comprising (today) five independent nation-states and several more or less autonomous regions. These countries have closely connected histories, and have developed from a shared cultural and linguistic background in the early Middle Ages.[1] The notion of civilization is used to sum up the common theme of this development. It also implies that we are dealing with an area with a well-known history and a long tradition of literacy, features that of themselves set a particular kind of frame for the anthropological investigation. In fieldwork this investigation has the nature of an exchange relationship between the ethnographer and the people studied, and like any other exchange this one carries the stamp of the context.

Generally, the context of the ethnographic exchange is cross-cultural. It has been suggested recently that in the course of cross-cultural dialogue differences are exaggerated and 'cultures' implicitly contrasted (Boon 1982; Hastrup 1985c). The question then arises of what happens to the anthropological discourse when the ethnographic exchange takes place between parallel cultures. It is to that question that my paper is addressed. The nature of my discussion is largely theoretical, but its substance is drawn from my field-experience in Iceland.

Like my own native country, Denmark, Iceland is one of the Nordic countries. I speak of the Icelanders as my friends for several reasons. First, and pre-eminently, they gave me all the benefits of their friendship while I worked among them.[2] This has probably also been the experience of many anthropologists working among the most exotic tribes, but there is another reason for stressing it here. Again, it is historical and linguistic; in Old Norse, *frændr*, homologous to 'friends' in Old English, denoted kinsmen. It has been reported as somewhat of an oddity that the Norsemen should use this notion of friendship in such a narrow sense of kinship (Cleasby, Vigfùsson, and Craigie 1975: 176); this argument could be turned upside down, allowing us to understand the wide range of kinship in medieval Scandinavia. Kinsmen *were* your friends, you could count on them (Grønbech 1931: 32). This, of course, is well known in the anthropological literature (Fox 1978: 66; Schwimmer 1974: 49). Thus, the Icelanders are my friends in the sense that they are a brethren people to my own, ever since the beginnings of history. These beginnings were marked, among other things, by a shared Nordic language – referred to as *dönsk tunga*, 'Danish tongue' (Haugen 1976: 135).

Today, Danish and Icelandic are no longer mutually intelligible. Modern Icelandic is still close to Old Norse, while Danish has departed very much from these roots. This linguistic fact carries an implicit cultural connotation: the Icelanders of today seem to be culturally closer to the cherished Viking ancestors than the rest of the Nordic peoples. I am not going to discuss the legitimacy of this view here, merely note an important aspect of (any) anthropology 'at home', that is, the implicit search for 'roots' and for cultural authenticity.

I have chosen to focus on fieldwork because it is in this context of direct exchange that, perhaps, the implications of doing anthropology among friends are the most conspicuous. Also, I believe that the discussion of fieldwork as such is as vital as ever in social anthropology.[3] My exploration of the general theme centres around two 'natural' aspects of the context of ethnographic exchange in the field: first, the sex of the anthropologist (translated into cultural categories of gender), and second, the dimension of time (expressed in a cultural discourse on temporal and historical issues).

Gender

There is an old notion in anthropology of female ethnographers becoming 'honorary males' in the alien cultures under study. This notion has been unmasked as an expression of a particularly Western, academic view of maleness – and of anthropology (Okely 1975: 176). However, the general question still remains whether the sex of the anthropologist makes a difference in fieldwork, and at what level. The very idea of the 'honorary male' covers more than a technical problem of data-collection, it also points to the implicit view of male spheres of culture being generalized (and hence 'larger'), while female spheres are specified (and 'smaller', and included in the male view) (S. Ardener 1984: 126).[4]

In the present connection the question to be discussed is whether the sex of the fieldworker changes its significance (within the ethnographic discourse) in cultures that are so close to one's own that gender-markers are the same as they are at home. While in exotic tribes the female ethnographers may, indeed, lack some or even most of the critical 'specification-markers' of women, in one's own culture this is not so (S. Ardener 1984: 126). The result is that the sex of the anthropologist, elsewhere so inconspicuous in relation to other and much more marked differences, becomes a primary element in the local classification of the ethnographer.

In Iceland, I stayed for some time on a farm inhabited by three generations. They formed three more or less independent households but were, nevertheless, one economic unit. I wanted to study the farmers' views of Icelandic culture and history (to put it very generally), and in order to do so I had to participate in their daily life. In this case the requirement of participation meant that I had to accept an age-old gender-role in Icelandic farming society, namely that of the *fjósakona* ('stable woman'). The farm-people knew very well that the purpose of my staying with them was to collect information about Icelandic culture, but to be able to do so without being a burden to them we agreed that I should be of some use. Hence I was allotted the work of *fjósakona*. In that capacity I had to milk and fodder the thirty cows of the farm, to clean the stable, and to take the cows out into the pasture. In addition to this I had some secondary functions in the kitchen and in looking after the children.

In the traditional division of labour, cows were under female supervision while sheep-rearing was a male task. Persons of either sex might cross this boundary, but the categories appear to be persistent. Even today, sheep-rearing is definitely an area of male dominance and pride, as testified by the annual ram-exhibitions.[5] Among the exclusively male tasks is the collection of the sheep from the mountain pastures in the autumn. In the area where I worked this involved risky excursions to the borders of a glacier, and lengthy ventures into inhospitable valleys and on steep slopes. As the snow began to cover the mountain peaks in the area, it became expedient to recover those sheep that were still at large. While it had been out of the question to ask permission to take part in the day-long excursions to far-away pastures (where my presence would certainly have been a burden), I was now eager to join the expeditions to the nearby slopes, to bring down the last sheep from those ledges where they had ended up, and from where they were unable to descend.

Eventually, having demonstrated my physical fitness in rounding up some stray lambs in nearby 'sands', I was allowed to join one of the lesser expeditions. One of the young wives of the farm (about thirty years of age) subsequently stated her wish to go as well. This woman, who became a very close friend of mine, is one of those fascinatingly articulate 'natural' feminists who seem particularly 'Icelandic' to me; on her own account she wanted to demonstrate that women were as capable as men. Her husband was slightly reluctant to accept the idea of her going (and was sceptical of her views upon sexual equality), but partly because of my presence he was forced to accept 'modernity' – and so we both went.

The party consisted of the male adult population of three neighbouring farms, amounting to some twelve men, a youngster of fourteen, and the two persistent women. As we gathered at the farmstead, all dressed in woollens and equipped with ropes, binoculars, and camera (the anthropologist's third eye), the old man of the farm came out to see the party off. On seeing me, so obviously dressed for the mountains, he was completely taken aback. 'Womenfolk in the rocks!' was all he could say. The degree of disbelief expressed made me in turn quite ashamed; I felt that the transgression of boundaries and my departure from the gender role allotted to me was perhaps inappropriate rather than adventurous. I was 'saved' by the appearance of my woman friend who, with much feminist self-consciousness, declared her own intention of going and thereby silenced her father-in-law, reducing his protests to mere headshaking.

Off we went, and it soon became obvious to me that I had actually engaged in a rather masculine endeavour. Already, on the lower slopes, I had difficulty in keeping up with the men (and my strong woman companion), but no one complained about occasionally having to wait. The men made a certain number of jokes about the women and displayed their own maleness in all sorts of ways. They were protective guides and boasting males at the same time. However, as we were about to negotiate the first really difficult, almost vertical, rockface, the entire context seemed to change; the 'signs' of the women present changed meaning (cf. Herzfeld 1983b). The male-show-off and the suggestive eye-winking attitudes were replaced by those of teachers and fathers. It seemed that we had reached a point beyond which 'females' could not go – but, in the 1980s you could no longer demand of women that they stayed at home. So, when the rope by which the unskilled mountaineers had to be lifted up was ready, the men called out: 'Now, come on you youngsters' (*krakkar*). The 'youngsters' referred to comprised the two women (including this ageing anthropologist) and the boy of fourteen, who was taking part for the first time. It was as 'youngsters' that we proceeded; we had to be taught and to be taken care of. Truly, we were in some ways a drawback to the expedition, but as the farmers were generally very loving and patient towards their children and took much effort in their training, no one ever complained about the additional weight upon their responsibility that the presence of the de-signified women entailed. They took a certain pride, even, and certainly much care in disclosing their techniques to the initiates; in more than one way the 'youngsters' were roped into the confidence of the men.

There are, of course, sequels to this narrative at many levels, but suffice it to note here that the sex of the anthropologist was very much part of her signification in the field. When, at a certain point, I attempted to internalize male spheres of experience, I was redefined – as an 'honorary child'.

In the fishing village, where I later spent a couple of months, my gender-role would become even more marked. In order to gain access to what seemed an incredibly closed community which was, furthermore, covered in darkness for up to twenty-one hours a day when I was there, I once again sought refuge in a proper woman's role. I obtained employment at the local fish-filleting factory where, for up to fourteen hours a day, I would cut and pack endless amounts of haddock, cod, and halibut. In this way I came very close to the women of the community with whom I worked, but I seemed very far from my own image of the hero-anthropologist, exploring the (sub-)Arctic. After all, there is nothing heroic about rubber-boots and freezing fingers, let alone in my poor score on the scale of the piece-work contract. In the eyes of the local people I was certainly neither a hero nor an honorary male. I was simply a female migrant labourer; by my act of seeking employment (necessitated by my anthropological aims) I had entered the well-known category of migrant fish-labourer, ranking lowest in any Icelandic status-hierarchy. It was somewhat out of season, so I was the only female migrant at the time, but the category was there ready to be populated, and the work was there as well.

Not only had I moved into a particular category of people (and of women), I had also taken up residence in one of those barracks built for migrant labourers in all Icelandic fishing villages. I shared this one with three young men, who worked incredibly hard five days a week to earn their wages, and let themselves go by drinking at the weekend. Life was almost cyclical: for five days we all worked between ten and sixteen hours a day, while at the weekend we relaxed and enjoyed ourselves. For a few days at the beginning of each week, the smell of fish glueing to our boots, clothes, and the entire house, was superseded by the smell of vodka and *brennivín* emanating from broken bottles.

As regards my sex-role, I soon came to realize that by living in this place I gave it a particular significance. I knew, of course, that I was classified as a woman. But I did not know that by staying in the barrack (*verbúð*) I was further classified as sexually accessible. At first, I failed to understand why my female workmates, to whom I gradually disclosed the purpose of my stay, and with some of whom I developed rather intimate friendships, would continually suggest that I went to live with some family or other. My own spirit of independence, and my not wanting to become associated with just one family, forbade me that, however. So I stayed in the *verbúð* in spite of the occasional outbursts of violence during the Saturday night parties, which attracted several local young people who, in this house, had their only 'safe' place – outside the ordinary authority structure.

It was only when violence was turned against me that I finally understood how I had been classified. At one of the usual Saturday night gatherings, some ten young people were drinking heavily in the room next to mine, where I was relaxing in my own funny way by reading Icelandic grammar. Suddenly some of the men burst in upon me, and displayed a degree of sexual aggression that I had never experienced before. It was only then that I realized how naïve I had been; by choosing these quarters I had marked myself out as proper 'game'.[6] In my faint knowledge of the cultural code, I had certainly 'asked for it'. Any idea of my being an 'honorary male' had no correspondence with reality in the fishing village; I was rather, and even more ambiguously, a prudish and therefore dishonest harlot.

I am not going to dwell on the details of the varied strategies I had to use in my continuous negotiations with the reality of the particular gender-role ascribed to me in the village. I shall merely note that because of my very wish to explore, from a neutral scholarly position, the lives and experiences of a closely related people within my own area of civilization, I could not escape involvement in village life as a very distinct kind of person. I had entered a paradox, not unlike the kind of paradox that mirrors may land you in (Fernandez 1980: 36–7),[7] and as it could not be solved, it had to be lived (cf. Boon 1982: 46). The only alternative would be to leave the place.

Anthropology itself is based on a paradox of a very personal experience of the field and of being 'at one' with the people studied, and the detached theoretical reflection. My field experience included a particular categorical affiliation and with it a particular set of role expectancies. Instead of general resistance to this and a facile withdrawal from the category (which I could have obtained by moving to a family house), I decided to exploit the position allotted to me in the local structure. By and large I would say that the kind of insight that I got into village life from this (conceptual) position, is in no way inferior to anything I could have obtained from other positions that a woman could have.

In general it seems to me that the most potent point of departure for solving the puzzles of local culture is the point where the locals actually 'see' your presence. Only there can the anthropological encounter turn into an exchange between subjects. In cultures close to one's own, the sex of the anthropologist seems to be an important element in the 'tribal' definitions of the 'scribe' (cf. Boon 1982). Perhaps this gives us less room for manoeuvring between distinct spheres of reality, and no possibility of acting as 'honorary males'. However, the advantages of being (for once!) unambiguously classified as female may easily outweigh any gain to be achieved behind the mask of maleness – or through the lack of any gender specification at all.

Time

We have to live with time in much the same way as with sex; both of them seem to grow out of nature, so to speak. However, just as the biology of the two sexes is transformed into the culture of gender, so 'time' may be read as a sign in a human discourse.

Of primary concern here is the question whether the ethnographer working within her own civilization reads the 'sign of time' differently from her colleagues working with remote primitive peoples.[8] As I shall seek to demonstrate, I believe that this is possibly so. Once we move into our own culture areas, it would seem that a new kind of awareness about the temporal discourse is required. If Fabian is right in his assertion that anthropology has largely treated its object within an implicitly evolutionist paradigm that has tended to express cultural difference in terms of temporal distance (Fabian 1983), should we then suppose that an ethnography of culturally similar peoples makes no recourse to temporal distancing? Or, if his argument appertains to the anthropological discourse in general, what kind of difference does it make to the scale used in this distancing?

In the field we experience coevalness; we live in a time *shared* with the others. In the monographs coevalness is replaced by allochronism (Fabian 1983: 31–2). If nothing else, this points to the fact that 'time' is a sign of ambiguous meaning.

The reason for the anthropologist's schizophrenic use of time is not only to be sought in the implicit evolutionism of the discipline, but also in the very nature of fieldwork itself. Fieldwork means a sharing of time, but once the anthropologist starts analysing she cannot escape a time-warp; the ethnographic present is part of her autobiographic past (Fabian 1983: 87 ff.). This, finally, provides me with the point of departure for my thematic reading of the ethnography of my exchange with the Icelanders, and our sharing the time. As hinted at in the introductory remarks, the Icelandic reality was implicitly conceived of as representing a shared Nordic history.[9] In this context it means that the notion of the ethnographic present as part of the autobiographic past took on a very particular meaning. 'They' came to represent 'us' in the past tense, not as a matter of evolutionary course, but as an effect of historical coincidence. I would argue that this probably applies to other anthropological studies of, say, village life in one's own society.

We cannot stop here, because the ethnographic exchange is an exchange with two subjects. The ethnographer herself is a sign open to interpretation (Herzfeld 1983b; cf. also Pouwer 1973), and for the Icelanders I was likely to represent an image of their past, being a member of the one-time oppressing nation. That is no novelty, of course; first exploited, then studied – the usual story of anthropology. Yet, in this case, the asymmetrical relationship had been replaced by a truly symmetrical one, and the one-time oppressed people had been literate for ages, and had a high degree of historical consciousness. From their perspective, then, the anthropologist's questions about matters historical (in one sense or other) were likely to be answered within a distinct frame of reference incorporating a particular version of our 'shared' history.

I was particularly interested in the use of history in the cultural construction of modern Icelandic identity, yet as it happened I also came to deal with the inverse process, that is, the cultural construction of the past from the modern perspective upon historical relevance (see Hastrup 1985d). Having studied Icelandic history for years, I was familiar with 'the old days' in the local reflections upon history, and with the supernatural inhabitants of earlier landscapes. There had been trolls (*tröll*), 'hidden people' (*huldufólk*), and ghosts (*draugar*), to mention but a few of these categories of beings.

Inevitably, we talked about them, and talked about the folk-tales (*þjóðsögur*) that we all knew, and which had been widely read and retold in Iceland until the present day. The youngest generation, that is the grandchildren of the old couple at the farm where I lived, was actually the first generation not to have been brought up with the telling of old stories and the singing of old verses in the evenings. Their parents would sometimes regret that they had failed to give their children a part of their cultural heritage, and instead had let them turn on the television – for some five years an inevitable element in farm life. With the two adult generations I was really treading common ground and sharing an interest in these stories, however, and I marvelled at the vitality of 'tradition'.[10]

Only gradually would I come to realize that tradition was still with us in a much more direct sense as well. Although talked about as a discourse on the past, the characters that inhabited this discursive space were still present. I had been caught in the trap of taking *statements that were made in the past tense* for *statements about past conditions* (Favret-Saada 1980: 64–5 n.1).[11] I believe that my falling into this trap was due both to my actual knowledge of the position of supernatural beings in Icelandic culture since the Middle Ages, and to my seeing the Icelanders as being much closer to their past (and mine!) than Danes, for instance, and therefore as better informants about the 'old days'.

The three kinds of beings mentioned above were not equal with respect to their position in time, however. Upon probing (carefully, of course), I learnt that trolls had effectively become extinct. Their one-time reality was not questioned. My question of *when* they had disappeared was answered with 'about two hundred years ago'. I suppose that other time-indications would have been possible, and that the two hundred years was a rather arbitrary choice, prompted by the wish to be precise – in a sense that was believed to be acceptable to the academic.

As regards the 'hidden people', it was an entirely different matter. The *huldufólk* represented a category of metaphorical humans, closely associated with particular features of the landscape. Around the farmstead there were two or three places in particular where *huldufólk* had been known to dwell, and these were all rather characteristic places, rocks or suchlike breaking through the flatness of the infield area.[12] The people stated that they did not know whether the *huldufólk* were still living there, because they had not been seen for a long time. My question of 'how long' was met with hesitant reflections and some internal debate. Clearly, we were moving within the limits of personal memories, and discussion centred upon the situating of particular events to which the appearance of *huldufólk* was tied. Eventually, the first answer produced was 'twenty years', and I was given details of an encounter. Further memorizing brought forward a more recent event. Ten years ago, a whole group of *huldufólk* had been seen at the corner of the farmhouse. The event was tied down to the arrival of a certain person, who had not been seen for a long time, and they were fairly certain as to when that would have been as, again, this was associated with other major 'historical' events. What I, much later and long since back behind my desk, came to think of as perhaps a main correlate, if not the actual cause, of the disappearance of the *huldufólk*, was the introduction of electricity. This had certainly been a major event on the farm, and one which had taken place about ten years before. Would it be unreasonable to suggest that the light cast by the enormous outdoor lamps would chase off a people who wanted to retain the most distinctive feature of their identity, that is, to remain a 'hidden' folk?

If not actually 'seen', the *huldufólk* were somehow still in evidence, as they would (sometimes half-jokingly) be accused of teasing the peasants by occasionally borrowing or hiding tools that were temporarily missing. Much the same applied to the third category of supernatural beings mentioned above, the ghosts (*draugar*). Ghosts, who were generally thought of as wandering revenants, were also still in evidence – even if talked about in the past tense as well. They were unpleasant, and they were sometimes seen as bad auguries, but they were harmless. If the *huldufólk* were conceived of as metaphorical humans, *draugar* were a kind of metonymical non-human, to paraphrase Lévi-Strauss (1962: 274–75). Earlier (and this is a statement of my knowledge of their past), people would have known the exorcizing spells, but I was unable to ascertain whether they were still in use.

Characteristically, *draugar* were also present in the fishing village, where there was little or no talk about the *huldufólk*. *Draugar* were not associated with the landscape but were everywhere, elevated from topography but belonging to darkness. In the village I would often wander about in the darkness; after all, it was dark most of the time. In connection with evening visits to the houses of my workmates and other informants and friends, I was recurrently asked whether I had no fear of *draugar*. The women I knew would rarely walk alone in the dark, and they were genuinely petrified on my behalf because of my behaviour. With my knowledge of *draugar* and with my recent farm-life experience I, myself, felt completely safe, however.

Once again I had to realize that my knowledge was like a veil over reality. The fear of the local women was not due to mere superstition (which, of course, may have been real enough), but also to the fact that, in the local context, the category of *draugar* was inhabited by real, living people. I stumbled upon at least one of them, namely a middle-aged half-wit, who (according to some reports, at least) was also a sexual pervert. He roamed about in the darkness, and on reflection it seems logical that he should be classified with the *draugar*, the metonymical non-humans. Only, I had been unable to foresee that this category could comprise living people. If my anticipation had failed, so also had my understanding of the warnings I was being given. Incidentally, this also contributed to my own ambiguous position in the eyes of the local men. I was a woman who could be 'picked up' under the cover of darkness.

There is more than one lesson to be learnt from this, I believe. First of all, it seems that the sheer amount of knowledge about the history and the lore of Icelanders made the ethnographer hear statements made in the past tense as statements *about* the past, to begin with at least. I believe that this is likely to be a general feature of doing anthropology 'at home', especially in Europe or other areas with long historical records.

Conversely, and this is the second lesson, because the people studied were brought up and educated in a social and cultural context which was seen in many ways as 'similar' to that of the ethnographer, the people would readily identify her as an academic and as a representative of the urbanized élite. This made them see themselves as a kind of 'backwater' population, and although the farmers were proud of being so, they would choose the past tense whenever they were talking about matters of 'folklore'. On 'my' particular farm, this tendency was probably further intensified, because the farm had been visited by a folklorist a few years before who had wanted to record old tales from the then oldest man (the father of the present senior) 'before they died out with him'.

Third, having eventually realized that some of the beings talked about in the past tense were still an element in present beliefs, I failed to discover the real content of this category. I still read it as a sign of the past, the meaning of which I understood. But in the fishing village (and perhaps elsewhere as well) the signified had changed. Because I considered it a matter of 'belief', and I myself did not believe, I failed to note this change, and so ran a real risk of colliding with a living signifier.

Returning now to the general problem of the anthropological discourse on time, I would argue that the matter is more complicated than that suggested by Fabian, when the 'others' are (largely) 'ourselves'. It may be that anthropological discourse in general violates 'their' time, and denies the experience of coevalness in fieldwork. But when the 'ethnographic present' is formulated in the past tense by people themselves, *they* are denying coevalness. They answer questions put by the ethnographer in her own autobiographic present in an ethnographic past. They know who *you* are, and they are left with no choice of grammatical tense. Thus, the verbalizing process iself *generates reality as folk-tale*, to be heard as 'tradition', even genre – when it is actually life itself!

Thus temporal distancing occurs in the ethnography of cultures 'similar' to our own, but it occurs partly on account of your friends textualizing you, and only partly on account of the inherent fallacies in the anthropological discourse. As for this second feature of distancing, I believe that the scale used is more finely graded than when dealing with (the rhetoric of) the 'primitives'. Also the grades refer to a well-known and well-documented history of a particular people, and not to speculative stages of the evolution of mankind.

The mirror of fieldwork

In the preceding pages I have suggested that doing fieldwork in a parallel culture may be different from doing fieldwork among more exotic peoples. There is a sense, of course, in which the ethnographer will always be both stranger and friend, wherever she works, but my point was more specific. From my own experience it seemed that the sex of the ethnographer took on a distinct meaning in the shared Nordic context of the ethnographer and the people studied; the sex was 'read' locally as an ordinary signifier of gender. In alien contexts the gender specifications are more likely to be lacking. Also, it appeared that in matters of time and of temporal discourse, the extensive historical knowledge of the ethnographer tended to introduce a certain deafness towards the proper meaning of signs; the signified was trusted, while in fact one could only take the signifiers for granted.[13] Knowledge blindfolded me, I took 'evidence' for granted (cf. Herzfeld 1983a: 101). In other words, the ethnographer of 'ourselves' is in danger of being too literal-minded (cf. Fernandez 1983: 329). It remains to be discussed whether this is a difference that makes a difference (Bateson 1972: 453).

To get beyond the looking-glass, one first has to identify the tricks played by the mirror of fieldwork. A mirror is the instrument of paradox *par excellence*, according to a recent assertion by Fernandez (1980: 36–7). It presents a completely recognizable image, which is yet an inversion, in one dimension at least. It teaches you about self-objectification, but it does not stop there because next it shows you that even objects are subjects (p. 36). To invoke the metaphor of fieldwork as a mirror, then, is just another way of dissolving the distinction between subject and object in the continuous exchange between the ethnographer and the informants (Parkin 1982: xxxiii). If 'cultures' interpenetrate symbolically as they are constituted (Boon 1982: x), so do the identities of the interlocutors in the cross-cultural dialogue.

Thus in fieldwork you will always 'see' yourself while studying others, just as the anthropological discourse is a discourse with two objects, 'selves' and 'others', materializing simultaneously. In recent years this fact of the anthropologist's presence in the discourse has been widely acknowledged, and there is no point in pursuing the matter further here. Rather, I shall pose a new kind of question and ask what happens if the dialogue is no longer cross-cultural but parallel-cultural?

To answer this question briefly, I would suggest that under such conditions your fieldwork is likely to reflect the situation of the one-way mirror; *you* will see only yourself and you will identify 'them' with your own image (of past and present conditions); *they*, on the other hand, will see through to 'you', and talk to you as if you were a real person in their world, absolutely distinct from themselves.

If I have now reached a point where it seems that I have passed judgement on doing anthropology at home, and found it inferior to anthropology elsewhere, it is not so. In actual fact I think that the difference, which I have here attempted to circumscribe in so many words, does not make a difference at the level of the anthropological discourse. If there are different experiences at the personal level, and if we may describe the initial stage of fieldwork among 'friends' of yours in terms of the one-way mirror (as opposed to fieldwork where both parties are looking into one and the same mirror and seeing each other's reflections) these are still differences at the 'technical' level, if you like. At the theoretical level, or the level of explanation, such differences give way to a fundamental similarity in a common pursuit of understanding humanity. What I am arguing is, in fact, that while fieldwork among your own people may provide you with an initially different 'context of situation', this context itself will eventually become textualized within the general context of anthropology. In this discursive context the initial differences are dissolved and replaced by others.

In short, and to terminate my paper, I would maintain that from the present perspective of our subject, anthropology is neither 'here' nor 'there'. It is everywhere, being actually a third culture in any cross-cultural dialogue, wherein the 'illusion of total truth is amended by the revealed discrepancies' (E. Ardener 1982: 12) – discrepancies that exist between the cultural codes of the two interlocutors.

In fieldwork, the representative of the third culture emerges as a third-person character.[14] The ethnographer is neither I nor you, but assumes a strangely unknown position as 'she' or 'he'. She is my reflection in the mirror, the subjectified object (cf. n. 7 above, and Fernandez 1980: 35 ff.). It is from this position that she may act as the enunciator even of silences in the cross-cultural discourse. Also in her own culture, or in a parallel culture, the ethnographer – as the representative of the third culture – will inevitably live and work in the third person. As such she is a friend to the locals and a stranger to herself.

This is the truly privileged position for ethnographic work. It is not solely a matter of both participating (assuming the role of you) and observing (keeping my professional aims intact), but also, and more importantly, to let go of both and live, feel, and experience from the position of the third person. Here, the silences of both you and I are heard, and the blank banners are readable.[15]

In 1950, Evans-Pritchard claimed that 'an anthropologist has failed unless, when he says goodbye to the natives, there is on both sides the sorrow of parting' (1964: 79). We have other measures of failure today, but not necessarily more precise ones. However, I would like to qualify the 'sorrow of parting', which we have all felt on leaving our friends in the field. The sorrow also emanates from the anthropologist saying goodbye to the 'she' with whom she had become so familiar at last. On parting we leave an experience behind which is the ultimate sign of the semantic creativity of anthropology, that is, the reflection of a subject, who is a mirror-image of no one, but who will for ever 'exist' as a language-shadow in the discourse upon our friends.

Notes

1 See for instance Foote and Wilson (1970), Haugen (1976).
2 Fieldwork was carried out over a total of thirteen months in 1982–83. The expenses were covered by grants from the Danish Research Council for the Humanities and the Icelandic Ministry of Education, which I gratefully acknowledge.
3 It is true that one ;an be an anthropologist without doing fieldwork, but fieldwork is much more than a way of collecting material. It is a particular way of relating to 'evidence', and as a collective experience it is part and parcel of the anthropological discourse.
4 The view upon the two sexes as representing the generalized and the specified gender, respectively, has been discussed in Hastrup (1978b). As it stands it is related to matters of dominant and muted structures (E. Ardener 1975; S. Ardener 1975).
5 See Hastrup (1985e).
6 Cf. Leach (1964: 44 ff.).
7 Part of the paradox consists in the subject experiencing herself as object, and then perceiving the object as subject in the next instance. Translated into the personal experience related here, I would say that I first came to see myself as 'object' in a discourse made by others, after which I began acting as a new kind of subject corresponding to my status as object.
8 The notion of 'primitive' is used for the (analytical) antithesis of civilization, being defined mainly by their distinct and radically opposed relationships to 'history' (Lévi-Strauss 1961: 45).
9 The idea of the Icelanders being closer to our shared Nordic ancestry is also widely entertained by themselves. At least, reference to the Middle Ages is constantly made in national rhetoric. A thorough anthropological analysis of medieval Iceland is found in Hastrup (1985a).
   Another way of conceiving of the dissimilar histories of Iceland and Denmark is to see them as alternative realizations of what once were equal and similar possibilities. Even using this perspective one would have to acknowledge different temporalities, though, or perhaps different 'levels of dynamism' (Hanson 1983) governing history.
10 I have discussed the concept of tradition in Hastrup (1985b).
11 This work by Jeanne Favret-Saada was the original inspiration to deal with the matter of time. Although I refer here only to a note of hers, I think that the entire book has had far more influence upon my paper, even if in opaque ways, than I had realized.
12 It is characteristic that they would thereby also shatter the 'social' quality of the 'inside'. In the tales of *huldufólk* these are associated with the 'outside', clearly, but in actual life these two spheres are not always topographically separated.
13 I am here using the semiological concepts in a purely linguistic sense, 'signifiers' referring to the sound image of the words.
14 Already Pocock speaks of fieldwork as a 'dialogue of three'–the anthropologist, the society studied, and fellow sociologists (!) (Pocock 1971: 105). My 'third culture' corroborates 'fellow' scholars, but not directly. It seems that Pocock is thinking very literally about the sociological community, while I use it metaphorically.
   In his recent 'experimental' monograph, Crapanzano also mentions a third person in fieldwork, but he refers to the interpreter, acting as mediator and neutralizer between the separate spheres of interest of the anthropologist and the informant (Crapanzano 1980: 143–51). In this work the mutual influence upon the life-histories of both the anthropologist and the informant is explicitly acknowledged,

and *Tuhami* thus provides an example of the self-reflexive tendency inherent in the anthropology of the 1980s.
15 The notion of 'blank banner' is due to E. Ardener (1971: xliii ff.).

References

ARDENER, E. (1971) Introductory Essay. In E. Ardener (ed.) *Social Anthropology and Language*. ASA Monographs 10. London: Tavistock Publications.
— (1975) The 'Problem' Revisited. In S. Ardener (ed.) *Perceiving Women*. London: Dent.
— (1979) Some Outstanding Problems in the Analysis of Events. In E. Schwimmer (ed.) *Yearbook of Symbolic Anthropology*, Vol. I. London: Hurst.
— (1982) Social Anthropology, Language and Reality. In D. Parkin (ed.) *Semantic Anthropology*. ASA Monographs 22. London: Academic Press.
ARDENER, S. (1975) Introduction. In S. Ardener (ed.) *Perceiving Women*. London: Dent.
— (1984) Gender Orientations in Fieldwork. In R. Ellen (ed.) *Ethnographic Research. A Guide to General Conduct*. ASA Research Methods in Social Anthropology no. 1. London: Academic Press.
BATESON, G. (1972) *Steps to an Ecology of Mind*. New York: Ballantine.
BOON, J. A. (1982) *Other Tribes, Other Scribes. Symbolic Anthropology in the Comparative Study of Cultures, Histories, Religions and Texts*. Cambridge: Cambridge University Press.
CLEASBY, R., VIGFÚSSON, G., and CRAIGIE, R. (1975) *An Icelandic-English Dictionary* (2nd edn). Oxford: Clarendon Press.
CRAPANZANO, V. (1980) *Tuhami. Portrait of a Moroccan*. Chicago: University of Chicago Press.
CRICK, M. (1976) *Explorations in Language and Meaning. Towards a Semantic Anthropology*. London: Dent.
EVANS-PRITCHARD, E. E. (1950/1964) Fieldwork and the Empirical Tradition. *Social Anthropology and Other Essays*. New York: Free Press.
FABIAN, J. (1983). *Time and the Other. How Anthropology Makes Its Object*. New York: Columbia University Press.
FAVRET-SAADA, J. (1980) *Deadly Words. Witchcraft in the Bocage*. Cambridge: Cambridge University Press.
FERNANDEZ, J. W. (1980) Reflections on Looking into Mirrors. *Semiotica* 30: 27–39.
— (1983) Afterword: At the Center of the Human Condition. *Semiotica* 46: 323–30.
FOOTE, P. and WILSON, D. (1970) *The Viking Achievement*. London: Sidgwick & Jackson.
FOX, R. (1978) *The Tory Islanders. A People of the Celtic Fringe*. Cambridge: Cambridge University Press.
GRØNBECH, V. (1931) *The Culture of the Teutons*. London: Humphrey Milford.
HANSON, F. A. (1983) Syntagmatic Structures: How the Maoris Make Sense of History. *Semiotica* 46: 287–308.
HASTRUP, K. (1978a) The Post-Structuralist Position of Social Anthropology. In E. Schwimmer (ed.) *Yearbook of Symbolic Anthropology*, Vol. I. London: Hurst.
— (1978b) The Semantics of Biology. Virginity. In S. Ardener (ed.) *Defining Females. The Nature of Women in Society*. London: Croom-Helm.
— (1981) Cosmology and Society in Medieval Iceland. *Ethnologia Scandinavica* 63–78.

108   Kirsten Hastrup

— (1985a) *Culture and History in Medieval Iceland. An Anthropological Analysis of Structure and Change*. Oxford: Clarendon Press.

— (1985b) Tracing Tradition. An Anthropological Perspective on *Grettis saga Ásmundarsonar*. In J. Lindow, L. Lönnroth, and G. Weber (eds) *Structure and Meaning. New Approaches to Old Norse Literature*. Odense: Odense University Press.

— (1985c) Anthropology and the Exaggeration of Culture. A Review Article. *Ethnos* **50** (3–4): 313–24.

— (1985d) The Cultural Construction of Icelandic Identity. Paper presented to the interdisciplinary symposium on 'Identity and Nationalism', Copenhagen, December 1984 (forthcoming).

— (1985e) Male and Female in Icelandic Culture. *Folk* **27**.

HAUGEN, E. (1976) *The Scandinavian Languages*. New York: Faber & Faber.

HERZFELD, M. (1983a) Signs in the Field: Prospects and Issues for Semiotic Ethnography. *Semiotica* **46**: 99–106.

— (1983b) Looking Both Ways: The Ethnographer in the Text. *Semiotica* **46**: 151–66.

LEACH, E. (1964) Animal Categories and Verbal Abuse. In E. H. Lenneberg (ed.) *New Directions in the Study of Language*. Cambridge, Mass.: MIT Press.

LÉVI-STRAUSS, C. (1961) *Entretiens avec Claude Lévi-Strauss* (edited by C. Charbonnier). Paris: Plon.

— (1962) *La pensée sauvage*. Paris: Plon.

OKELY, J. (1975) The Self and Scientism. *Journal of the Anthropological Society of Oxford* **6**: 171–88.

PARKIN, D. (1982) Introduction. In D. Parkin (ed.) *Semantic Anthropology*. ASA Monographs 22. London: Academic Press.

POCOCK, D. (1971) *Social Anthropology*. London: Sheed & Ward.

POUWER, J. (1973) Signification and Fieldwork. *Journal of Symbolic Anthropology* **1**: 1–13.

SCHWIMMER, E. (1974) Friendship and Kinship. In E. Leyton (ed.) *The Compact: Selected Dimensions of Friendship*. St John's: Memorial University of Newfoundland.

Martine Segalen and Françoise Zonabend

7 Social anthropology and the ethnology of France:
the field of kinship and the family[1]

Birth of an ethnology of France

The ethnology of France is not really a new field but has roots in several traditions. There is a direct line of descent from the folklorist movement which developed, in our country, after the middle of the nineteenth century. The folklorists were fine fieldworkers and they collected a great number of traditions, customs, and practices, thereby building up a precious body of material for the understanding of present-day France, without which ethnology could not have developed to its present state. However, they were concerned above all with the study of the 'prejudices' and the 'superstitions' of a supposedly 'traditional' civilization that they thought they could see disintegrating under the impact of industrialization, which came later in France than in England. Hence they were more interested in the past than in the present, in the exceptional and the spectacular rather than the ordinary or everyday. Moreover, this body of material was gathered independently of any historical or sociological context, so that we cannot know for sure whether the folklorists observed the rites they describe or whether they relied on verbal accounts, nor do we know who the social actors were who practised them – rich peasants, agricultural workers, or townspeople? These methods of the folklorists explain in part the absence of theoretical reflection and scientific analysis that is noticeable in most of their work. It is true too that, in France, the 'folklorist' movement was put to one side, even rejected, by the university scientists, who were ignorant of it for a long time, as indeed they were of social anthropology as well. Even today there is not a single chair in any French university devoted to the ethnology of France (Cuisenier and Segalen 1986).

Let us recall that great folklorists such as Pierre Saintyves, Paul Sébillot, or Arnold Van Gennep developed their ideas in the framework of learned societies, and so outside French university circles.

Another feature of the ethnology of France is the link with museums. At the time of the founding of the first Trocadéro museum, in 1889, the ethnology of France and general ethnology were mixed together: the 'French room' was on the same footing as the 'American room', the 'Asian room', and so forth. The old Trocadéro was succeeded by the Musée de l'Homme, and this was the base from which, in 1937, Georges Henri Rivière founded the Musée des Arts et Traditions Populaires. It was from here that the whole of ethnographic research on France came to be guided and organized. This close link between museums and ethnography led to an emphasis on the collection and documentation of material objects. Between 1945 and 1970, fieldworkers collected material objects as much as cultural evidence (i.e. oral literature, music, and dance), but this time set in their appropriate socio-economic context. From this 'museum' perspective, questions of diffusion, technical invention, and cultural innovation were treated as the key issues, while at the same time classification systems were refined with a view to the presentation of objects in museum galleries. The collections undertaken before and after the last war, covering the whole field of rural culture, without doubt made possible the rescue of a heritage which is today highly valued but which, at that time, was of interest only to specialists.

This association between ethnology and museums did, however, bias the approach to social and cultural facts, in so far as their relationship with material objects is neither self-evident nor adequately self-explanatory. While it is true that marriage, for instance, can be displayed through the ritual signs that it uses – costumes and jewels, ceremonial objects – many of its social or symbolic aspects are not explained by objects, and we can only understand it by means of a whole set of questions and analyses. Similarly, facts pertaining to witchcraft or to healing practices cannot be reduced to a collection of magical dolls, or of recipes designed to cure such and such a disease. Thus it was necessary to sever, in part, this strong link between the ethnology of France and museum studies; and this is what happened when researchers trained in classical anthropology turned to the study of France. Moreover, at a very early stage, there were great anthropologists such as Lucien Bernot (see Bernot and Blancard 1953) or Louis Dumont (1951) who did their own first fieldwork in France. But for them it was more a matter of experimental, didactic research than of true anthropological reflection, and it was not until the 1960s that a real social anthropology of France was born. This new field which opened up for ethnological research posed some specific problems of its own.

The exotic illusion

Some claimed that the principle of distancing, which is normal in classical anthropology, was an absolute prerequisite for the ethnological method. Today there is agreement that the distancing of the object, supposedly productive of objectivity, is an illusion. Whether one is familiar with or a stranger to the culture one is working on, there are no absolute grounds for considering the degree of cultural difference between object and observer as either an obstacle or an advantage with regard to its objective description. Certainly it can happen that, to the observer who is close to the culture which he or she is studying, the object can seem at first to be profoundly familiar, forming part of his immediate universe. In that case facts, attitudes, behaviour patterns seem hopelessly self-evident and so indescribable, because colourless, insipid, without precise contours, as if bathed in the implicit. In these extreme situations, the first imperative, which is only the obverse of that which applies to the ethnologist of the exotic, is to defamiliarize himself with the object, to re-create artificially that distance and perspective without which any perception is impossible. This distancing, this externality to the object, can be achieved when observer and observed come to know and take into account their respective positions.

The ethnologist of the exotic must become familiar with his ethnographic field: the difficulty of grasping a different, foreign culture, the place which one assigns to the Other and which the Other assigns to oneself, understanding the language, are so many obstacles to objective knowledge. Exoticism certainly offers data which are immediately and easily descriptive because they are new, whereas familiarity blurs the object to be described. Both can prove to be deceptive. If one rejects the complicity of the strange and the illusion of the known, then ethnographic 'fields', distant or near, are revealed as on an equal footing. For it is necessary to understand fully that, in his or her own culture as in another, the ethnologist is never neutral; he or she is a member of a social class, bearer of university learning and of a certain view of the world. In that respect he is not and cannot be in a situation of equality, and this marks the relationships between the ethnologist and the group he studies. For if the ethnologist who is foreign to a group is excluded from it at the outset, the ethnologist who has come from inside the group will always be in a marginal position; he will be excluded from the group by having internalized its own taboos *a posteriori*.

The discourse of the observed is always transmitted by the observer and bears the observer's mark, whatever the latter's position may be; and in both cases there are lasting theoretical problems which are inherent in all scientific research: problems of unremitting critical reflection on the knowledge acquired, and beyond that problems of an ethical kind concerning the restitution of knowledge which has been collected in this way.

Thus one should not oppose exotic ethnology and 'ethnology at home', and in our own field of interest, kinship and the family, it is the encounter with general anthropology that has permitted us to restructure our enquiries. Kinship and the family were not unknown to earlier ethnologists of France; they were especially interested in rites of passage (Van Gennep 1909, 1946) but alliance structures were outside their field of research. It was only after

112   Martine Segalen and Françoise Zonabend

Claude Lévi-Strauss had distinguished societies with elementary systems of kinship from those with complex systems of kinship (1968) that it was possible to look at marriage in a new light. Similarly, Jack Goody's comparison (1976a and b) of different systems of property transmission enabled a fresh anthropological look to be taken at modes of inheritance, a field of study which formerly (in the case of our own societies, at least) came under the heading of law.

The contemporary sociology of the family has therefore progressed since the dialogue with anthropology began. Under its influence, the over-fluid concept of 'the family' has been replaced by analytical concepts such as the domestic group and kinship, whose transformations can be followed through modes of filiation, residence, and the transmission of property. The European family is no longer singled out as the specific product of Western society, but is restored to the continuum of societies studied by anthropologists. There is a methodological continuity, too, in the need to study, as in any society, the vocabulary of kinship, to observe how the genealogical and familial memory of interlocutors is organized, and to analyse the social practices of kinship.

Difficult concepts to transpose

There are, however, limits to parallelism in this field between general anthropology and the anthropology of European societies. Is it possible to transpose a conceptual vocabulary forged by and for societies exotic to ours? How can we build up a working vocabulary to understand the specificity of our own societies?

Anthropologists of Europe borrow from general anthropology some concepts which fit very imperfectly the kinship groups with which they have to deal. Clan and lineage relate to kinship groups with a strong genealogical depth, uniting kinsfolk through a single line of filiation to a common ancestor, whether mythical or real. There is nothing similar in European societies: one can certainly speak of lineages, but they are not at all deep genealogically; they are never institutionalized as corporate groups. Moreover, the use of these terms makes one think of society in unilinear terms, whereas, although our own societies present a patrilineal or matrilineal emphasis, they are in reality deeply undifferentiated.

Does the concept of *parentèle* (or kindred) work better? The classical description given by Freeman for the Iban of Borneo (1971) certainly grasps some of the facts of kinship observed in our societies: cognatic filiation, fluidity of kinship ties, *ad hoc* and temporary constitution of kinship groups to achieve such and such a task in such and such a situation. The *parentèle* of numerous modern rural or urban societies can be described in this way. Yet there is one essential datum which distinguishes our societies: they are multi-dimensional, 'interleaved' (*feuilletées*) as Lévi-Strauss has said; we have to take account of the emergence of the state, the church, the role of economics as it connects with kinship or becomes autonomous from it. In peasant societies especially – where the way of life is linked to access to land – the system of land tenure and farm ownership, price and market conditions must be known both independently from the facts of kinship and also in their relationship with kinship. From this perspective, the neologism 'patrimonial lineage' (Lamaison 1979) seems to be useful because it allows us to locate within each sibling group the individual among the children who will be his or her father's successor. From such units, we can start to look for 'matrimonial regularities'.

Is it possible to go beyond that vague expression and study the structuring of the matrimonial field in European societies? Can we locate – as has been done in alliance theory – units of exchange between which there is a circulation of spouses? It is often difficult, notably in societies where there is high mobility and a high incidence of tenant farming, and where farms cannot be assimilated to discrete units. Nor can one easily identify any circulation of women in these generally cognatic societies; on the contrary, there are often documented cases of what are locally known as 'son-in-law marriages', when the son-in-law instals himself on his parents-in-law's farm.

Françoise Héritier, arguing a continuity between elementary, semi-complex, and complex societies, has postulated that 'traditional cognatic societies with matrimonial prohibitions practise, systematically if not preferentially, marriage by "looping" within the circle of blood relations beyond the point where prohibitions operate; moreover, they simultaneously practise the exchange of sisters and the reinforcing of alliances by blood relatives of the same sex' (1981: 149). Marriage in complex societies, or at least in peasant societies, would on this reading be connected with kinship by means of loopings within consanguinity, restricted exchanges (in Lévi-Strauss's sense), and the creation of cycles.

Many research projects are currently exploring these hypotheses, which call for the building up of genealogies from state archives. In fact, the memory of informants seldom goes back more than four generations, and also certain lines are privileged in relation to others, so that oral genealogies are always truncated. Because of the bilaterality of the kinship system, and also because the location of these cycles and loops necessitates in-depth knowledge of genealogies, recourse to the archives is always vital.

As for the 'loopings', or more simply marriages between consanguines, we can observe their frequency from ecclesiastical archives which give dispensation for marriages, in principle forbidden, for up to 4 – 4 cousinship – that is to say, the children's children of first cousins, or between spouses whose grandparents were cousins. Beyond that prohibition, one cannot verify the statistical and preferential importance of marriage between consanguines without assembling a vast body of genealogical data and then devising simulation programmes to compare the actual frequency of these unions with their possible frequency, taking account of the number of 5-5 cousins that the average individual possesses according to the demographic pattern of the population under study. With the exception of some findings concerning an area in Brittany (Segalen 1985: 146), it is not yet possible to negate or confirm this proposition.

As for cycles, Pierre Lamaison (1979) has discussed some of these in the course of his analysis of the marriages of heirs belonging to the patrimonial lines of a village in Gévaudan. Studying the circulation of dowries, he has noted that dowries which 'leave' a house end by returning there after several generations, sometimes covering more than two centuries. Such matrimonial patterns are quite unconscious and the social actors have no real hold on them. By contrast, conscious strategies are clearly expressed in the matrimonial figures that are attached to various forms of restricted exchange: these are often documented in peasant societies. Thus there are marriages which unite sibling groups, and these are found in very different socio-economic contexts. Certainly the simultaneous marriage of two different male heirs with each other's sister allows a resolution of the problem of dowry in impartible (*préciputaire*) societies: each family gives its daughter the same dowry but this remains fictive, so the money does not leave the house. But one can equally well see that marriage between sibling groups is spread through-out 'egalitarian' or partible societies, though in that case, the dowries really leave the patrimony of each family. One is obliged to conclude that matrimonial patterns do not necessarily have patrimonial ends, or that in any case marriage is not solely a corrective to the system of inheritance. The causes must be found in factors which are political – such as rivalries for control of local power – or else symbolic – the fact of staying within one's kinship universe, between lines of the same status.

Another type of marriage answering to conscious strategies, and also very common in European societies, is the pattern designated by the term 'chaining or renewal of alliance', as the anthropologists called it when they encountered and identified it for the first time (Jolas, Verdier, and Zonabend 1970). This describes the marriage between two lines which 'renews' a marriage that had taken place some generations previously: the second union reties, in a sense, the knot between lines already allied. This pattern of alliance is not exceptional, indeed it seems to be widespread as more research is carried out. But it would be hard to include it within the general theory of alliance, except as a variant of the category of generalized exchange. To what ends does the pattern correspond? Is it a means of staying within one's own kinship universe while getting round the church's prohibitions – for such unions keep the same lines united, while at the same time avoiding con-sanguineous marriages? Is it a way of avoiding incest, of resolving the dilemma of proximity versus distance, exchange versus endogamy? Should we think of special social, political, or economic motivations? It is important that research on our contemporary societies should develop and that it should refine our knowledge of these 'chainings of alliance' that seem to be encountered in numerous social groups. Moreover, they can take several forms. Thus we can find chainings of alliance that are linked to a widowhood or to a remarriage: here the chaining seems to be a way of preserving bonds with the deceased's family or of reinforcing bonds with the family of a second spouse. Equally, special attention needs to be paid to building up a vocabulary and concepts relating to modes of property inheritance.

In France there is a great diversity of systems of property inheritance: *préciputaire* (or inegalitarian) systems in the centre and south of France, egalitarian systems in the north and west. This crude distinction has to be refined considerably; we must take account of practices and norms, examine the modes of property-owning – freehold or leasehold – which mould attitudes and strategies. Jack Goody, however (1973, 1976b), does not take account of this distinction when he contrasts the system of 'bride-wealth' or 'bride-price' – matrimonial prestations circulating from the group of wife-takers to the group of wife-givers – with the Eurasian system of 'dowry' associated with a method of diverging devolution. However, the French example invites us to reflect on this contrast, because the same term 'dowry' embraces two quite different systems. In an 'egalitarian' regime, the dowry is a sum of money given by the parents to both parties to the marriage in order to allow them to set up house, immediately or later; and it can be brought back or not, as the case may be, to the estate on the death of the parents. Thus the dowry is often a sum paid in instalments, more a hope of inheritance than a tangible asset, and the husband as well as the wife is the recipient.

Under the 'inegalitarian' system, the term 'dowry' describes quite another mode of property transfer. The dowry is a sum of money paid to those of the children who will not inherit: it serves to pay them off from the family patrimony. If the son is the heir, he will say that he has 'paid his sisters' (Collomp 1983), meaning that they have received their share and have no further rights to the family patrimony. Families were very reluctant to impoverish themselves by paying these sums, hence the frequency of the double brother–sister marriages mentioned above, which avoided any diminution of the family capital. Here again, developments in the anthropology of kinship in European societies show the necessity of devising an adequate vocabulary to characterize specific phenomena. Can we really continue to call by the same name modes of inheritance which can be opposed conceptually to each other, detail by detail?

Dowry under egalitarian systems	*Dowry under inegalitarian systems*
All members of a sibling group receive one	Only non-successors receive one
Generally supplemented at the point of inheritance	Not supplemented at the point of inheritance
Consists of money but also of land and cattle	Cash only

| Both husband and wife receive it | The son who stays within the family house does not get one; daughters are generally endowed and excluded |
| Marks the link with family property which is shared among everyone | Marks the break with the family property, which is transmitted to a single heir |

Recent researches have shown, moreover, that it is not sufficient to confine oneself only to the forms of transmission of patrimony if one wants to study structures of matrimonial alliance. It seems to be necessary to examine the social practices of kinship, that is to say, the roles and functions of kinship within each group studied.

The social practices of kinship

Such practices can be grasped in the first place through the vocabulary that each society has developed to 'talk' of its relatives.

Alongside the current terminology used everywhere in France, there coexists a regional vocabulary which, when it can be reconstituted, allows us to see the structure of local systems of thought and grasp more adequately, for example, the relative weighting attributed in a given society to, say, alliance versus consanguinity, or descent versus siblingship (Zonabend 1981; Segalen 1985).

We can still try to understand these practices through forms of reproduction which any system of kinship borrows to ensure its perpetuation. Take the case of ways of transmitting individual names. Everyone carries a surname (*nom de famille*), a patronym transmitted from father to daughter and son for generations, constituting a real symbolic patrimony which gives its bearers their unity and their identity. The given name or names sometimes play the same role, in so far as they are drawn from among those borne by members of the paternal or maternal line, living or dead. The most frequent usage ascribes to the eldest boy the given name of his paternal grandfather, and the eldest girl that of her maternal grandmother; the younger son or daughter receives respectively the given names of the maternal grandfather and paternal grandmother; as for other members of the sibling group, they bear the given names of collaterals chosen in turn from one line or the other. But there are many other norms for choosing given names (Bromberger and Porcell 1976; Zonabend 1979; Formes de nomination en Europe 1980), all of which reveal cycles, repeats of the same name, regular transmissions. Given names are thus perpetuated within family lines and ease the entry of new members into the family. But this same name, once accepted and used continually, is charged with the presence of all the dead relatives who bore it. Such names have the role of uniting the living and the dead, providing a kind of survival for past generations as if, within the family group, real human losses were perpetually being compensated for by these new members bearing the old names.

The study of the forms assumed by family memory is another way of understanding the roles and functions of kinship. This memory can be located by means of the places and spaces where families live.

Thus, if one looks at the place where a married couple and their unmarried children live, their intimate domestic life is enacted in a space where a set of quasi-ritualized behaviours can be observed, tracing the unique character of each unit. This space gives an indication of the social rank, cultural milieu, and regional origin of the group which resides there, and it constitutes, now as before, an anchorage for family memory.

The furniture, ornaments, knick-knacks – all these objects have a history that can be recounted in detail. Each has a meaning to be deciphered within the family, a story to be narrated. There is precise accounting for property received, shared, passed on; genealogy is tangibly recollected by means of these objects whose origin, history, and future are known. Thus the role of kinship relationships is illustrated, thus the perpetuity of the family is shown. In these ordered spaces representing family values, everything is evidence of the different stages in the constitution of the family, along the generations and within a single generation.

Distancing and restitution: some specific methodological problems

The study of vocabulary, names, memory, and the discourse on kinship which each social group conducts, presents special difficulties to the anthropologist at work within his or her own culture. This distancing of the object of study proves particularly thorny where kinship is concerned, for two reasons.

The situations that the social anthropologist must study are practically identical to those which confront him daily in his personal life, or which involve him recurrently. He or she must then reach a new understanding of phenomena that seem to him nonetheless to be self-evident. The difficulty is especially serious because the phenomenon 'family' is intensely familiar, and the discourse linked with it is profoundly internalized. When one 'talks family' with any interlocutor, one is always approaching a secret, hidden, intimate realm which borders on sexuality and affectivity, sometimes on social morals. To surmount these difficulties, research must be undertaken slowly and time must be allowed for the relationship between observed and observer to develop. Here as elsewhere there should be no attempt to economize with time.

These methodological and epistemological difficulties once resolved, there remain ethical problems. What should one make public from one's findings? What words can be contributed to the general fund of information, without the persons who have uttered them recognizing themselves? How can one present the ethnographic description which is necessary to all anthropological theorizing without embarrassment to those who have provided its elements?

The problems of returning findings to the field can be formulated in analogous ethical terms, whether one is studying exotic societies or not; but geographical proximity, the sharing of a single culture and language, and the insistence of the subjects of investigation that they read a report in preparation – all these factors pose the question in very different terms when one is working in one's own society. In our own societies, whom are we writing for? To begin with, we have to account to our scientific employers who finance our research, and to our university colleagues– hence the production of a certain type of text. But we also owe to our subjects in the field some account in which they can find themselves or learn the results of our research. We must take care not to impoverish our analysis to the point that the impression given is that the researcher is only describing what everyone knows by virtue of sharing in the culture. We, both, in our own fieldwork, surmounted the difficulty by organizing exhibitions in villages where research had been conducted, in Burgundy and Brittany respectively: the exhibitions dealt with the social history of the community with the help of photographs, and all kinds of archival documents and maps. With these exhibitions, accompanied by local lectures, the reciprocity of exchange between anthropologist and informant was established.

Many researchers who style themselves social anthropologists impose on themselves as a constraint – or perhaps it is a refuge – the rule that as far as kinship is concerned they gather only material relating to the past, only that which is strongly formalized and dying out: bygone rituals, biographies of ancestors and so forth, which present, at first sight, an innocuous aspect. We would not wish to belittle these data-gathering projects, only to point out their limitations, and above all how necessary it is to reflect collectively on the difficulties inherent in this field of study, so as to formulate clearly the ethical problems that are likely to arise.

Note

1 Translation by Jonathan Benthall (who would like to thank Simon Roberts for his advice with regard to some technical terms).

References

BERNOT, L. and BLANCARD, R. (1953) *Nouville, un village français*. Paris: Institut d'Ethnologie.

BROMBERGER, C. and PORCELL, G. (1976) Choix, dation et utilisation des noms propres dans une commune de l'Hérault: Bouzigues. *Le Monde alpin et rhodanien* **1–2**: 133–51.

COLLOMP, A. (1983) *La maison du père*. Paris: Presses Universitaires de France.

CUISENIER, J. and SEGALEN, M. (1986) *L'Ethnologie de la France*. Paris: Presses Universitaires de France, Que Sais-Je.

DUMONT, L. (1951) *La Tarasque. Essai de description d'un fait local d'un point de vue ethnographique*. Paris: Gallimard.

Formes de nomination en Europe (1980) *L'Homme* **XX** (Oct–Dec.): 4.

FREEMAN, J. D. (1971) The Family System of the Iban of Borneo. In J. Goody (ed.) *The Developmental Cycle in Domestic Groups*. Cambridge: Cambridge University Press.

GOODY, J. (1973) Bridewealth and Dowry in Africa and Eurasia. In J. Goody and S. J. Tambiah (eds) *Bridewealth and Dowry*. Cambridge: Cambridge University Press.

— (1976a) *Production and Reproduction: A Comparative Study of the Domestic Domain*. Cambridge: Cambridge University Press.

— (1976b) Inheritance, Property and Women: Some Comparative Considerations. In J. Goody, J. Thirsk, and E. P. Thompson (eds) *Family and Inheritance. Rural Society in Western Europe, 1200–1800*. Cambridge: Cambridge University Press.

HÉRITIER, F. (1981) *L'exercice de la parenté*. Paris: EHESS, Gallimard/Le Seuil.

JOLAS, T., VERDIER, Y., and ZONABEND, F. (1970) Parler famille. *L'Homme* **X** (July–Sept.): 5–26.

LAMAISON, P. (1979) Les stratégies matrimoniales dans un système complexe de parenté: Ribennes en Gévaudan (1650–1830). *Annales ESC* **34** (4): 721–43.

LÉVI-STRAUSS, C. (1968) *Les structures élémentaires de la parenté*. Paris: Mouton.

SEGALEN, M. (1985) *Quinze générations de Bas-Bretons. Parenté et société dans le pays bigouden sud 1720–1980*. Paris: Presses Universitaires de France.

VAN GENNEP, A. (1909) *Les rites de passage*. Paris: E. Nourry.

— (1943, 1946) *Manuel de folklore français contemporain*, Tome I, Vols 1 and 2. Paris: A. Picard.

ZONABEND, F. (1979) Jeux de noms. Les noms de personnes à Minot. *Etudes rurales* **74** (April–June): 51–85.

— (1981) Le très proche et le pas trop loin. *Ethnologie Française* **XI** (4): 311–18.

Maryon McDonald

8 The politics of fieldwork in Brittany

Different cultures

The main geographical focus of this paper is on Brittany, France, and the main theoretical thrust, if such it can be called, concerns the question of moving between different groups and different sets of values – we might even say different cultures. There is nothing particularly novel about that, one might say: it is, surely, what anthropology is doing all the time. Quite so. Sometimes, however, the situation can get quite complicated.

As anthropology has come closer to home, so, too, has ethnography become finer in detail. This is partly attributable to a shift from the large unit categories which we have allowed to be stretched over the belly of the globe, to the finer distinctions, in categories of time, space, and 'ethnic' identification, for example, which we know to crowd the more temperate zones (on this general point, see Ardener 1985). For some anthropologists, this has meant a fascination with internal variety and a shying away from the study of large unit categories at home, on unstated moral and political grounds, or in some positivistic fear of inexhaustiveness. The finer grain of modern ethnography, however, can allow us to grasp heterogeneity in categories of identity (including, for example, 'the English' and 'England') in a way which is quite compatible with, and demands, a sensitivity to local context, and which lifts us out of simple geography and positivist innocence. There are different constructions of, say, 'England', of 'France', of 'Brittany', and so on, and different notions of what is, or of what it is to be, 'English', 'French', or 'Breton'. My initial research project in Brittany, the subject of this paper, could be described as a study of France, of the French, and of French culture, and it could be described also as a study of Brittany, of the Bretons, and of Breton culture, and all these notions were drawn up differently by different sectors of the population, according to how they defined themselves. I also gained an ethnography of different perceptions of England and the English.

As anthropologists we can no longer, I think, slap a political or ethnological label on to an area, read it backwards and forwards in history, and demand the identification of the people in that particular place with a particular language and culture. This is, interestingly, a still common practice in educated circles, and particularly so in areas of 'ethnic' or 'minority' interest (of which Brittany is one example). It supplies its own tautological ways of imposing homogeneity and excluding the undesirable intrusions of different and perhaps conflicting views. Anthropologists have traditionally been rather good at this practice, at throwing their own boundaries around the world they have wished to study, at ironing out the differing cultural content, and contextual arbitrariness, of the categories of identity they impose, and at rendering invisible anything from administrators to modern tourists or local academics. They may well have had to negotiate the different realities involved when actually in the field, but the problems are usually invisible in the final ethnography.

A not unrelated problem has cropped up now that anthropology is closer to home: friends, often academic friends, can visit the anthropologist during fieldwork, and it is not always easy to change one's whole manner, conversation, and persona, and accommodate what are often two different worlds. One simple solution has been to ask friends not to come, or to meet them elsewhere. This could be an arrangement of simple courtesy, trying not to mix people who risk offending and misinterpreting, each through the structures of their own world, the other's proprieties. What happens, however, if you are actually studying both worlds – if you are actually studying, say, intellectuals, on the one hand, and relatively uneducated people who hold very different values, on the other? And what if they actually live next door to each other? You could, of course, just note the encounters and watch the occasional fireworks, but it is likely that there will come a point when the fireworks start exploding round you. That, roughly, is the point I shall get to at the end of this paper. Before going any further, however, I want to make a more general point about moving and translating between different worlds, and we can start off with one very obvious division between 'home' and 'abroad', between Britain and France.

Symbolic boundaries

France is not far from Britain. It is possible to go there for a day's shopping trip, and, similarly, there are French shoppers who come to Britain. This two-way traffic, with its attendant thrills, is not a simple emanation of either geographical propinquity or some economic base. Much of the excitement derives, rather, from the crossing of a known boundary, British on one side and French on the other. The crossing of this boundary, and the shopping trip image, can serve us as a useful metaphor for understanding certain aspects of the way in which identities are created and confirmed, and structurally arbitrary boundaries are drawn and redrawn. We could, of course, find boundaries, and excitement in their crossing, without all the back-up of passports, customs officials, money and language differences, and so on, which (for the time being at least) mark so clearly a line between Britain and France. For example, this paper was first drafted for a conference in Staffordshire, and this, for a 'southerner' such as myself, has long been a place of dark and devious, murky and mysterious goings-on. I still cannot avoid a slight thrill when the train crosses an unseen line somewhere after Birmingham. Insecurities crowd in, anything could happen, the people even talk oddly, they are warmer perhaps, or lacking in manners, different anyway, and I always knew they were. The boundary is not drawn on the ground, it shifts around, and if I met a 'northerner' in a London hotel foyer, it could pop up in the cartoon bubbles of mutual perception. I am over-condensing some important issues here, but I hope one simple point emerges clearly enough: we can find symbolic boundaries right on our doorstep (and often quite literally so) and they are nonetheless 'real' for that. We can, and do, pack moral, political, economic, linguistic, geographical, biological, historical, and other social, cultural differences into the divide, and we both perceive the divide as these differences and perceive these differences in the divide.

Before this starts to sound more complicated than it need do, let us come back to the perhaps more attractive image of a crossing to France. This divide has a tried and tested capacity to bring national identities alive, in the ferry port, on the boat, anywhere. Fred Bloggs and Sir Henry may feel quite at home with each other over a drink at the bar, although they had not spoken a word to each other before and probably never will again. British football supporters may be in no doubt that they are going to an 'away' match, and determined to show the foreigners what they're made of. Stuff the wine, let's have some real booze, and down goes one can of beer after another. And so on. While some make themselves thus at home in a big way, and only quite so at home because away from it, others savour the delights of being away from home by endeavouring to go native. Home-grown images of the 'French' world then commonly reappear, with the areas of food and wine providing the most obvious examples. 'French food', we all know, is jolly good stuff. The French always did know how to eat. So they do, but it is interesting that what counts as 'French food' can be as special to rural French people as it is to the British traveller, and the urbane British traveller is often far more at home with it. The phenomenon of 'French wine' bears some structural similarities to that of 'French food'. As shopping caddies testify, this, to many British visitors, is what France is all about: wine. It is not a simple *rouge* or *vin ordinaire* that these travellers bring back with them, even if that is what it says on the labels of their six litre bottles: it is 'French wine'. The structural mismatch is such that what, in many French localities, would spell alcoholics or uncouth masculinity, may well be about to become, in Britain, various expressions of sophistication or of femininity.

If it can sometimes seem odd to French people that the British should concentrate so fiercely on wine, the reverse shopping trips can also offer surprises. One woman whom I came to know well in Brittany proudly returned from a shopping trip to England with her several shopping caddies packed with – lamb chops. Such a prize was not uncommon, and the return shoppers entertained regally with, and received compliments and thanks for, their lamb chops. They were not, of course, lamb chops, any more than 'French wine' is or was *du rouge*. They were variously 'English meat' or *côtelettes d'agneau* or *côtes d'agneau*. What, for me, figured as common fare was here, in France, the stuff of a rather special dinner party (and not necessarily cooked any differently, ketchup and all). Clearly, the same objects can, in different worlds, have very different values. To invoke economic determinism here would be to miss the point.

By a perhaps circuitous route, I hope I have made it clear that just where is 'at home' and where is not, and what constitutes the boundary between the two, does not necessarily entail crossing international frontiers; and that, wherever we go, an entire return trip can easily be made with a home-spun cultural baggage intact. Apparently 'going native' does not necessarily mean that, in your cultural baggage, home categories and values have been notionally exchanged for, or set against, a different, indigenous set; it might just mean that the home baggage has assumed greater conviction, or been, as it were, well fed. One has no more captured French reality by bringing home bottles of 'French wine' or packets of *croissants* (or, more accurately perhaps, kwassonce), than one has captured British life with *côtes d'agneau*. In some respects, such items are structural translations of each other. It could be said, for example, that the French for 'kwassonce' is *le toast*.

All this might seem rather trivial, and so perhaps it is, but the points I am making are not far removed, I think, from some hoary old problems of anthropology which we might imagine we had got rid of some time ago, but which might merely reassert themselves now that anthropology, or some of it at least, has apparently come closer to home. We now realize, I think, that some anthropology never actually left home, or never really returned with its home categories and values seriously challenged in any way other than that in which we might expect them to be disturbed. We expected the natives to have lots of ritual, religion, kinship, metaphor, marvel, myth, and meaning, and that is what we found. (And then to give them politics, economics, law, science, and rationality, while a well-meaning compensation, is often merely to work with the same structures.) I am not saying that this was, or is, necessarily 'wrong', and there are some very good reasons why, in the experiential reality of the observer at least, this kind of presentation might be deemed quite right. What I am saying is that, while I love to drink 'French wine', I also want to know why I am drinking it (there is nothing naturally good-tasting about it, after all); and I want to know why it is that, at the crossing of some unseen and shifting line between 'British' reality and 'French', I now stop drinking it, and might turn instead to tea, or, rather, *le thé*, and would not feel at home in France if I did not.

I am not going to answer such questions literally here.[1] I have used these issues as a fairly easy, and perhaps topical, way in to certain questions that the general subject of 'anthropology at home' raises, and which my own work in Brittany has raised for me quite specifically. I want to move on now to Brittany, therefore, and shall deal with it in the following way. First of all, I try to situate Brittany in France, and give some idea of its image and attraction; second, I outline my fieldwork in Brittany, and the different groups with whom I was based; and, third, I give a brief account of reactions to the written results of this fieldwork.[2] If all this seems rather removed from 'lamb chops' or 'French wine', and so on, let me just say that, conceptually, it is not.

The attraction of Brittany

I think I was attracted to France in the first place by things of the order of 'French wine', with the odd Gauloise or two thrown in. It is perhaps enough said here if I just point out that, as we all know, France is both civilized and exotic, and, above all, jolly sophisticated. (Why else would we have tolerated all those 'epistemological ruptures' and Lacanian in-jokes?) I had already carted my cultural baggage round much of the rest of the globe, and France seemed as good a place, and as exotic a place, as any. Once within France, however, there is much which, within the structures of the French world, would direct attention to Brittany.

Certainly, much internal French attention has been focused on this far west peninsula. France has taken a sometimes guarded, sometimes enthusiastic, interest in its provinces since the 1789 Revolution, when a new and single nation was to be created – and the authorities were keen to know just who all these people were who were now meant, somehow or other, to be turned into free and equal 'citizens'. Generally speaking, whatever the provinces were felt to have, good or bad, Brittany had more of it. For example, in the search for national origins, a common ancestry for the new nation, France was felt to be Celtic, and Brittany supremely so. There was the Breton language to prove it, and no doubt all kinds of odd things still went on in that distant peninsula that could be seen as survivals of Celtic mysteries, fairies, druids, and the like. Visits and enquiries naturally proved this to be the case. We can imagine the thrill sensed by travellers throughout the nineteenth century when they crossed some imaginary line that separated civilized rationality from whatever it was not. This line could begin anywhere west of Paris, but certainly made itself felt the nearer one got to Lower Brittany, or the western most,

Breton-speaking area. For every fashion of romanticism, for the folklorist right on to the modern visitor, tourist, or social scientist, Brittany has regularly been required to yield special interest and excitement, and so it does. This is not simply because visitors might see only what they want to see, or because indigenous actions and categories confirm any sense of mystery, irrationality, riot, splendour, or spangle as they dance around those of the visitor; it is also because visitors' expectations are sometimes willingly confirmed by local aspirations, and some hollow categories filled: there may or may not have been druids in Dark Age Brittany, for example, but there are certainly a number of them now.

Interest in Brittany, and the various images of it, have not been without their political context. In the nineteenth century, certain Breton noblemen, priests, and scholars, some of them openly ultra-Catholic and legitimist, constructed a chaste, traditional Brittany in moral and political opposition to the Republic that was threatening their traditional seats of power and corrupting the populace; the Breton language was to be promoted as a guard against French and its republican depravities; they now felt that Breton was, in any case, not proof of Brittany's Frenchness, but of its distinct unFrenchness, and the 'Celtic' category was filled with flesh and blood that traced the Bretons back, not to the French Celtic Gauls, but to the insular Celts, the ancient Britons. However, the French nation was, by definition, French-speaking and, in the Republican view, if all citizens were to be truly free and equal, then they should all – and not just the clergy and noblemen who had ruled under the *ancien régime* – have access to French. For the authorities, the nineteenth-century scholars and legitimists evoked images of the clerics and nobles who had unwillingly surrendered their privileges at the passing of the *ancien régime*, and of events such as the *chouan* revolts, which became associated with Brittany. The nobles and scholars themselves did not object to such a collapse of history, and actively contributed to it, reading their own Breton/French divides back into these other, different, battles of the past. All this combined to give Breton and Brittany enduring images of clericalism, religious fanaticism, and political reaction, and to make the Republic ever more determined to spread French in the province.

While a small group of noblemen, clerics, and scholars now promoted Breton and its new Celtic poesy, song, and mysteries as an unFrench culture threatened with immorality and violation, other erudites and folklorists found, in the same source, edifying popular song and poems for Republic and Empire, and various curiosities that should be collected and noted before they were, rightly if sadly, eclipsed by positive thinking or civilized rationality.[3] For many, Brittany remained, both in external image and self-image, a particularly backward area in need of schooling.[4] While some administrators, at both local and national levels, may have sharpened their efforts, therefore, and may still imagine themselves to be facing the *chouans* in every peasant unrest, there are, on the other hand, self-consciously 'Breton' enthusiasts who, in their own political collapse of history, have tried deliberately to conflate King Arthur, the *chouans*, Celtic impetuosity, the thickness of Breton skulls, and every peasant demonstration with their own modern protests demanding a politically autonomous and Breton-speaking Brittany.[5] A more moderate 'legendary stubbornness' of the Bretons is now a common image in social science, and it has occasionally been appropriated by members of the Breton workforce themselves and used as a slogan in modern strikes and demonstrations, but without nationalist or separatist implication (see Lovecy 1982).

The air of archaic resistance to change that all such images have given to Brittany has helped to make the region all the more attractive to certain brands of modern social science, anthropology included. Added to this, Brittany is still a rural area, with a sizeable active peasantry, and it still has the Breton language. Set in the demographic and linguistic context of France, these factors have had the capacity to inject new, symbolically dangerous excitement in recent times. It was only in the 1960s that French social science began to note 'the end of the peasantry', to talk of the 'vanishing peasant', to find this feature of exotica and revolution right at home, and a modern ethnography of rural France was launched.[6] Brittany, where the rural population fell to under half the total only in the 1960s, was one obvious site for such an ethnography.[7] Such is its appeal that a rather jovial, urban-dwelling classics teacher has been able to turn his Breton-rural-roots autobiography into a national (and international) best-seller, and find it classified as ethnography and published by the same Paris publishing house, and in the same series, that had earlier produced Claude Lévi-Strauss, and his *Tristes Tropiques* (Hélias 1975; 1975/1978).

While this last work – the work of Per Jakez Hélias – has been tremendously popular not only in France overall but also among the Breton peasantry itself, it has come under heavy fire, in writing and in speech, from one particular sector of the Breton population: from the modern Breton movement. This movement, publicly united around a defence of Breton language and culture, entertains various visions of political nationalism and separatism. It is largely made up of well-educated people who have been brought up in French, but who have learnt Breton and use it with some enthusiasm. University departments are important recruiting-grounds for members (or 'militants' as they prefer to call themselves, 'activists' having, in their circles, some pejorative connotations, including that of mindless bomb-throwing). There are a number of social scientists (including anthropologists) in the movement, and there are many others who might not consider themselves Breton militants, but who nonetheless write and rewrite the militants' discourse for them. Since, as my fieldwork with the Breton movement made clear, all youthful and modern, politically radical metaphors of educated, moral right have been discursively stacked on the movement's side, it is not easy to do anything else.

The two major criticisms that Breton militants have made of Hélias' book are that it is 'folklore' and that it is written in French. Hélias claims he wrote much of it in Breton first, but this has not satisfied the movement, and the appearance of an English version before any sign of the promised Breton text has certainly not helped to endear him to militant circles. The vast majority of the Breton-speaking population of Brittany would have difficulty reading it if it were published in Breton, but the politically symbolic Breton text will nevertheless be forthcoming as required. As implied in the pejorative classification of the work as 'folklore', Hélias' book seems, unforgivably to the movement, to present a disappearing world without any obvious sign of the political commitment that is now required in both historiography and epistemology. His book even suggests that he and others quite enjoyed learning French at school at times, and there is no claim to being either 'traumatized' or 'alienated' (common terms in militant vocabulary) by the experience, or by the fact of speaking French.

After the events of 'May '68' in France, and with influences such as Algeria and Third World peasant movements, the peasantry, the regional languages they speak, and decentralization, all shifted from being the property of political reaction in France to being the property of the political left. Within a very short time, left-wing political parties were, at the national level, taking on such causes as decentralization and more Breton in the schools, and radical Parisian chic became devoted to France's 'minorities' (see, for example, *Les Temps Modernes*, 1973, nos 324–26). The Breton movement itself shifted, in the 1960s, from such safe preoccupations as Celtic dances and Breton costumes to being a very different animal, much larger, younger, and, above all, politically committed – in a post-1960s framework. (Within which, the spiritual, formerly Catholic, Celt became the natural, and often Marxist-Leninist, anti-capitalist.) Many French intellectuals have found political excitement and mileage in attacking French and writing about Breton, and in a Republic which had, since its inception, made the French nation and the French language synonymous, there could be no better stick than a regional language, such as Breton, with which to beat the government on the head.

The modern Breton movement has taken much of its vigour from opposition to a largely right-wing Fifth Republic. My own fieldwork with the movement covered the end of the 1970s and the beginning of the 1980s, a time of the heyday of political counter-culture in France, and when the Breton movement was, in many ways, at its height. I was then one of many who were researching or writing theses and books about Breton language and culture. Since the 1960s there has been an explosion of such works, and many, in the full flood of enthusiasm, have been written in Breton.

My own thesis is written in English. In pragmatic mood, Breton militants were pleased about this, and it is clear now that I was meant to be part of their publicity machine. Other anglophone researchers whom I met in Brittany have written up their work in English (e.g. Hewitt 1977; Kuter 1981) and have then followed it up either by setting up international groups for the 'defence' of Breton language and culture, or have stayed on in Brittany itself and become important figures in the ranks of the movement. Their written work accepts, in each case, the broad outline of Breton reality as put forward by the movement. My work differs from theirs in that I considered the views of the movement as part of the ethnography. This does not mean that I did not believe the militants, or that I did not accept that their values and beliefs about the world were rational, or had objective reality for the militants themselves. I treated their views ethnographically, and no more threw myself into their world as one I would readily take on as my own any more than I might seriously consider sticking it out for life in, say, some South American jungle. Or so I told myself. However, I had very much in common with the intellectuals of the Breton movement. Moreover, they have a cause, a reality, a story, that the literate, educated world at large can recognize, and which is posed in terms of self-evident praiseworthiness. To treat their views ethnographically is not to lapse into moral relativism, or to turn the world into a jelly, but it does mean treating ideas that one might well be accustomed to using as analytical tools, or living as social and historical truth, as, instead, social facts and interesting theories that people have of themselves. This, I think, is one major point, and one from which others follow, about doing anthropological research in, and about, a milieu in which one could easily feel quite at home.

Within and between different worlds in Brittany

My field-research was based with two groups in Brittany. The first group with whom I based myself, chiefly in the regional capital of Rennes, for over a year, was the Breton movement. Through participant observation, I was able to give an ethnographic account of some of the arguments, debates, and activities of the movement. History is important to the movement, and especially important is a history of the position of Breton in the schools. Taking my cue from this, and also wishing to give (as had become customary) some historical introduction to my work, I investigated national, regional, departmental, and municipal archives on the question of Breton in the schools. I had access to archives, administrative offices, and schools, and meetings and discussions with teachers, politicians, and administrators at various levels. From this, I was able to gain an ethnography of the official 'French' point of view against which Breton militants ostensibly conduct their activities.

From the archival sources, a different story also emerged. When the historical documents are, as in modern historical anthropology, granted their own historical context, there emerges a story of struggles to establish a French-speaking nation, through an all-important French language education system, in the name of popular emancipation. This is not, however, the history written or lived by the modern Breton movement; their history was also subject to my anthropological gaze, and became part of the ethnography. Breton militants also cite archival sources, but cite them as if they were speaking today. Realities of the past are more obviously forgotten or traduced, in the preoccupations of the present. The Bretons have been oppressed by the French, with French imposed in the schools, and Breton gratuitously and cruelly excluded. Militant perceptions, of the past or the present, are regularly organized around a structural opposition of Breton/ French, and there is a very general tendency in the movement to locate outside Brittany the source of all its problems. The Breton/French duality –with the language difference providing a structure that gathers up other issues, and through which they can be posed – is an opposition that structures militants' readings of history and this history, in turn, determines the way they perceive the present, the way they order their moral, political, economic, and linguistic argument, and the actions and activities they undertake.

A second area of influential historiography in which the Breton/French opposition is particularly evident is the conviction, now dominant in the movement, that the Bretons are, indeed, insular Celts in origin, and their language, historically and in essence, Welsh. This shares much with our own commonsense understandings of what history, and ethnicity, is all about. Like the Breton militants, we have been quite at home with historicist, essentialist understandings of the world. A historicist, essentialist presentation of a people, and of their identity with a particular language and culture, can be used to argue away the events of history, to reassert its proper course and the autonomy that time has apparently failed to conserve. In the Breton case (as elsewhere, and much closer to home), the minority identity always comes from the present, from the contemporary structural context, and turns to history, a history drawn up from contemporary structures in which self-definition is sought. Breton militants draw up an unFrench origin, a period of Breton independence, and a Breton-speaking Brittany, all threatened or distorted by French intrusion and oppression, and all located in a time when the contemporary opposition which demands and shapes this past was irrelevant or non-existent. An anthropological approach to ethnicity cannot now, I think, join in this pursuit of identity through the construction of an autonomous minority history, any more than we can search for the 'true' meaning of a word in, say, its earliest attestation or etymology. Rather, the history becomes part of the ethnography and, like the ethnic identity it describes, assumes its meaning from the contemporary context.

The modern, self-conscious 'Celtic' identity posed some interesting problems during fieldwork – ranging from rather delicate political encounters and alignments to having to drink vast quantities of alcohol (especially Guinness) or dance Celtic dances from dusk to dawn. I also had to assent, for my own preservation and acceptance, to a 'Celtic' identity – which I learned to accept instead of, or myself to substitute for, any 'English' categorization, especially when the going got rough.[8] The insular Celtic identity places Brittany in a political taxonomy in which national autonomy is conceivable. The mismatch between the political contexts of France and the UK is such that one does not easily translate into the other, there being, for one thing, no comparable component units. The invocation of the British context usefully makes France appear gratuitously oppressive, but it also imbues the relevant internal boundaries of Britain (e.g. between Wales and England, Welsh and English) with a mutual hatred that is, in many ways, foreign to them, and helps to make 'English' a rather unpleasant thing to be. A further aspect of the 'Celtic' business which posed problems was the fact that the two universities of Brittany, one at Rennes in the east and the other at Brest in the west, each of which has a Celtic department, disagree strongly on the Celtic origins of Brittany. For Rennes, and those associated with it (and these are the dominant faction in the movement), the Bretons are Welsh in origin; for Brest, on the other hand, the Breton is still a scion of the Gaul, or the French Celt. The two sides cannot tolerate each other, and it is wise for any field-worker not to get caught in the cross-fire. Different spoken forms of Breton, and different political constructions of Brittany and Breton culture, are taught or used in the two departments, and each side has its own Breton orthography. Trying not to give offence demands a certain studied agility. A recent anthropological textbook, offering guidelines for fieldwork, suggests that a fieldworker can and should take a restful break from the field in some nearby university department (see Hicks in Ellen (ed.) 1984: 199). However, if your 'field' includes these departments, this is clearly not possible. When, later in my fieldwork, I moved from the university centres into rural Brittany, and came across the further meeting of different worlds there, it often felt as if there was no rest available; the only solution seemed to be to make myself notionally at home, as far as was possible, with whichever group I happened to be with.

By 'making myself at home' here, with whomsoever I happened to be with, I do not mean giving up and letting all the old categories and values from home reassert themselves; I mean, on the contrary, trying to attain that difficult ethnographic ideal whereby we become able to speak and behave in a way that would be considered indigenously appropriate in that context. This is no simple 'when in Rome . . .' policy (which can commonly lead to a form of 'French wine' syndrome). To add complication, it might just require the anthropologist to act out a form of 'French wine' ritual, but one seen through the eyes of your hosts: for 'That's what you English (or southerners, or people from X village, or academics, and so on) like, isn't it?' What you are then required to eat, drink, or do might well be wholly foreign to you, although your hosts might imagine they are making you feel totally at home.

During my fieldwork with the movement, I became aware that this was happening in all sorts of ways within Brittany. I shall just cite one example. Learning and speaking Breton is an important aspect of militant life. Once you have attained a certain standard, it is possible to move on to what is considered to be the acme of Breton-learning courses; this involves staying for a week or so with a Breton-speaking family on a farm, where Breton can be learned in exchange for helping out with farm work. The families are asked to speak only Breton to us and we, the learners, are advised beforehand, by our militant leaders, that we should speak only Breton, always and everywhere, to the families. Apparently, we will all benefit in this way: not only will we learn Breton and become properly Breton and at home in Brittany, but so, too, will the families. They will be able to shed their French exterior, relax, be liberated, and just be their true, Breton, selves. In my experience, however, the families concerned are commonly left in a state of socio-linguistic exhaustion at the end of the week, and are glad when the time is up and they can stop being 'Breton' in the image required of them, and use both Breton and French (and often predominantly French) again, as they normally do.

During such events, the families are required to change from being Breton-speaking peasants to being 'Breton-speaking peasants' or true 'Bretons' in the militants' image. In some respects, it is the difference between, say, *du rouge* and 'French wine' in the French/British example to which I have already alluded. If we can imagine guests (especially female guests) from Paris being handed glasses, then the bottles, of ordinary red and not only expected to drink it as a special drink, and with great savour, but to drink only that, any time, day in and day out, and to take it with kwassonce (which they also like) and 'French bread' and anything else we might have to make them feel at home, then we are perhaps on the way to picturing some of the confusions involved and the efforts and politeness, and deference to you, that are required if it is all to pass off without incident. Luckily, those Breton-speaking peasants are often very glad of the help on the farm, and are fully prepared, in exchange, to entertain your bizarre enthusiasms and image of their world. It is an image which, ignoring and muddling as it does the structures of the world it claims to represent, can easily seem alien, capricious, or daft. In some ways, they knew what they were in for on the farm, having been told in advance, but it is understandable if, during your stay, they burst into unexplained fits of laughter at it all, as they sometimes do, momentarily unable to control themselves any longer.

We have no linguistic analogy which can convey this kind of meeting of militant enthusiasms and the values of the 'people' in whose name they claim to speak. Perhaps the image of enthusiastically learning Cockney or Yorkshire, and then going to the native-speakers and solemnly taking notes, asking for vocabulary, repeating it, and wanting to speak nothing but this tongue all day, everywhere, to everyone, might convey a few (but only a few) more features of the situation. It may be a measure of the easy familiarity and powerful persuasiveness of the discourse, aspirations, and realities of intellectuals such as the Breton militants in France that anthropologists will sometimes unquestioningly live out what are, in some ways, the fantasies of such nationalist movements. It has been noted (Davis 1977: 3) how anthropology can be, and has been, used in the service of nationalism, and in very recent years, and perhaps still, there are anthropologists stepping enthusiastically into certain 'minority' areas and, with a great sense of virtue, insisting on a use of the minority tongue, no doubt believing – just like the Breton movement – that they are getting at the 'real' culture of their 'people'. So they might be (although not in the way they imagine). Their resultant work is very attractive, sells well, feels like 'real' anthropology, and thrills us all; they have made a very successful shopping trip, and may even have managed to smuggle a few extra bottles back.

The second major group with whom I based myself in Brittany consisted of a native Breton-speaking village in central Finistère, in the westernmost part of Lower Brittany. The views of the native Breton-speaking peasants had inevitably cropped up already in various ways, although largely as 'Breton-speakers', in other people's images of them. Now I was able to see their own image of themselves, and their own aspirations. The village in which I finally came to rest, for over a year, was situated in an upland area particularly noted for its isolation, backwardness, and Breton-speaking. It was an area where Breton militants had often suggested that I might eventually go to do my fieldwork, my 'real' fieldwork, with the 'real' people. Indeed, one section of the movement, known as *Diwan* ('seed' or 'germination'), had selected it as a site for one of their newly established Breton-medium schools (a venture to which I also paid close attention throughout my fieldwork in Brittany); and many other post-1968 back-to-the-landers have chosen to make it their 'alternative' home, with windmills, weaving, pottery, organic farming, and Breton all part of much the same enthusiasm.

Within the local world itself (self-consciously 'local' in the face of 'those people', or the militants), there were other divisions and difficulties, which included moving between the different activities, values, and organization of time in the 'bourg' and *campagne*, and among the young and the old (and sometimes having to be awake for twenty-four hours as a result); having to eat lots and lots of cakes (that's what ladies and special visitors do, and I often seemed to be both); coping with a high rate of male celibacy and of alcoholism; trying to visit both presbytery and town hall, and both private and public schools, in a world of Clochemerleian politics; and learning when Breton was possible, and above all – a novelty after the militant world – when *not* to use it. I had to learn to follow local sanctions and to know that (in an aged, symbolically all-male gathering over alcohol), a use of French could be smirked at, although not for the same reasons, or in the same way, as in the militant world; and to know, importantly, that a use of Breton, by Breton-speakers among Breton-speakers, was sometimes not simply to be derided but positively laughed at. After working in the militant milieu, this was difficult to take, and could easily seem fascist and immoral. However, I did not feel it was my task to quarrel with native-speaker sentiment. I listened to views about Breton which sometimes included the idea that it should be stamped out altogether; and to enthusiastic tales of French schooling. When militants were present at any such discussions, it was occasionally obvious that local views were statements about what they thought of the militants rather than statements about the past. The militants themselves were ever ready to explain away such tales, among themselves, with explanations of the 'they're-all-alienated' and 'it's-all-to-do-with-French-oppression' variety. I considered it my task to note the different points of view, of the local people on the one hand and the militant incomers on the other, and to understand how each group coped with the contradictions posed it by the other. The militants' explanatory frameworks formed part of the way they coped.

The contradictions played themselves out in several areas, in politics, farming practice, language-use and language evaluations, and evaluations of 'traditional' culture. Local attitudes to the militants varied contextually, but could include angry hostility. Not only were there very different levels, and images, of education involved, and different socio-linguistic rationalities and aspirations, but also different notions of right/left politics, and different conceptions of the peasant life; and there was also the spectre of *Breiz Atao* ('Brittany Forever'). This was a (now defunct) section of the Breton movement which had seen, in co-operation with Germany in the last war, a way of achieving Breton independence from France. In the post-war years, it had come to represent collaboration in popular opinion, and many local people, former Resistants or not, now choose to revivify *Breiz Atao* in the modern militants, to the horror of the latter. I am not pretending to set out all the details of my fieldwork here, but I hope it will be clear that there was far more than any simple question of different language use involved in any one situation, or with any group, or between groups, and my interest in Breton, my knowledge of Breton, and my use of French or my use of Breton, and the kind of French or the kind of Breton I used, could easily be misinterpreted, or say more than I wanted it to say.

I always liked to imagine, during my fieldwork, that I was being fair and even-handed. Thus, for example, I visited not only Breton-speakers but also those in the local world who could now master only French – trying as I did so to educate myself out of the impatience I sometimes felt to move on elsewhere, to speak to people who might perform in Breton as required. Within the militant world, I tried to please both Brest and Rennes, and I also tried to show interest not only in the Breton movement but also in what is, in many ways, a late back-formation: the 'Gallo' movement, a relatively new movement which seeks to 'defend' the Gallo interests of Upper Brittany (and with some resentment of the Breton movement's appropriation of the entire 'minority' and 'Breton' space). I also tried, in my dealings with representatives of the administration and officialdom, to impress on them my genuine interest in French, France, and education – as well as Breton. There was never any great difficulty in access to officials, documents, and schools, but there was often an obvious worry that I was in some way part of the Breton movement and, like many others before me, there to amass glamour and virtue by writing yet another thesis or book about the oppression of the 'Bretons' by malicious 'French' authorities. I found teachers, and educational and administrative authorities defensive and sometimes over-enthusiastic to help. They apparently had centuries of oppressive activity to live down. The French authorities have had a knack in recent decades of confirming, through various ham-fisted exercises or administrative failures, the movement's required image of two hundred years of unmitigated genocide.

I had expected there to be a divide between state authorities and the Breton movement: indeed, the militants' own cause and self-definition depended on it. In 1983 my recently awarded doctoral thesis, containing the results of my research, came to the attention of the French press. Another divide, that between the Breton militants and the local native-speakers, was, through my work or press images of it, given new expression.

Reactions to the thesis

It is not possible to recount here the full story of publicity given to the thesis, the reactions it has evoked, and the ways in which it has been appropriated by the different groups involved. Luckily perhaps, and of interest in itself, there is now a published bibliography available listing many of the articles and responses so far published on the matter.[9] In this same publication, the whole matter is referred to, as it often has been, as 'l'affaire'.

'L'affaire' began in June 1983 with a headline (in a newspaper claiming the highest circulation in France) which read, in translation: 'Breton peasantry accepted French with open arms'. Much of the thesis was ignored. The headline, and at least part of the article, offered a summary of my archival findings. It was enough, however, to make the movement bound high and react fast.

Over the next few months, I was thoroughly redefined by the movement as an outsider. If I had been accepted as a 'Celt', I was now 'English' once more, and a 'fascist'. I was 'reactionary' and working for figures and bodies as various as Thatcher and Marchais, the CIA and the KGB, and (no doubt with Falklands overtones) the Royal Navy. I was also a 'royalist', or, rather, royaliste, which is insult indeed. In many respects, the monarchy is the stability of the UK, and allows Celtic minorities to flourish in a way they have not been able to in the unstable French Republic; however, the British monarchy is assimilated to that which France rid itself of some time ago, and, more than this, is made a symbol of the majority 'England' which oppresses the Celts.

Local reactions, within the village where I lived, were nervous but supportive. I had placed a copy of my thesis in the local *mairie* or town hall. As things started getting rough, it was gently hinted that perhaps I should remove it, so I did. I think there were fears that the town hall might go the way of part of Versailles. Also, no one particularly relished the thought that they might find themselves before a journalist, microphone, or camera and expected to speak out on the subject. The most vociferous peasants were immediately on my side, and others slowly let me know their views, too, but there was always a worry that I might name them in public and that they would find themselves under the same kind of fire as me, but unable to defend themselves in the same way. They knew they could not match the militants' French if there was to be a debate, and in Breton they did not have the same neologistic vocabulary to cope if required. There was also the point that publicity previously given to Breton-speakers had tended to be from the Breton movement, or its sympathizers, and some local people had learned how to perform for that. Now, suddenly, there was a different story blazing in the papers, and the prospect of exchanging external glamour for bombs was not very appealing. At the same time, these people told me that what was in my thesis was 'true' and had, in any case, been what they had told me themselves. A self-consciously 'local' identity became very much alive, asserting its own authenticity and excluding the militants (or 'those people'). I was offered the electric fences normally used around the fields: I could use them, it was suggested, to keep away any threatening characters. For a while, it was woe betide even the most innocent friend who might try to visit me in the village; any stranger was one of 'those people' who had come to get me. Militants actually living locally were reticent, and I contacted them to apologize for the way in which a divide between themselves and the local population was being sensationally concretized, and without the full context of the rest of my work. Their own views were being given no autonomy, but presented as silly, 'wrong', or deliberately deceptive. In general, the militants living in the rural area where I worked took no public part in the controversy. Their own daily lives, and their local acceptance, were deeply implicated in the affair, and they were not always pleased when militant colleagues elsewhere carried on a public battle that could so easily erode their own hard-won, and still fragile, integration.

My own public debate with the movement consisted, much of the time, in my restating the real content of the thesis and in pointing out that every militant attack, in its structure and the categories used, was predictable, and confirmation of the authenticity of my work. On the militant side, on the other hand, the Breton movement seemed to be caught up in its own autonomous discourse of oppression and tried to use every occasion to make me yet another instance of it. Within the movement, I was appropriated, predictably enough perhaps, by the metaphorical Gauls. There has been ample room to turn me into a political football. Another axis for this possibility came in the form of letters from *deputés* of the French National Assembly asking for copies of the thesis. The government was engaged in negotiations with the Breton movement over funding for certain cultural activities. This funding was to be given on the grounds of 'historical reparation'. According to press reports of my work, however, it seemed there might be no historical reparation to be made. My thesis was made unavailable for loan at the Bodleian, where a copy had been deposited.

The flurry of debate since the fieldwork and thesis has made me aware of one point which is, I think, particularly relevant for the theme of this volume. Although I am now taking militants on as an anthropologist and, if necessary, will argue my case with them as such, I now realize that I had never done so during fieldwork with them, except on the most banal of points. I had, as part of my fieldwork, sat through discussions, at university level, of such old anthropological favourites as colour categories and politeness, for example, and how they differed between Breton and French, and what this might mean. I had noted such discussions, and they appear in the thesis (McDonald 1982: chapter 9). I treated them as part of the ethnography rather than intervening, and becoming part of the discussion, as an anthropologist, and one who would probably have disagreed strongly with the way the issues were dealt with. Right or wrong, my attitude in such discussions ought perhaps to have encouraged militants to believe me when I told them, as I often did, that I was there to do an ethnography of them. There is, it seems, no easy way to react to such a statement, and militants usually passed it off as a joke, and pretended to be savages or monkeys, and so on. Anthropologist I might be, but it was very difficult for them to believe that I was doing an ethnography of them. Like any other researcher, I was naturally coming to them first for analysis and a grasp of what was really going on, and then I would eventually move off to see this reality for myself. They never believed I was treating their views (including their history) ethnographically. My ethnography was going to begin when I got to the 'real' people (which in this context meant the peasants, and for which one equivalent in the UK has been the urban working class). It was going to begin, indeed, when I crossed some unseen line west of Rennes. Anthropologists will readily understand the weight of such prejudice, I think, for we have shared it for so long. Close to home, however, the anthropologically naïve becomes the ethnographically interesting. And I must admit, I did experience an enormous thrill when I first changed my fieldwork site, and sped off from my home-base in Rennes into deep, dark, mysterious Finistère.

Notes

1 Some of the wider problems of divides such as lamb/*agneau* and different drinking habits can be found in McDonald (1982), chapters 8, 14, and 15; Snyder (1985); McDonald and Chapman (1985); McDonald (1986c).
2 The written work referred to here is my doctoral thesis: McDonald (1982).
3 For some examples see issues of *La Revue des Traditions Populaires*, 1885–1916, in which Brittany regularly figures. Further details of the ethnographic and folkloric

interest shown in Brittany during the Revolutionary period and the nineteenth century can be found in Gourvil (1960); Tanguy (1977); Bertho (1978); and Burguière, Ozouf, and Bourguet (1977/1982); also McDonald (1982), chapter 6.

4 Quiniou (1973) gives an account of how French literature in the nineteenth century, including the works of Balzac, Stendhal, and Flaubert, helped to create such an image of Brittany as a country of savages. Such an image, however, is simply the other side of the coin, the other face of the wonderful, unspoilt naturality that modern Breton enthusiasts such as Quiniou herself would see, and have seen, as the 'true' Brittany (for related comments on the image of Highland Scotland, see Chapman 1978).

5 See, for example, an article by the Breton psychiatrist/ethnologist, Yann Daumer (1983).

6 See Mendras (1970), and Lévi-Strauss and Mendras (1981).

7 This is obvious from the fact that a vast CNRS-funded team arrived in Brittany in the 1960s: their work, which involved anything from head-measuring to gathering popular song, is written up, in its more sociological aspects, in Morin (1967) and Burguière (1977). See also the modern journal *Etudes Rurales*, where Brittany occupies a significant place. Other features of this special attraction of Brittany are outlined in McDonald (1984/1986a).

8 Some of the reasons for, and implications of, such a contextual shift from being 'English' to being a 'Celt' are set out in McDonald (1982, chapter 6) and (1984/1986b).

9 See Broudic (1984), especially pp. 253 and 272–73.

References

ARDENER, E. (1974) Social Anthropology and Population. In H. B. Parry (ed.) *Population and its Problems*. Oxford: Clarendon Press.
— (1985) Social Anthropology and the Decline of Modernism. In J. Overing (ed.) *Reason and Morality*. ASA Monographs 24. London: Tavistock Publications.
BERTHO, C. (1978) Les livres consacrés à la Bretagne au XIXe siècle: les enseignements d'une bibliographie. *Revue française d'histoire du livre* **8**.
BROUDIC, F. (1984) Bibliographie des publications consacrées à la langue et à la littérature bretonnes. *Bulletin de la Société Archéologique du Finistère* **CXII** (2): 253–91.
BURGUIÈRE, A. (1977) *Bretons de Plozévet*. Paris: Flammarion.
BURGUIÈRE, A., OZOUF, M., and BOURGUET, M.-N. (1977/1982) Naissance d'une ethnographie de la France au XVIIIe siècle. In J. Le Goff and B. Köpeczi (eds) *Objets et méthodes de l'histoire de la culture*. Paris: CNRS.
CHAPMAN, M. (1978) *The Gaelic Vision in Scottish Culture*. London: Croom Helm.
— (1982) 'Semantics' and the 'Celt'. In D. Parkin (ed.) *Semantic Anthropology*. ASA Monographs 22. London: Academic Pres.
CNRS (1977/1979) *L'Anthropologie en France. Situation actuelle et avenir.* (Colloque du Centre National de la Recherche Scientifique, en collaboration avec L'Ecole des Hautes Etudes en Sciences Sociales: La Délégation Générale à la Recherche Scientifique et Technique, Paris, 1977). Paris: CNRS.
DAUMER, Y. (1983) A la découverte d'un mythe: la tête dure des bretons. In *Recontre de cultures et pathologie mentale en Bretagne*. (*Cahiers de L'Institut Culturel de Bretagne*, no. 1.). Rennes: Skol Uhel ar Vro/Institut Culturel de Bretagne.
DAVIS, J. (1977) *People of the Mediterranean. An Essay in Comparative Social Anthropology*. London: Routledge & Kegan Paul.

ELLEN, R. F. (ed.) (1984) *Ethnographic Research. A Guide to General Conduct*. ASA Research Methods in Social Anthropology I. London: Academic Press.

GOURVIL, F. (1960) *Théodore-Claude-Henri Hersart de la Villemarqué (1815–1895) et le 'Barzaz-Breiz' (1839–1845–1867)*. Rennes: Imprimerie Oberthur.

HÉLIAS, P. J. (1975) *Le Cheval d'orgueil. Mémoires d'un breton du pays bigouden*. Paris: Plon.

— (1975/1978) *The Horse of Pride* (translation of Hélias (1975) by J. Guicharnaud). New Haven, Conn. and London: Yale University Press.

HEWITT, S. (1977) The Degree of Acceptability of Modern Literary Breton to Native Breton Speakers. Linguistics diploma thesis, University of Cambridge.

KUTER, L. (1981) Breton Identity: Musical and Linguistic Expression in Brittany, France. Ph.D. dissertation, Indiana University.

LÉVI-STRAUSS, L. and MENDRAS, H. (1981) Rural Community Studies in France. In J. Durand-Drouhin, L. M. Szwengrub, and I. Mihailescu (eds) *Rural Community Studies in Europe*. Oxford: Pergamon Press.

LOVECY, J. (1982) Protest in Brittany from the Fourth to the Fifth Republics: From a Regionalist to a Regional Social Movement. In P. Cerny (ed.) *Social Movements and Protest in France*. London: Frances Pinter.

MCDONALD, M. (1982) Social Aspects of Language and Education in Brittany, France. D.Phil. thesis, University of Oxford. (Forthcoming, London: Tavistock Publications.)

— (1984/1986a) Tourism in Brittany. Paper presented to RESSG (British Sociological Association), October 1984. In M. Winter and M. Bouquet (eds) *Who From Their Labours Rest? Conflict and Practice in Rural Tourism*. London: Gower.

— (1984/1986b) Celtic Ethnic Kinship and the Problem of Being English. Research paper. *Current Anthropology* **27** (4).

— 1986c Social Drinking in Brittany, France. Research paper.

MCDONALD, M. and CHAPMAN, M. (1985) A Study of Two Breton Villages, with Particular Reference to Local, Regional, and National Identities. London: ESRC Report.

MENDRAS, H. (1970) *The Vanishing Peasant* (translated by J. Lerner). Massachusetts: MIT Press.

MORIN, E. (1967) *Commune en France: La Métamorphose de Plodémet*. Paris: Fayard.

— (1967/1971) *Plodémet. Report from a French Village* (translation of Morin (1967) by A. Sheridan-Smith). London: Allen Lane.

QUINIOU, A. (1973) Images de la Bretagne dans la littérature française du XIXe siècle. Mémoire de Maîtrise, Université de Bretagne Occidentale, Brest.

SNYDER, F. (1985) The Political Economy of EEC Law: The Sheepmeat Regime. Draft paper presented at Annual Conference of Rural Economy and Society Study Group (British Sociological Association): 'Agriculture in Advanced Societies', Oxford, January 1985.

TANGUY, B. (1977) *Aux origines du nationalisme breton*, 2 Vols. Paris: 10/18.

Chris Hann

9 The politics of anthropology in socialist Eastern Europe

This paper is concerned with 'anthropology' in Eastern Europe, both as it has been practised over a long period by native scholars, and as pursued in the socialist period by Anglo-Saxon anthropologists. In arguing that the two approaches should now be complementary I reach the same conclusion as Hofer (1968) who was, to my knowledge, the first to draw attention to the basic differences between the cumulative and introspective discipline of national ethnography (*Volkskunde*) in Eastern Europe and the generalizing, essentially comparative discipline in the West. Hofer himself is one of the few native ethnographers who has attempted to bridge the two, and the discussion in his essay is relevant to many other societies where Western anthropologists work alongside native researchers. In this paper I concentrate on one facet of the division of labour which may arise in the case of the socialist countries. These are, of course, complex societies, in which much valuable 'anthropological' work has been carried out by native scholars who seldom acknowledged the label 'anthropologist'. Hence the risks of 'naïvety' for the outsider are as great here as elsewhere in Europe, where cultural self-knowledge has been profoundly influenced by nationalist movements. However, political considerations have posed extra problems for native social scientists in socialist countries, and may even dissuade some of the most talented from engaging in serious enquiries into their own societies. Here there is at once an obvious potential for the Western anthropologist, simply at the level of accurate reporting of political phenomena. However, for a Western anthropologist to study any aspect of these societies must itself be a highly political undertaking. There has been understandable concern among those working in this region, mostly citizens of the non-socialist superpower, as to what methodological and ethical stance to adopt.[1] I address these issues in Part III where, drawing on my own fieldwork in Hungary and Poland, I try to show how political 'neutrality' can be preserved in this minefield by accepting certain parameters of the systems and arguing for policies to meet the needs of the populations within them. Part I is a brief outline of the achievements of one native tradition and the problems it faces today, while Part II shows how foreigners can help to solve these problems, though there may be some research areas in which they can hardly hope to compete with natives.

I Native anthropology in Hungary

The institutional beginnings of something akin to Western anthropology in Hungary date back only to 1969, when a subgroup to specialize in 'social ethnography' was set up within the long-established Ethnographical Research Group of the Hungarian Academy of Sciences. Its small membership, about half a dozen, is outnumbered by colleagues at the Academy who specialize in what are, in the Hungarian context, the more familiar branches of national ethnography, notably folklore and material culture. All these scholars are primarily researchers (though some may choose to become involved in teaching outside the academy). In addition to pioneering modern fieldwork investigations within Hungary, members of the 'social ethnography' subgroup also endeavour to keep abreast of developments in anthropology outside Hungary. While they have not found it easy to gain fieldwork experience abroad (not all were keen on this anyway), some have been able to travel widely to conferences and for extended periods of study in established anthropology centres. Interest in both the British and the North American traditions in anthropology is strong. It has increased in part as a result of the general climate of *détente*, which has enabled not only a flow of personnel, but also of journals and ideas.

The members of this small group which most closely corresponds to our notions of anthropology would not themselves see their work as something entirely novel, without native precedent. In the institutional sense the discipline of ethnography in Hungary can look back upon a distinguished past, linked in the nineteenth century with a political movement that placed a high value upon the distinctive culture of the Hungarians in the past, and even upon the folk culture of the rural Hungarians in the present. In addition to a certain amount of speculative or sensational writing, many lasting works of scholarship were produced by Hungarian ethnographers about the Hungarian people, at a surprisingly early period.[2] The further consolidation and professionalization of this tradition in the twentieth century guaranteed that the output in the *Volkskunde* genre was of high quality in Hungary.

Hungarian ethnographers, then, conducted exhaustive enquiries into the folklore and material culture of the Hungarian people. Most of those professionally engaged in ethnography at the present time, including university and museum staff as well as researchers at the Academy, are working consciously in this tradition. Those branching off in more novel, anthropological directions may prefer to look back to some of the maverick figures of earlier ages – to outstanding individuals who declined to be constrained by the *Volkskunde* tradition. Some of these included evolutionists of the Morgan mould, others were anthropologists in the Frazerian style, while others combined their speculations with the active life of the explorer, and some produced superb travel literature that ranks among the foremost achievements of anthropology before Malinowski.[3]

Hungary also produced outstanding scholars whose impact on Western anthropology was as great as their impact on the native tradition: Géza Róheim and Károly Polányi are perhaps the names that spring immediately to mind.

Although today's native anthropologists are obliged to site their fieldwork within their own country, and although they have shifted away from the ethnographers' concerns towards an interest in social structure, they too can reach back to native antecedents. It is true that, lacking the stimulus provided by the national reform movement, and often handicapped by an unfavourable political environment, enquiries into such subjects as the system of social stratification were few and 'sociology' did not acquire institutional consolidation until well into the twentieth century. Many amateurish analyses, or merely descriptive, documentary works, were published in earlier periods, and these are of value to the historian.[4] There were also a few more ambitious studies, whose authors may legitimately be viewed as the precursors of today's anthropologists and sociologists. Curiously, the earliest work produced in Hungary was by the French sociologist, LePlay. His thorough analysis, according to the pattern of his other monographs, was poorly received by the Hungarian intelligentsia of the time, apparently because his moralizing, sentimental tone was felt to reveal a failure on the part of the Westerner to grasp the realities of Hungarian conditions.[5]

One more important movement of the pre-socialist period should be cited, in view of its far-reaching consequences for politics and society as well as anthropology. In spite of the conservative regime which dominated political life between the World Wars (and which had become a fascist regime by the end of the Second), writers associated with the populist parties produced work of the highest quality, especially in the years of depression, when conditions in the countryside were at their worst. Some of these were themselves of peasant origin, early beneficiaries of mass education. Many more originated in the liberal intelligentsia; they also went out into the villages to discover precisely what was happening, and even their most sophisticated theoretical analyses were solidly grounded in empirical investigations. It is easy to dismiss all this as radical journalism (cf. the widespread contempt for the basic populist stance); but, given the rather apolitical character of academic ethnography by this period, and the continuing absence of any wider social science school, the best of these writers also contributed significantly to the 'prehistory' of native anthropology.[6]

I shall be equally brief on post-war developments. The populist school lost its political battle, neither radical journalism nor academic sociology managing to flourish in the first decades of socialism. Ethnography was, of course, more securely established, but there were no opportunities to document the momentous changes taking place throughout the society. Researchers chose safe topics within the *Volkskunde* tradition, and the peasantry was frozen in time (i.e. before collectivization). The outstanding work of this type is Fél and Hofer (1969).[7]

The period since 1969 has been one of general relaxation in the political, economic, and cultural life of Hungary. This favourable climate has enabled writers of many kinds to attempt to come to terms with the most recent changes in Hungarian society. Most prominent has been the resurgence of the populist tradition, at the hands of a new generation of rural writers and journalists. Official tolerance of, and even support for, such endeavours is shown in the encouragement of publications, including explicit revivals of pre-war series.[8] The authorities have not censored this literature, in order to emphasize only the positive transformation of rural and urban life that has taken place since the years of pre-war depression. On the contrary, much of the detail in these new volumes has revealed just how limited the trans-formation has been in many regions, and for many sections of the 'under-class'. It seems to me, however, that these volumes have not sought to link empirical description ('sociography' is the standard term in Hungarian) so closely to an informed theoretical analysis, as the best of the pre-war populist writers did.

For such theory one should be able to turn to the academics and research workers, but here the position is perhaps less satisfactory. Sociology has been inhibited from developing 'macro' critiques of existing socialist society.[9] Among those who have come closest to doing so are those who have studied the situation in the countryside. Hegedüs (1977) has provided a general survey, while Simó (1983) is a re-study of a community which was the focus of a *cause célèbre* when depicted by a populist writer in the 1930s. However, although these sociologists have gone some way towards developing a general theoretical approach to rural society, this has so far been lacking in the works produced by the anthropology group set up in 1969. They have since that period conducted very detailed fieldwork in two contrasted rural com-munities: only one of these projects has been fully written up (Bodrogi 1978; a brief introduction in English can be found in Durand-Drouhin and Szwengrub 1982). The method has been based on teamwork, i.e. each member of the group has taken a particular topic of investigation and written up his research (e.g. into economic changes, or family structure) independently of the others, though of course conferring with them, and frequently conducting the field-work jointly. The anthropologists are city dwellers (and for the most part of city background) and they tend to do their fieldwork by short visits to the village (seldom lasting more than a week; some of the anthropologists preferred never to reside on the spot, but always to visit from a local urban base). This should not necessarily be read as a reproach. The native anthropologists still enjoy a number of advantages in comparison with any foreigner on the scene, in terms of their 'observational sensitivity' (Fél and Hofer 1969: 5) and potential insight into the cognitive world of the rural dweller. Moreover, as improving communications have helped to narrow the gap between town and country, it can be claimed that the city-dwelling anthropologists of today have an easier task in comprehending the village life of today than did the populists of the pre-socialist generation.

A more serious criticism might focus on the excessive degree of compartmentalization and the failure to develop a theoretical (which means also a *political*) analysis in the manner of Simó (1983). Although several chapters of Bodrogi (1978) are of very high quality, particularly those which eschew the quantitative approach of a sociologist such as Simó, perhaps the lack of productivity and slowness in publishing of this group of anthropologists indicate a real problem. It could be that the relative familiarity of the rural scene makes it seem uninteresting to the native anthropologists. At any rate, either because they do not like doing it, or because they do not think it is worth doing, or because they think the sociologists can perhaps do it better, the native anthropologists in Hungary are not in the forefront of the efforts currently being made to achieve a better understanding of Hungarian society – not even in the limited context of the rural community.

II The privileged Westerner

There is a potential in this situation for a useful division of labour to develop between the native and the foreign anthropologists. Foreigners specializing in social or cultural anthropology, particularly those who carry out a long period of intensive fieldwork, have produced detailed and comprehensive rural community studies that no individual native has matched.[10] Some of the most revealing insights have been in the economic field, for the era of liberalization has witnessed a burgeoning of the 'second economy', which is centred for most rural dwellers on the household plot. In this sort of field comparable evidence can be gathered and similar conclusions reached by native researchers of several disciplines, and the sociographers have been particularly prominent. It may be disconcerting to the foreign researcher, but the astute native anthropologist or journalist may be able to gather such evidence much more efficiently, perhaps over a wider area, and reach the same or more interesting conclusions than those painstakingly worked out in one locality by a foreigner. The advantages of working *within* one's native culture are also amply demonstrated in some of the more academic studies, particularly when such topics as value systems and cognition are involved. I am suggesting that there may be fields in which no amount of prolonged immersion on the part of the outsider is enough to achieve what the native enquirer may accomplish in the space of just a few weekends in the field. Of course the native may remain blind to certain details that the 'objective' outsider may choose to stress, and he may well be unable to place his knowledge firmly in any comparative framework. Nevertheless, there may be questions where no quantitative increase in the number of field observations or qualitative effort on the part of the foreigner can allow him to approach the intimacy available to some insiders (though not all insiders: I am well aware of the subjective factors involved here, and by no means all of the native anthropologists I have known in Eastern Europe have easy rapport with the villagers of their own culture). A prime example would be the analysis of changing norms and values in the socialist period. Here I find Jávor (1983) more satisfying than either Bell (1984) or Hann (1980).

Yet, despite these problems, I feel there is an important compensating field in the socialist countries in which the Western side is privileged, and here Bell (1984) is a fine example. This concerns the ability to describe and analyse the political system. I think there are two distinct points to be made here. The first is perhaps obvious. Despite the very considerable changes which have taken place, above all in the economic mechanism, some aspects of Hungarian life, including academic institutions, are still very tightly regulated. Those with posts in social science institutions or universities are, in effect, precluded from delving into certain taboo areas of contemporary society; when sociologists have in the past transgressed these ill-specified boundaries, the consequences have been serious.[11] Those working in more journalistic fields may enjoy greater freedom to work in 'sensitive' areas; and a consequence of this tends to be that some in the academic institutions take this division of labour for granted, and even look down on the study of social and political relations as a subject fit only for ephemeral journalistic analysis.

But I would argue that politics is, apart from these pragmatic reasons, in any case an area in which the outsider is better placed to make informed, comparative analyses. His very detachment from the society he is studying, which makes his task so difficult when a common cultural identity is a precondition for the effective probing of value systems, enables him to identify the workings of the social and political hierarchy more clearly than any native.

Politics is, then, the field in which the Western anthropologist has the greatest opportunity to excel in a socialist country such as contemporary Hungary. Partly this is because, even if an ideal political climate prevailed in intellectual life, the native researchers would not be able to attain the same objectivity. Partly it is because ideal conditions do not prevail. The foreigner in Hungary thus has the unique chance (and even duty) to report and describe honestly the political phenomena which he has ample opportunity to observe. Alongside Bell (1984), Hann (1980: chapter 6) is a contribution in this field.[12]

To suggest that a Westerner can achieve high standards of objectivity in the reporting, let alone the evaluation, of political matters in a socialist state may seem paradoxical. Overall the record of Western social science in improving our understanding of socialist societies is not impressive; as Hough (1977) has argued, far too much research is constrained by the unhelpful models of 'totalitarianism'; instead of moving beyond 'cold war' journalists, we too often apply their categories and concepts without reflection, even to countries such as Hungary, today as in the past so very different from the particular socialist society for which this body of analysis was developed. How can the anthropologist rid himself of the prejudices drilled into him over many years, and can he perhaps offer any alternative models that the political scientists themselves would be advised to take seriously?

We know that objectivity is not possible, that the Kremlinologists are not likely to start communicating with anthropologists; but I would like to show how an anthropologist may try to follow a 'neutral' path, to maintain clear distinctions between his description, his evaluations, and his policy pre-scriptions; I shall illustrate the requirements with reference to my own, quite highly politicized, work in Hungary and Poland.

III Neutral utilitarianism

Hungary, where I began a research project in 1975 after short visits pre-viously, is often regarded as the success story of the socialist bloc in recent decades. Whatever the truth behind this image, whether or not one can reach agreement on definitions of 'Kadarism' or 'market socialism', it is clear that since 1968 the economic mechanism has deviated substantially from the Soviet model of central planning. Nor can it be disputed that within a few years of the 1956 trauma, Hungary was able to collectivize the vast majority of her peasant farms, and that by the 1970s the agricultural sector was making a healthy contribution to hard currency earnings, in addition to satisfying domestic demand. These were the basic facts about the country which had stimulated my interest before going into the field in 1975. I still believe them to hold ten years later, though neither the national economy nor the agri-cultural sector is quite as buoyant as before the impact of the current economic depression.

My particular project centred upon the problem of how collectivization could be accomplished in zones of scattered settlement: the 'tanya problem' (Hann 1980: chapter 2) is a characteristic feature of the Great Plain, extensively studied by geographers, both native and foreign. After almost a year in Budapest affiliated to the anthropologists of the Academy, I inde-pendently selected an appropriate area of the Plain, and lived there for a further ten months. During the micro research I found it useful, apart from investigating the problem of the scattered farms, to keep in mind the main features of the 'macro' situation, as summarized above. The farmers of Tázlár belonged to the minority that had not been fully collectivized, merely formally enrolled in a loose, so-called 'specialist co-operative'. This socialist institution offered limited help with supplies and claimed a monopoly over most marketing, but it left the members free to carry on looking after their own enterprises and their own land in something akin to the old peasant ways. Their products were the typical ones that the country needed, both for internal and external markets. And these farmers were certainly producing at something close to maximum potential in the booming years of the 1970s, motivated by the incentives of an unprecedented consumer goods market, and also, in many cases, by the pressing need to find resources to construct or improve housing in the expanding village centre. Over the ten months I had plenty of opportunity to see how much effort most families were putting into their farm work in order to attain their consumer goals. In the macro framework it seemed to me that these members of the specialist co-operatives represented, in an exaggerated form, the predicament of the mass of the rural population, i.e. the members of the more familiar collective farms, who are well known to put in similarly long hours on their household plots. My conclusions were that the market mechanism had certainly been exceedingly successful in expanding agricultural production and raising living standards for the whole nation, but that the social costs of this reliance upon 'overtime' or 'self-exploitation' on the part of the rural population were very high (stress consequent upon lack of leisure, etc). In order to reduce these costs and to improve the general welfare of rural dwellers *vis-à-vis* the city dwellers, it would be appropriate – so I argued – not merely to raise the prices paid for farm products, but to move towards a fuller realization of the original col-lectivization programme. In other words, it would be desirable if policy-makers acted to eliminate or reduce the country's reliance upon high levels of commodity production in all parts of agriculture's 'non-socialist' sector, as exemplified by the specialist co-operatives.

Hofer (1968: 313) takes a rather harsh view of the 'slash and burn' style of comparative anthropologists. In defence, I have at least revisited this village every year since fieldwork ended. I am happy to report that the regionally specific anomaly of the specialist co-operative has been largely eliminated. The short duration of recent visits does not allow me to say that rural attitudes to work and leisure now approximate more closely to those of townspeople. I suspect not: the wider problems of the household plot and of urban–rural imbalance are still far from resolution, as Simó (1983) and Vásáry (1983), among others, have recently confirmed.

Poland was deliberately selected in order to provide maximum contrast with successfully collectivized Hungary. As the basic facts are perhaps better known, I shall be very brief. Fieldwork was begun at the end of the 1970s, when Gierek still held power. The economy was already on the brink of collapse; its disintegration was accentuated by the political turbulence of the early 1980s. It is widely recognized that, alongside other economic and political causes, the structural problems of the agricultural sector also played some part in the gestation of this crisis. These problems resulted from the failure to permit any alternative form of modernization in the countryside, collectivization having been ruled out for political reasons after 1956. As in Hungary I had the opportunity, over two years equally divided between city and independently selected rural community, to form some impressions about state policies and citizen needs. It was clear that the productivity of the mass of independent farmers was very low, that they had great difficulty in obtaining modern equipment and in expanding acreage. Many peasants, and especially the younger generation, had ceased to believe that they had a viable future on the land: however, adopting the life-style of the peasant-worker did not solve the problem of efficiency in the agricultural sector. At the same time it was obvious both from national statistics and from micro observations that even this demoralized private sector compared favourably with the perform-ance of the socialist sector. Yet only the latter enjoyed the support and subsidies of the authorities. In this situation it was obvious that acceding to the basic demands expressed by *Rural Solidarity* (such as improved access to material inputs, constitutional guarantees of private property rights, etc.) would be in the interests not merely of the peasant landowners but of the nation as a whole, otherwise condemned to rely upon a rationing system for a wide range of foodstuffs. I suggested further (Hann 1985: chapter 8) that these policies, if adopted, might have important repercussions for rural social structure, but would be unlikely to threaten the basic socialist character of society. My conclusion in this case would be that for both rural and urban populations to pull themselves out of the crisis, some significant modification of previous, ideologically inspired hostility towards the peasantry was warranted.

I have also returned to this village each year since fieldwork was completed in 1981. Sadly, there is as yet no sign of significant modification of past policies; all the main structural problems remain unsolved, and frustration and mutual mistrust characterize both the rural and urban populations.

In preparing the two monographs (Hann 1980, 1985) I was therefore addressing the political dimension at two levels. First, I was seeking to provide authentic descriptions of local political processes. Second, and this too is a level at which native researchers are effectively unable to work, I also tried to grapple with some of the major 'macro' implications of the rural micro-study, including the fundamental tenets of development policy. In each case the basis of evaluation, and consequently of policy prescription (though recommendations may not have been made explicitly enough) lay in the problems, needs, and aspirations of the people I was studying, both in a specific locality and in the wider society. That I did not seek to impose some *a priori* evaluative basis of my own is indicated by the fact that the ideological character of my policy prescriptions is quite different in the two cases.

In Hungary I found that large-scale reorganization of agriculture along socialist lines had been accomplished to the advantage of the mass of the population; but I also found that the strains imposed upon certain sections of society by the new divisions of labour, and particularly certain regional imbalances, were such as to justify even larger investments in the collective sector – the authorities should be *more* committed to their own ultimate ideological goals, in other words, more socialism. I am fully aware that such a prescription would be unlikely to find endorsement in the village where I resided, that it must rest on a claim (supported by long periods of observation) to be in a better position to interpret the needs of the rural population than they are themselves ('false consciousness').

In Poland, by contrast, where socialist reorganization has not been achieved and the large peasant sector remains thoroughly frustrated in all its aspirations, in both production and consumption, I argued against rigid adherence to socialist dogma, and in favour of opening the road to more 'capitalist' development; the general grounds were that the benefits this would confer on all sections of society would, in Polish conditions, far outweigh any threat to the basic, highly egalitarian character of the system. In this case my own position was roughly congruent with the demands being made by the mass of the rural population, but it was not shared by the authorities; whereas in the Hungarian case, the rural constituency remains on the whole rather satisfied with the 'self-exploitation' that the government is anxious to encourage, and only a few academics, both native and foreign, are voicing reservations.

If there is any consistency behind my arguments in these two cases, it lies in the attempt to place the interests of the populations studied (at various levels – the bias towards the inhabitants of the small rural community is justified by the numerical dominance of the peasantry until the very recent past) above ideological dogma, either a government's or the anthropologist's. Many objections to this might be raised. It is perhaps a rather short-term assessment of welfare, since the contrasting prescriptions for Hungary and Poland result from only one generation of politically induced divergence. Thus it might be objected that the virtues of the small plot are such that its final disappearance in Hungary would mean untold psychic damage to the population; similarly, that the virtues of public ownership and the large-scale farm are such that any commitment to maintaining the private sector must be detrimental to the long-run interests of society. I would suggest that such statements imply a dogmatic judgement which the anthropologist should be wary of introducing.

It might also be objected that, short term or not, this is a rather vague kind of utilitarianism. I think I would be reasonably happy with this sort of label, but I repeat that sometimes the anthropologist alone may claim to have the best knowledge of how to set about raising the quantity of happiness; and it should also be added that the anthropologist is not inhibited in other parts of his work from looking outside the narrow utilitarian perspective, to paint a picture of the society under study that is consonant with his own inclinations and moral values, however inappropriate and ethnocentric they may seem to others. Hence the importance I attach to describing political systems; although my own descriptions purported to be 'factual', my 'pluralist' values are doubtless clear enough to any reader. Similarly, I have gone to some trouble to highlight the particular grievances of an ethnic minority in Poland, though the group is nowadays so small as scarcely to influence any over-all welfare calculations.

Perhaps the most serious objection would be that to follow these guidelines would place extreme and unreasonable demands upon the competence of the anthropologist. Specializing, as traditionally, in the intensive study of one small segment of society, he is being asked first of all to provide the authentic descriptions that no native can provide, and so to construct some model to facilitate understanding of the larger unit; but second, he needs directly to tackle that larger unit itself, grasping its empirical diversity, and reaching a theoretical understanding of the whole that cannot possibly be supplied by anthropology alone. Though one may utter fine words about transcending disciplinary boundaries in the study of complex societies, in practice the anthropologist must rely heavily upon other specialists; particularly, I would suggest, upon historians and political economists. What matters is not that the anthropologist should necessarily serve as part of a team whenever a project for a socialist country is set up, but that, in addition to the usual requirements for technique, language study, etc., he should be able to apply a critical intelligence to the work of other scholars, native and foreign, in a variety of related fields.

IV Conclusion

'All art is propaganda' declared one of the great native sociographers of twentieth-century Britain (Orwell 1961: 73). This may be an exaggeration in the case of some lyrical poetry, but it is a truism for social science. The best anthropological works in socialist Eastern Europe, as elsewhere, will be those which hold out some hope of separating out comparative scientific data from propaganda. My argument has been that there is not much to be gained from denying that, in some contexts, sensitive political problems face the Western anthropologist. I think that one can observe a basic rule of 'sympathy' with villagers, who represent the largest and least privileged group in all socialist populations, thereby reaching conclusions about major policy issues, and improving the quality of one's propaganda so as to render it suitable for cross-cultural comparisons. I have not worried much about whether any ideal conception of anthropology is compromised in this process. Dissatisfaction with the understanding of socialist societies provided by other academic disciplines, which seemed often to be grossly ethnocentric, was my prime reason for trying to approach them from the inside, through fieldwork; this was most easily accomplished by assuming the guise of an 'ethnographer', as I did initially in Hungary. I have argued equally pragmatically that this kind of work was seldom undertaken by native researchers; so, without bothering with any more intellectual arguments, I would argue the case for more empirical work by Westerners in Eastern Europe in terms of the political realities. The situation might even be compared to the 'colonial encounter'. There is obviously a descriptive and comparative job to be done, and native researchers are, in important respects, unequal to the task (through no fault of their own, of course). Western anthropologists are in a position to make good this deficiency, and I would like to see more of them doing it. It would be nice if later generations could agree that we made fewer mistakes than the anthropologists of the colonial period, and managed even a fraction of their insights.

However, whether or not these great opportunities exist, the approaches have not so far been uniform. There is a danger in adopting without reflection the concepts of Western political scientists and journalists, which may be unhelpful for comparative understanding. There is a danger of an opposite sort in the uncritical acceptance of the ideological position of the ruling power in the host country. Clearly I was lucky in the relatively liberal character of the regimes in the countries where I worked, and my position has been influenced by this fact. In my experience the authorities pay no more attention to the work of Western anthropologists than the Hungarian authorities in the nineteenth century did to LePlay. Why should they? Would our governments? Our writings are inevitably political, but most of the time we are writing for narrow academic audiences. The best we can realistically hope for is to influence policies and stereotypes in our society, not in theirs. If my work should become a *cause célèbre*, perhaps this would be the greatest compliment. But I do not think it would lead me to change my methodological guidelines. I would probably have little trouble obtaining a visa for the country next door. The states of Eastern Europe may all have elements of the 'police-state'; but they are often less efficient than those of the West; there is likely to remain tremendous scope for anthropology, and I expect it to be a growth area in the discipline for many years to come.

Finally, I concede that I have been advocating only a very short-term horizon for this 'sympathetic' anthropologist. The greater challenge, if we really are to banish relativism, must be to reach evaluative conclusions over the longer term. I have so far avoided such issues. Hungary seems to have satisfied the needs of its population more adequately than any other socialist state considered in this paper. But what if ideological hostility towards peasants were to cease in Poland: might the non-collectivized variant then take the prize? I am not ready to answer this sort of question; but for the moment the anthropologist in Eastern Europe can afford to leave aside such 'ifs' and get on with the overdue comparative enquiries into actually existing socialism.

Notes

1 The views of some of these anthropologists can be explored in successive volumes of the *Newsletter of the East European Anthropologists' Group*, published from 1982 at the Department of Anthropology, University of Michigan. The sharpest debate so far arose over the work of a group in Romania: a complaint that the work of this group was politically suspect was levelled by a Hungarian-American anthropologist, and apparently inspired primarily by the ethnic tensions between Romanians and Hungarians in Transylvania (see the controversy in the pages of the 1979 *Current Anthropology* **20**: 135–47). The complicating factor that a lot of the work by Americans in Eastern Europe is carried out by people of East European descent, and who may therefore be neither entirely foreign nor entirely native, is not examined here; it is important, but it is not my own case.

2 First to use the term 'ethnography' in Hungary was János Csaplovics, writing early in the nineteenth century. Most of his works dealt with the country's ethnic minorities. It is a sign of the nationalist times that, as the discipline developed, so more emphasis came to be laid on specifically Magyar culture. Prominent late in the nineteenth century were the folklorists Lajos Kálmány and Lajos Katona; the latter has a good summary of early researches into the ancient religion of the Hungarians in volume 8 of the journal *Ethnographia* (1897 – in Hungarian). But this, and the works of Bernát Munkácsi based on fieldwork among the related Siberian peoples, were also an interesting opening towards a wider, comparative view of the subject. For a short historical guide in English, see Sozan (1978).

3 Frazerian in scope was the work of the Catholic Bishop Arnold Ipolyi: *Magyar Mythologia* (1854). Later Zsigmond and Ákos Szendrey applied Frazer's theories of magic to Hungarian data.

Antal Csengery and Leo Beöthy were major figures in the dissemination of evolutionist theories in the second half of the nineteenth century (the latter is the subject of a monograph by Gábor Zsigmond: *A Magyar társadalomnéprajz kezdetei Beöthy Leo 1839–86*. Budapest: 1974).

For examples (with modern annotation) of the writings of the great Hungarian travellers and explorers, see the two volumes edited by Tibor Bodrogi: *Messzi Népek Magyar Kutatói* (Budapest: 1978). These include excerpts from Arminius Vámbery's accounts of his travels in Asia, János Xanthus in Borneo, and Lajos Biró in New Guinea. A notable Hungarian predecessor of Malinowski in London was Emil Torday (*On the Trail of the Bushongo*. London: 1925).

4 See, for example, the critique of feudal conditions and an early attempt to compare European peasant societies by Gergély Berzeviczy: *De conditiore et indole rusticorum in Hungaria* (1806); even before this, Sámuel Tessedik had analysed some of the internal social relations of the Hungarian peasantry: *Der Landmann in Ungarn, was er ist und was er seyn könnte* (1784).

5 LePlay's case study of a single peasant family was researched in 1846 and apparently published in Hungarian in 1850 (Hegedüs 1977: 84).

6 The outstanding work of this school is Ferenc Erdei: *A Magyar Paraszt társadalom* (1941), in which the author adds theoretical insight to the monographic results of more than a decade of empirical research. Among the major monographs by other authors in the 1930s were Géza Féja: *Viharsarok* (1937) and Zoltán Szabó: *A Tardi Helyzet* (1936); less significant ethnographically, but still an interesting autobiographical work by one of the major literary figures associated with the populist movement, is Gyula Illyés: *The People of the Puszta* (Budapest: 1967 – in English).

7 It is remarkable that the finest native monograph of the post-war period has not been published in Hungarian. Since it does not comment on socialist transformation, this can scarcely be put down to politics. The research, conducted with

many short periods of research spread over some fifteen years, has been published in two parts in the West: in addition to the rich analysis of social structure offered in Fél and Hofer (1969), a detailed description of the material culture of the community is available – *Bäuerliche Denkweise in Wirtschaft und Haushalt* (Göttingen: 1972).

8 *Magyarorszag Felfedezése* (*The Discovery of Hungary*) is the title of the principal series, nowadays including fine urban studies in addition to rural sociography; it is a pity that so little has been translated.

9 Some of Hungary's best sociologists, including members of the so-called 'Budapest School', have had to leave the country to be able to work and publish freely. Those who have left include not only distinguished theoreticians, but the country's leading empirical sociologist, Iván Szelényi.

10 In addition to Hann (1980) and Bell (1984) it is to be hoped that Vásáry (1983) will be published in due course. Further examples of Anglo-Saxon and native anthropology in Hungary can be found in Marida Hollos and Bela C. Maday (eds): *New Hungarian Peasants: An East Central European Experience with Collectivization* (New York: 1983). For a comprehensive survey of recent English language anthropology in Eastern Europe see Halpern and Kideckel (1983).

11 See n.9 above.

12 Among the responses to an earlier draft of this paper I received interesting comments from two young East European anthropologists. One felt that my claims on behalf of the Western anthropologist were exaggerated, and that the most illuminating theoretical analyses of his own country had been written by natives who were not known as specialist anthropologists. However, it appeared that they lived in exile and could publish only in English. My other friend felt that in his country far-reaching criticisms could be made by authors who did not emigrate, but who wrote in a sort of code which at least some sections of the native intelligentsia could crack (i.e. detect meanings in allusions etc.). These are important points, but I stand by my argument that 'neutral' Westerners also have a contribution to make, alongside that of natives and exiled natives. As to the second point, Westerners may even be rendering a service to later generations of natives, who may forget how to read between the lines of their indigenous forbears. I guess that neither of my correspondents would appreciate being named in this paper, and the substance of their comments to my mind confirms the disabilities under which those who do not emigrate must work.

References

BELL, P. D. (1984) *Peasants in Socialist Transformation – Life in a Collectivized Hungarian Village.* Berkeley, Calif: University of California Press.

BODROGI, T. (ed.) (1978) *Varsány: tanulmányok egy észak-Magyarországi falu társadalomnéprajzához.* Budapest: Adadémiai Kiadó.

DURAND-DROUHIN, J. and SZWENGRUB, L. M. (eds) (1982) *Rural Community Studies in Europe*, Vol. 2. Oxford: Pergamon Press.

FÉL., E, and HOFER, T. (1969) *Proper Peasants: Traditional Life in a Hungarian Village.* Chicago: Viking Fund Publications in Anthropology 46.

HALPERN, J. M. and KIDECKEL, D. A. (1983) Anthropology of Eastern Europe. *Annual Review of Anthropology* **12**: 377–402.

HANN, C. M. (1980) *Tázlár: A Village in Hungary.* Cambridge: Cambridge University Press.

— (1985) *A Village without Solidarity: Polish Peasants in Years of Crisis.* New Haven, Conn.: Yale University Press.

HEGEDŰS, A. (1977) *The Structure of Socialist Society*. London: Constable.

HOFER, T. (1968) Anthropologists and Native Ethnographers in Central European Villages: Comparative Notes on the Professional Personality of Two Disciplines. *Current Anthropology* 9: 311–15.

HOUGH, J. F. (1977) *The Soviet Union and Social Science Theory*. Cambridge, Mass.: Harvard University Press.

JÁVOR, K. (1983) Continuity and Change in the Social and Value Systems of a Northern Hungarian Village. In M. Hollos and B. C. Maday (eds) *New Hungarian Peasants: An East Central European Experience with Collectivization*. Brooklyn College Press (dist. Columbia University Press).

ORWELL, G. (1961) *Collected Essays*. London: Secker & Warburg.

SIMÓ, T. (1983) *A Tardi Társadalom*. Budapest: Kossuth Könyvkiadó.

SOZAN, M. (1978) *The History of Hungarian Ethnography*. Washington: University Press of America.

VÁSÁRY, I. (1983) Social Change in a Hungarian Village: From Peasant Farm to Agricultural Collective. Ph.D. thesis, University College, London.

Tamara Dragadze

10 Fieldwork at home:
the USSR

In the USSR, doing fieldwork in one's own country is probably not very different from the situation elsewhere. What differs significantly is the degree to which particular aspects – political control, the nationalities policy, and a high literacy rate – dominate the situation there. I have selected some data and a few anecdotes which I think would be helpful for comparative reflection. I have no intention of offering a comprehensive analysis of the Soviet system itself.[1]

The constraints imposed by a political system affect directly the way in which fieldwork is done and reported. In an indirect way this also affects the nature of what anthropologists are interested in. Soviet scholars might not be so aware of restrictions as some of their Western colleagues would be.

Being a British anthropologist myself, though, I could not presume to be able to see things entirely through their eyes. Their perceptions anyway vary among themselves a great deal. This account will be based on my own observations. My first visit to the USSR was in 1968, so my involvement to date with Soviet anthropology has spanned seventeen years. Nearly sixty months have been spent in the USSR, including a three-year postgraduate course in the Ethnography Department at Tbilisi University in Soviet Georgia, where I had to take the same examinations and train in similar fieldwork methods as the Soviet students. I worked for over a year with the anthropologists in Moscow at the University and the Institute of Ethnography and visited colleagues in Leningrad. I have also done research with the anthropologists of the Department of Ethnography of the Academy of Sciences in Tadjikistan. It is, however, the length and variety of the experiences themselves which increasingly inhibit me from generalizing with confidence.

The background

ORIGINS

Anthropology in the Soviet Union has an established, venerable pedigree: learned societies were founded in the nineteenth century in the Russian Empire, at around the same time as in Great Britain. Their members shared many of the same foibles, in particular a fascination with the general principles of the origins and history of all mankind. From 1917, however, Marxist doctrine incorporating the intellectual fashions of the time alone became acceptable. Later, when in the West the interests and approaches of early twentieth-century anthropologists began to change, in particular with the so-called Malinowskian revolution which rejected historicism, Soviet intellectuals were cut off and isolated by Stalin. Today their main interest is in historical reconstruction, and this reflects an attitude not only derived from Marxist piety but also from a pre-Revolutionary, uninterrupted cultural tradition (see Dragadze 1975).

Unlike some other disciplines (e.g. sociology: see Weinberg 1974), anthropology was not suppressed in Soviet times. Lenin himself had been interested in the Siberian minorities. Later on, anthropologists persuaded Stalin of the usefulness of the subject and the impeccable pedigree of some of the pre-Revolutionary anthropologists who had even been exiled to Siberia by the tsars (see Dragadze 1978b). Fortunately for the Soviet anthropologists, Miklukho-Maclay himself (1846–88), a most illustrious and daring scholar (see Lienhardt 1964), had at one stage been inexplicably expelled from school. They surmised that it was for his Revolutionary, anti-tsarist activities (see Tokarev 1966). They even succeeded in having the USSR Academy of Sciences Institute of Ethnography named after him.

In recent years, history as a discipline has widened its scope, sociology has been resuscitated and, partly in reaction to this, J.V. Bromley, the Director of the Institute of Ethnography in Moscow, has claimed for anthropology a unique skill: the study of ethnic processes. Theoretical works on this theme have been written. Under the name of 'ethno-sociology' some vast surveys were done which I will return to below. The majority of field-studies, however, whether directed from Moscow or by the Institutes of the minority republics, are not *explicitly* concerned with ethnicity.

INTELLECTUAL CONCERNS

A Soviet anthropologist is a historian, not a sociologist. The contrast in the thought-styles of many anthropologists from the West and the Soviet Union when they set out to do fieldwork can best be illustrated by the following example.

A Russian anthropologist who specializes in the study of Central Asia was complaining to me about the tediousness of fieldwork. He had taken as gifts a hundred wooden spoons from Moscow to a Turkmen village where he had worked the previous summer. To his dismay his host, a local schoolmaster, did not let him out of the house for three days until all the plans for the allocation of the spoons were completed. The teacher needed time to divide and redivide the spoons into groups, according to the importance of each family in the village. He would allocate, for example, seven spoons to one family and only three to another, then change his mind and allocate six and four respectively. The anthropologist told me that he nearly lost patience because he had just begun thinking that he could detect some Indo-European influences in early Turkmen religion which he wanted to check out at the village's shaman seances. He resented his work being held up for three days and was very surprised when I said that I would, so to speak, 'have given my right arm' to see the social reality of village ranking and prestige in quasi-numerical terms through a local person! Our concerns were very different, we agreed. Had I studied shamanism, one of my interests would have been to understand it in the village context and to see how it was perceived by the villagers. He, instead, wanted to use his observations of the ritual alone to reconstruct early Turkmen history.

All the main works on the nature of anthropology by Soviet anthropologists have stressed the closeness of anthropology and history. In Leningrad, as in Moscow, during the early Sovietization of the subject, it was moved from the faculty of geography to that of history.

Later, in 1945, S.P. Tolstov, Director of the Moscow Institute of Ethnography in the post-war period, wrote:

> '*Etnografia*[2] is a branch of history, which researches the cultural and customary particularities of different peoples of the world in their historical development, which studies the problems of origin and cultural-historical relations between these peoples and which establishes the history of their settlements and movements.'
>
> (Tolstov 1946)

A later *doyen* of Soviet anthroplogy, S. A. Tokarev, has written much the same thing in terms of anthropology and history, stating it to be 'A historical science, studying peoples and their way of life and culture' (Tokarev 1968). Two years previously he had affirmed that:

> 'Historicism is one of the basic principles of the Marxist method. Any subject, any phenomenon can only have its reality understood and known by approaching it from a historical point of view, by revealing its origin and development.'
>
> (Tokarev 1966)

There is also a sense of urgency among Soviet anthropologists in the field to record customs and the reminiscences of elderly people before they are lost. This information is seen to provide the key to reconstructing the past history of a particular people; in no other way can a people be understood.

Occasionally, the government authorities have commissioned the services of anthropologists to go to rural areas and to publish descriptions, in appreciative terms, of progress and modernization. They must demonstrate how people have benefited from the Soviet state over the years and how official, secular ideology and customs are ever-increasingly accepted. The objective is to write about what is to be approved of at the official level, not to investigate the real attitudes of contemporary villagers towards their world. In contrast to the restrictions placed on the study and publishing of data on contemporary rural life, there is much more scope for focusing on ancient customs and cultural history.

FIELDWORK METHODS

To gain people's trust to talk about their reminiscences and their traditions is not easy in the Soviet Union, as elsewhere. Fieldworkers need to develop great skills to engage people in conversation and, especially, to be allowed to observe traditional rituals. The environment in which these skills are used will be discussed below and form the main subject of this paper.

The basic approach in fieldwork centres around recording what people tell the anthropologist. Except for watching rituals and ceremonies, it is what is *said* (by the informant) rather than what is *observed* (by the anthropologist) that is used for reports – apart, of course, from the study of material culture. As many informants in as many places as possible within a particular region will be interviewed. This is generally thought to provide substance for the veracity of data, regardless of context.

Most work is done by anthropologists in the field on their own, especially their major, thesis work. However, 'complex expeditions' are also organized. Under a leader, a group of researchers, each with a particular interest – in religion, marriage traditions, old ploughing techniques, and so on –go to a particular region for a few months. At the end of each day they meet to compare notes and receive guidance. They usually live together, in a vacant building or by setting up a campsite, with a strict rotation of duties and considerable internal discipline.

Anthropologists do field research mainly during the 'expedition season', in the summer months. Those who stay out for longer return to their homes or institutes more frequently than a British anthropologist going overseas. Being in their own country, they resemble more closely a Londoner studying a community in Yorkshire, for instance, who would be unlikely to resist the temptation of going home rather than enduring an uninterrupted period of fieldwork for eighteen months. Many Soviet anthropologists return every summer to the same research area over a long period – twenty or thirty years, or more. Although they may not have considered it a prime objective when doing fieldwork, many eventually establish relationships of close friendship with some of their informants. A few scholars earn the respect and affection of people in a whole area where they do fieldwork. I remember how the male choirs of several mountain villages came to the capital to sing dirges at the funeral of a distinguished Georgian anthropologist, Vera Bardavelidze, all visibly upset by her death.

Fieldwork at home

For the purposes of comparison, it is important in assessing 'anthropology at home' to differentiate between those characteristics which derive from studying one's own people and those from publishing in the same country as well. It should be noted that a description of the Soviet case always includes both.

RESTRICTIONS AND AMBIVALENCE

There is a complex network of constraints which form an important part of the environment within which Soviet anthropologists work. These overlap to such an extent that it would be erroneous to isolate particular features under different headings. Two facts, that political control is keenly felt, and that the Soviet nationalities policy is significant for anthropology, are both interlinked in a way which precludes separate analysis.

Soviet anthropologists are well aware of the basic contradiction between official doctrine and their fieldwork experience, which they must conceal, regardless of its causes. Sanctions are severe compared to those experienced in many other countries.

Officially, there is supposed to be equality between the sexes and harmony between the generations throughout the Soviet Union. There must be 'love' between all the ethnic groups and regional groups within the country, and mutual respect between city and village. Furthermore, there should be definite indications of a convergence of thought and custom by all Soviet peoples, characterized by secularization, even though it is conceded that the different nationalities have for a long time had particular ways which are 'national in form' although 'socialist in content' (Stalin's formula). All evidence to the contrary is officially considered to be a sign of 'backwardness', while evidence supporting the fulfilment of these directives is applauded as 'progressive'. Anthropologists are unlikely to witness a great deal of success here; their concern with tradition will unveil the opposite. Moreover, they share with their informants the knowledge that they could all be severely reprimanded and punished, the villagers for being 'backward' and the anthropologists for publishing damaging information (if it is published) or collecting unpublishable material. I have been told of local officials being asked to investigate the sources of information published by anthropologists in the capital city who had claimed, for example, to have witnessed a particular ritual officially considered harmful or 'backward'. Local pride must also be reckoned with, and anthropologists must avoid the wrath of their informants who might themselves read what has been written about them. With such a high literacy rate as there is in the Soviet Union, especially among the minorities who have an intense interest in their own national culture, anthropologists can expect some of their work to be read and inspected locally. Signs of criticism, as well as any indication of the possibility of a reprimand, or worse, from zealous officials, will be looked for by the local people.

Anthropologists respond to such tensions by writing about *past* traditions and reassuring the informants of their intention to do so. They are often vague about actual dates when describing a custom and, if admitting that it was witnessed recently, a catchphrase is used such as 'this custom is dying out' or 'it has ceased to exist'. A good measure of self-censorship is used, not only about what to publish but also about which questions to ask. Throughout the Soviet Union informants are quick to appreciate the quality of discretion in an anthropologist.

Were it not for the necessity to be brief, I would also comment on the subject of individual moral conscience among Soviet anthropologists, especially concerning what they write to be published. Suffice it to say, here, that there is a lot of variation between what is written in Russian and in the minority languages. As far as Russian anthropologists are concerned, especially in Moscow and Leningrad, they usually display confidence and suffer fewer personal inhibitions, whether writing about fellow-Russians in rural areas or minority peoples. Perhaps this is because they are better informed about what is officially 'permissible' and what is not, at any one time. Being the dominant nationality, too, they are less likely to be aware of the same tensions that are felt by the minorities. For their part, indigenous anthropologists in the minority republics have told me that their sense of common identity with the village informants directs them in choosing what to write. When indigenous anthropologists in Central Asia, for example, write in Russian about contemporary observations, they embellish their descriptions with comments about 'progress', no doubt to present their informants in the best possible light. They display what appears to be an ambivalent attitude, which in their keenness to describe 'progressive' features may dampen their enthusiasm and national pride in the uniqueness of their customs.[3] When they write in their own languages in scientific journals a different approach can be discerned, characterized principally by an effort to display a wealth of detail unlikely to appear in Russian language publications.

On reflection, I think that when comparing the Soviet example with others, the sanctions and constraints mentioned above are noticeable not only because of a particular political system. It is not state Marxism which is different but the efficiency and extent of the bureaucracy which upholds official precepts and confirms people's expectations of its reactions.

DISADVANTAGES AT HOME

Research institutes throughout the Soviet Union are ultimately controlled centrally by the highest authorities in Moscow. There is much uniformity, therefore, throughout the country, regardless of regional differences in organization and implementation structures. Except for short visits to Eastern Europe students cannot train abroad. Moreover – whether imposed from above or desired anyway – in the minority republics in particular anthropologists must only study within their own borders.

The shortcomings of studying your own people are not unique to Soviet anthropologists. In keeping with their claims of 'knowing your own people' and 'being one of them', for example, most anthropologists are singularly unapprised of the tremendous differences between urban and village people. Even scholars whose parents live in villages tend to disregard the consequences of their own long residence in a capital city to complete their higher education. Despite paying lip-service to the contrary, there exist throughout the Soviet Union both patronizing attitudes of city dwellers towards villagers, and suspicion and resentment towards urbanites by villagers who are relatively disadvantaged (except for food). Paradoxically, however, the urban intelligentsia in minority republics usually take the romantic view that the repository of authentic national culture is in the village. On the other hand, the very fact of their identifying so closely with the people studied, especially in the nationalistic intellectual climate among the minorities, can occasionally obscure particular aspects of their research. It can cause regional insularity. At a staff meeting I once attended, an anthropologist was so intent on proving that, in his own region, it was ingenious in the windy climate to hold down a roof with rocks and stones that he was unaware that in all the neighbouring provinces this symbolized the barrenness of his region. He vehemently denied it when he was told.

In the minority republics anthropologists are so keen to record their own history that, even if they were allowed to, they would consider they did not have the time to study the peoples in other Soviet republics. I cannot but regret this fact, although I know that, because of the importance of ethnic identity, it is difficult to be accepted by a Soviet minority other than your own when doing fieldwork. Even regional differences can count: in Tadjikistan, for example, someone from Southern Tadjikistan can find it difficult to be accepted easily by local people when doing ethnographic fieldwork in Northern Tadjikistan.

The single exception to the rule of only doing fieldwork among your own people are the Russians. From the main institutes in Leningrad, and especially Moscow, Russian anthropologists have gone to study in all the Soviet republics. Some, through devotion and skill, have eventually been able to do good fieldwork. Others, unsurprisingly, given the antagonisms towards them, have done but superficial research without even mastering the language.

The ethno-sociologists of the USSR Institute of Ethnography in Moscow have done mass surveys offering fascinating data and revealing excellent and original scholarship. Such is the delicacy of the situation in the USSR that my reservations about some of their findings are based on the shortcomings of the work in minority republics that has been organized by Russians. Even though an Armenian directs much of the work, albeit based in Moscow, his very ethnic origin is likely to prejudice his chances of obtaining accurate information, except in Armenia. This applies particularly to the study of 'ethnic self-awareness', where his team asked leading questions of villagers in minority republics such as, 'Would you be happy for your daughter to marry a Russian?' In other areas, the ethno-sociology team do competent work. Yet it is interesting to note that the minority republics' local scholars have not applied themselves specifically to the study of their own 'ethnic self-awareness'.

Inescapably, we are alerted to the fact that the complexity of the Soviet nationality question, on the whole, precludes a straightforward and succinct commentary on many of the interests and practices of Soviet anthropologists.

ADVANTAGES AT HOME

It is possible to be brief here because, once again, the most obvious advantages of doing fieldwork at home are not confined to Soviet anthropologists. The knowledge of the language, a partly shared culture and religion (despite urban–rural and regional differences), the absence of pressure on time in the field, and the possibility of returning at will for further research because of the geographical proximity of the area are helpful to all anthropologists working 'at home'.

Other advantages, however, are more noticeable in the Soviet Union than in some other countries:

First, you can gain a particularly rewarding kind of trust from some informants because they know that you both share the same political system, run the risk of the same kind of sanctions against making certain revelations, and so on. People usually know where to find you in the capital when you leave the area and, in a way, do not feel they have no control over you or your knowledge. This is not to deny some drawbacks in this very situation, but these would invariably depend on the individuals involved and the issues being studied.

Second, in the Soviet Union centralization is a general feature of administration and the distribution of goods. Relevant decisions are taken and valuable items are purchased only in the capital. Many villagers have to travel to the capital for this reason. They often call upon anthropologists whom they have befriended in the course of fieldwork to offer 'return hospitality'. Over the years some genuine friendships are formed and this offers the chance of continuous contact with the field, throughout a lifetime. This is particularly the case in the minority republics, although similar instances are not completely excluded with the Russians.

Finally, in view of the strains inherent in some aspects of the Soviet nationalities question, a few pitfalls in doing fieldwork are avoided by studying your own people, as has already been indicated. Given the vigour of ethnic and regional prejudices, admittedly overcome by some anthropologists (for example, in the affection for the Russians, Sukhareva and Snesarev, who worked admirably well in Central Asia), little relatively better would be achieved in anthropology if Soviet anthropologists reversed the policy of, by and large, studying their own people exclusively. Furthermore, the tensions between honest reporting and official demands are such that it is the indigenous anthropologist who best can master the Soviet art of subtle double-talk and symbolic representation.

Conclusion

It would be a mere truism to state that it is the quality of the fieldworker and not the choice of field which makes for good anthropology. Unlike colleagues in the West, however, Soviet anthropologists cannot have the choice of whether to do fieldwork at home or not. Whether that hinders or helps the discipline there in its development is open to question. I would nevertheless suggest that, given the circumstances and orientations of Soviet anthropology which I have described in part, fieldwork at home is more suitable in that kind of environment than among 'strangers'.

I have tried to argue consistently, throughout the paper, that one must resist the temptation of seeing the political and social situation in the Soviet Union as unique and exotic. What differs is the *degree* to which certain elements of policy and political control are significant and effective.

In other words, it is not Soviet policy which is so different but the capacity of the bureaucracy to uphold the policies of central government authority, whatever these may be, which causes the greatest differences between the experience of Soviet anthropologists and those anthropologists who have contributed to this volume from other countries.

Notes

1 Also, I do not want to repeat myself too much. I have already written on the subject of fieldwork in the USSR on several occasions, in particular Dragadze 1978b and 1984.
2 I recognize that some of the nuances are lost by translating *etnografia* as 'anthropology' in English. For the limited purposes of this paper, however, it is the most suitable term.
3 An example is Annaklychev's article on the Turkmen in Dragadze (1984).

References

BASILOV, V. N. (1984) *Izbranniki dukhov* (*Chosen of the Spirits*). Moscow.
BROMLEY, J. V. (1973) *Etnos i Etnografia* (*Ethnos and Ethnography*). Moscow: Academy of Sciences.
CHITAIA, G. S. (1957) Printsipi i metod polevoi etnograficheskoi raboty (Principles and Method of Ethnographic Fieldwork). *Sovetskaya Etnografia* **4**.
DRAGADZE, T. (1975) Response to Gellner. *Current Anthropology* **16** (4).
— (1978a) A Meeting of Minds: A Soviet and Western Dialogue. *Current Anthropology* **19** (1).
— (1978b) Anthropological Fieldwork in the USSR. *Journal of the Anthropological Society of Oxford*.
— (1980a) The Place of 'Ethnos' Theory in Soviet Anthropology. In E. Gellner (ed.) *Soviet and Western Anthropology*. London: Duckworth.
— (1980b) Comment on Soviet Anthropology. *Royal Anthropological Institute Newsletter*, June.
— (ed.) (1984) *Kinship and Marriage in the Soviet Union*. London: Routledge & Kegan Paul.
GELLNER, E. (1975) The Soviet and the Savage. *Current Anthropology* **16** (4).
ITS, R. F. (1974) *Vvedenie v etnafiu* (*Introduction to Anthropology*). Leningrad: University Publishing House.
LIENHARDT, G. (1964) *Social Anthropology*. Oxford: Oxford University Press.
TOKAREV, S. A. (1966) *Istoria russkoi etnografii* (*dooctyabrskiy period*) (*History of Russian Anthropology*) (*The Period before October*). Moscow.
— (1968) *Osnovy Etnografii* (*Basic Anthropology*). Moscow.
TOLSTOV, S. P. (1946) Etnografia i sovremennost (Anthropology and the Present). *Sovetskaya Etnografia* **1**.
WEINBERG, E. (1974) *The Development of Sociology in the Soviet Union*. London: Routledge & Kegan Paul.

A. P. Cheater

11 The anthropologist as citizen:
the diffracted self? *

'Instead of being a full-time member of one "total and whole" society,
modern man is a part-time citizen in a variety of part-time societies . . . to
each of which he owes only partial allegiance.'

(Luckmann 1978: 282)

'It is not profitable first to separate the two terms of a relation in order to try
to join them together again later. . . . The concrete is man within the world
in that specific union of man with the world which Heidegger, for example,
calls "being-in-the-world".'

(Sartre 1969: 3)

Introduction

If I read him correctly, for Malinowski the 'problematic' of being
simultaneously anthropologist and citizen, of studying one's own society as
anthropological professional, did not exist. He was quite clear in his own mind
about the distance separating anthropologist from informants of lesser intelligence, in whatever society (1922: 11–12); and he regarded the understanding
of the exotic as justified not least by the understanding of his own 'human
nature' (society? culture?) that such a pursuit potentially conferred upon the
anthropologist (1922: 25, 518). Today, polite astonishment and raised eye-
brows may still greet the anthropologist who chooses to work in his own
society. The premise that we will work in other societies seems to me to
underlie and sustain the Malinowskian separation of anthropological pro-
fessionalism from citizenship.

As the world changes, however, this premise becomes increasingly unrealistic. Research funds shrink while foreign costs escalate; national
governments define their own priorities and, in developing states, are

increasingly unwilling to admit foreigners for research purposes; civil unrest and war render any kind of fieldwork inadvisable. In socialist and under-developed countries in particular, anthropologists themselves may have little inclination – even if it were possible – to focus their attention outside their own national boundaries, when so many research opportunities exist within them. The separation of anthropological and citizenship roles thus becomes increasingly difficult to sustain, even as an ideological premise.

In contrast, the conflation of these roles raises problems which social anthropology seems to me to have preferred to avoid in the past, but which have been faced squarely in this century by philosophy, phenomenology, and sociology. Today, I think we are now forced within our own profession not merely to question whether there is a conflict of roles between citizenship and anthropology. At a more fundamental level, we are also challenged among other things to confront the dimensions of 'self' and 'other' in our own professional consciousness; to re-examine the issues of subjectivity and objectivity in our research methods; to question the effectiveness of our communication of a whole intellectual discipline to our students. These challenges, which I shall consider separately in detail later, arise from the disparate expectations of citizenship and profession for those practising anthropology in their own societies.

Let me try to clarify, at this point, what I mean by 'citizenship'. A formal definition based on the rights and obligations of deciding on the mode of government and deployment of resources, in the ritual of voting, is in my opinion less helpful outside Western democracies than is a concentration on 'constructive engagement' in society. Academics certainly vote and may be political activists; but they have a far greater significance in societies where their intellectual skills carry an exaggerated scarcity value, through their power as teachers and writers to construct social reality in a particular con-ceptual image for their students and readers. This construction of reality for a particular society feeds into the development process, and must therefore be regarded as a responsibility – as well as a right – of intellectual citizenship in such a system. Certainly politicians regard it as such, in their recognition that intellectuals carry the mantle of ultimate legitimacy even while they them-selves wield power, and that independent ideas are more dangerous than physical violence. In this respect, anthropologists are but part of the larger intellectual community, of social scientists in particular, whose constructions of reality may be unacceptable to political controllers; and it seems to me that the historical debate about anthropology and colonialism reflects precisely such unacceptability as the political controllers changed while the academics remained constant. But now, a decade and more later, in the Third World at least, the academics have also largely changed. They share citizenship with their own politicians, even while their respective constructions of reality may remain distinct.[1]

In two intellectual generations, then, the locus of responsibility for anthropology in the Third World has turned full circle. Metropolitan academics such as Radcliffe-Brown spent the 1920s and 1930s establishing social anthropology in the colonial periphery. Many able practitioners born into citizenship of these societies were later attracted into anthropology and cut their professional teeth on their own societies, but then moved into the 'centre' (Firth, Fortes, Gluckman, and Hilda Kuper are perhaps the most notable examples among many). Those who chose to remain in their own systems professionally (Stanner, Eileen Krige, Monica Wilson are some names who come to mind), seem to have exercised less influence on the directions in which anthropology developed at the centre, and notably were not involved in the debate about colonialism (cf. Asad 1973). In the mid-1980s, however, mobility into the centre is practically impossible and, for some, ethically undesirable, and so the younger generation of Third World anthropologists must confront problems which their seniors appear to have avoided, ignored, or conceptualized differently. In this paper, therefore, I shall speak specifically to the problems of Third World anthropologists working in their own societies, while recognizing that much of what I have to say may be more widely applicable.

These problems are born of citizenship in polyethnic, racially differentiated, and class-structured societies in which the anthropologist, as intellectual, is by definition of a class different from many – but not all – of his research subjects, even if he is not also from an ethnic or racial minority in the total society. In this situation, we have arguably moved beyond the familiar colonial depiction of the anthropologist as spokesman and broker for 'his people' to the outside world, to a more overtly political and politicized context in which such brokerage may be irrelevant and even damaging (cf. Cheater 1985) and the anthropologist himself may be torn by 'cross-cutting ties' arising from his own social commitment to the system he is studying. What has changed most, perhaps, is the anthropologist's own definition of the situation and conceptualization of the locus of his professional responsibility, as a permanent member of that society.

Concomitantly, as Clammer (1984: 82–4) indicates, 'styles' of anthropology change too. The colonial anthropologist may be regarded as having practised in his own 'backyard', like those who study Gypsies, peasants, and ethnic minorities in the West.[2] The citizen anthropologist of an independent Third World state is, in contrast, often working in his own 'front room', along with Western sociologists, social workers, psychiatrists, and F. G. Bailey! Increasingly, then, we are being asked to confront ourselves as 'other', alienated from our own social identities by the fact of others' existence; and to recognize others as in many ways congruent with ourselves in some categorical or even personal sense, as class actors, state bureaucrats, students, and citizens. In such circumstances, it seems to me inevitable that we must consider the subjective, personalized dimensions of our own professional behaviour, in order to understand the apparently widening divergence between the interests of Western and non-Western anthropologists who, on the rare occasions when they meet at international conferences, seem to have increasingly little to say to one another. I am not suggesting that the themes which I shall address are in any way new in themselves, but in considering them from a particular existential perspective[3] I believe that we may transcend the content of our past discourse concerning such matters. This 'existential' dimension of our professional behaviour is problematic, however, for, as Mary Warnock notes:

> 'Existentialism does not recognize the boundary between ethics and epistemology, or between either and ontology (as for logic, it has no interest in it). Just as there is no sharp distinction between knowing and acting on one's knowledge, so there is none between perceiving and feeling.'
>
> (In Sartre 1969: xii)

Self and other

In considering our ability to operate as professionals within our own societies, the obvious starting-point is to understand our own constructions of 'self' and 'other' in a system to which both are committed. Sartre (1969) distinguishes four different refractions of being. The first, being-in-itself, exists effectively only as a non-conscious potential which is extinguished in its conscious realization as the second, being-for-itself. Being-in-itself may therefore be ignored for our purposes. Being-for-itself, in contrast, is fundamental to my argument, even though it is almost impossible, except for purposes of classification and analysis, to separate it from being-for-others, Sartre's third refraction of being. Being-for-others views the self as object, or other, from the perspective of others; and I shall argue that these others' views of self are extremely important to the citizen anthropologist, in ways that differ from the importance of other-constructions to a visiting anthropologist, for whom they are in any case very much more limited. Finally, the constructions of being-for-itself and being-for-others occur in specific contexts: Sartre argues that the fourth refraction, being-in-situation, allows being-for-itself to define itself in relation to others through behaviour, while remaining ultimately founded on being-in-itself. The situation itself is neither subjective nor objective: as 'total facticity' and 'absolute contingency' (Sartre 1969: 548–49), the situation relates being-for-itself to being-in-itself so that the limits to individual freedom are defined by the self in situation-specific behaviour. For Sartre, therefore, the self can equally be subject or object, either from its own perspective or that of others, a view which overlaps with Schutz's (1978a: 127) notion of a 'founding intersubjectivity' which links ego and alter-ego, hic (here) and illic (there), and, in my own view, more generally self and other.

The consciousness of self simultaneously from the perspectives of oneself and others is, as Sartre (1969: 429) notes, marked by conflict, the essence of all relations between consciousnesses'. As anthropologists, we are often aware of this conflict in our concern for what colleagues will think of our published ideas. Sometimes this awareness extends to a sensitivity to what respondents will feel about seeing their actions in print. (Should we disguise the actions or the actors? Is Latin a sufficient cover for the former?)[4] But rarely, in my own personal experience, are we conscious of the process by which we are incorporated into the historical facticity of those we study. Perhaps only when the 'normal' roles of anthropologist and respondent are reversed, only – for example – when we are greeted by hosts of village photographers and interrogated closely about our professional descent in order to be fitted into the local experience of the genus 'anthropologist', do we really perceive our status as 'other' *in our own eyes*. Maybe I am a little slower on the uptake than many colleagues, but I learned some unexpected things on my recent fleeting visit to Kaixian'gong, things which I had never previously experienced during research within my own system.

And yet, in other ways, one is sensitized working within one's own society to the problems of self and other, and their reflexivity within the roles of citizen and intellectual. Policy, reflected in legislation, always intrudes into research, especially in one's own society, and while the evaluation of policy can be objective in its orientation, in the context of local research, the goals of such policy evaluation form part of the situational contingency by which being-in-situation is constructed. In such contexts, being-for-itself is more often constructed within the encompassing frame of citizenship rather than the more limited context of profession, for policy issues are not isolated from, but form part of, the total context of life lived in a particular system. Certainly the issue of how fish are marketed has a contextual specificity; but the connection between marketing systems and rewards to labour and capital respectively form part of the contextualization of the citizen anthropologist's own work and life, even if his particular professional analysis does not favour such a wider frame of reference. If the citizen anthropologist addresses such issues as a professional, he must take the consequences which an outsider can often escape if his analysis falls from political grace: we might remember here the experiences of Fei Hsiao-Tung (1983) and others. We might recall, too, that the punishment for dissent of whatever kind often takes the form of intellectual harassment designed specifically to subordinate being-for-itself to being-for-others. Manual labour and even physical torture may have less effect on being-for-itself than the intellectual humiliation of self, as Chinese colleagues know from their experiences of the past three decades. But if the citizen anthropologist refuses to engage professionally in the political discourse of his own society, he inflicts on himself a different kind of self-humiliation, as students especially will demand to know by what personal philosophy he can justify withholding his knowledge and experience from his own people, most of whom in the Third World are singularly less fortunate than himself.

Doing anthropology in one's own society thus more easily creates being-for-itself through the contingencies of professional practice than is possible through professional practice in another system. Indeed, one might without malice draw the old parallel (with a new twist) between visiting anthropologists and tourists, both 'doing the natives' in ways that have little impact on their own selves within their own life-worlds. Of course, for Malinowski (1922: 517–18) 'our final goal' was 'to enrich and deepen our own world's vision, to understand our own nature and to make it finer, intellectually and artistically', and this personal enhancement was expected to follow automatically from 'grasping the essential outlook of others' through anthropological fieldwork.[5]

But this view says nothing of the mechanics of functioning as citizen anthropologist within a particular system, and may therefore be regarded more as an article of faith (or perhaps advertising) than a guide to behaviour. One might even venture, with Sartre (1969: 59), to suggest that, in his separation of aspects of his professional life from his total existence, the visiting anthropologist is merely 'playing at' anthropology: that he is in bad faith with himself.[6] Is there not, in Malinowski's (1922: 2–25) semi-ironic but in Sartre's (1969: 580) sense 'serious' description of method, a positivist resonance of 'the priority of object over subject', together with a suspicion that roles are being staged?

'Let us consider this [anthropologist] in the [village]. His movement is quick and forward, a little too precise, a little too rapid. He comes toward the [villagers] with a step a little too quick. He bends forward a little too eagerly; his voice, his eyes express an interest a little too solicitous. . . . All his behaviour seems to us a game. . . . The [anthropologist] in the [village] plays with his role in order to realize it.'

(With apologies to Sartre 1969: 59)

'Imagine yourself suddenly set down surrounded by all your gear, alone on a tropical beach close to a native village, while the launch or dinghy which has brought you sails out of sight. Since you take up your abode in the compound of some neighbouring white man, trader or missionary, you have nothing to do, but to start at once on your ethnographic work. . . . Imagine yourself, then, making your first entry into the village, alone or in company with your white cicerone. Some natives flock around you, especially if they smell tobacco. Others, the more dignified and elderly, remain seated where they are . . . .'

(Malinowski 1922: 4)

Unfair and irreverent it may be for me to single out Malinowski for the purpose of turning his own words against him. The point is not to pillory our ancestors, but to draw attention to aspects of our professional behaviour which those of us who are less gifted than Malinowski was, tend to overlook and suppress in ourselves. Malinowski was an inductivist, trained at the turn of this century in mathematics, physics, and philosophy, with interests that branched out into the social sciences, notably psychology, before he became an anthropologist (Paluch 1981: 278). As Paluch (p. 279) notes, Malinowski's positivist epistemology runs consistently through his anthropological works from beginning to end. Yet his posthumously published diary reveals that his collection and analysis of anthropological data involved a very different kind of behaviour, overwhelmed quite frequently by his subjective inclinations and structured very firmly by his perception of the intellectual inequality separating anthropologist from respondents. Doubtless we, his descendants, suffer the same problem; but I find many more indications of an existential dimension to Malinowski's anthropology[7] than are apparent in more recent work, with the obvious exception of F. G. Bailey. Perhaps because we lack the philosophical background of European scholarship, as well as holding historically a professional lack of interest in our own societies, social anthropologists since Malinowski have generally emphasized his positivism rather than his subjectivity, and most, I think, have experienced no cause to query his assumptions about inequality.

Subjectivity and objectivity

Given the contextualization discussed above, how is it possible to construct social reality in such a way that others will accept it as objective? To answer this question, we must begin by differentiating professional colleagues from other others, for the positivist criteria of reliability and replicability by which objectivity is judged within the profession will differ from the criteria used by fellow citizens, which generally refer to opposed national and sectarian interests. In this latter context, specifically anthropological analysis is questioned by the existence of multiple interpretations of the shared 'life-world': it is one among many interpretive possibilities. Here we are concerned not so much with the differences between magical, theological, and scientific interpretations which, as Schutz (1978b: 270) notes, may simultaneously be brought to bear on the same reality, but for example with the divergence between an emphasis on national unity, integrity, and equality, and the specific requirements of local communities. The latter may be regarded within the wider society as promoting 'tribal', 'class', and other politically unacceptable behaviours. By definition in the past, anthropologists have tended to accept their respondents' versions of local social reality. For the citizen anthropologist, however, there may be a real conflict between his sympathetic desire to repay locally incurred debts by supporting such local versions of reality, and his own understanding, from a different class perspective, of the future outcome for his own society of supporting such views. Here the anthropologist is faced not with a simple conflict of views or even of roles, but with what Schutz (1972: 8–9) calls the 'fundamental difference' between the anthropologist's interpretation of his own subjective experiences, as researcher and analyst, and his interpretation through 'parallel streams of consciousness' of the subjective experiences of his research subjects, whose own 'naïve understanding' (Schutz 1972: 140) creates the categories of subjective understanding which are analysed by the anthropologist as 'objects of thought'.

There is a further refinement of this problem when the research field includes, as economic or political competitors, actors of different races, classes, and languages, whose divergent interests may create incommensurable views of the 'same' reality, each of which is in turn further subjectively constructed by the anthropologist's analysis. Horton's (1962) construction of the concept of a 'triangle of forces' to explain behaviour with reference to the assumed relationships between three different categories of free spirit in Kalabari belief, can perhaps stand as a model here. In practice, the precise alignment of these forces would, I presume, be open to interpretation through divination. However, where such forces are not Kalabari spirits, but rather white capital, black government, and black labour (or American capital, Asian government, and guest labour, or similar permutations), infused by the 'spirits' of knowledge, policy, and subsistence respectively, divination is not an adequate tool of analysis and interpretation. So when his research field covers such conflicting elements, which are integral to one another and inseparable, with which of his respondents should the citizen anthropologist empathize or identify? Under what circumstances? At which time? For what purposes? How should he respond to requests for advice from everyone? As he becomes a participant himself in such an arena of conflict, drawn into it by his acceptance as a researcher of more and more information from all sides, how might he avoid his own subjective response of 'a plague on all your houses'? Short of going insane or turning politician, how can the anthropologist cope with these explicit subjectivities of himself and others?

If he does nothing, then there is, as Clammer (1984: 65) observes, 'the grave danger of fieldwork creating a subject–object relationship between the fieldworker and those observed'. While this danger may arguably apply to citizen and visiting anthropologists alike, there is less chance that the citizen anthropologist will be allowed to duck what his fellow citizens being studied define as his moral or ethical obligations to themselves. For one thing, he is spatially close at hand, and the long-distance strategy of writing letters to remind him of moral obligations (cf. Firth 1967: 12) may well be supplemented by personal visits of supplication, letters to the local press, the use of network links, and so forth. In short, the citizen anthropologist is 'trackable' and accountable, where the visitor is not, precisely because his research subjects can assume that he is subjectively 'one of us', an equal in terms of citizenship obligations, if not in terms of race, class, or language.

That there is an intermingling of these two different subjectivities, of observer and observed, is perhaps the fundamental reason for our disciplinary emphasis on participant observation as our main research tool. Subjectivity is useful. Malinowski (1922: 4–7) explicitly recognized the importance of his own subjectivity as something essential but to be subdued, even subordinated, in the process of becoming a 'natural' part of the society under study, able to participate in its patterns of etiquette and to appreciate the subtleties of its language. To observe fully, it is necessary to participate, though, as Clammer (1984: 68) rightly notes, there are limits to the extent to which this is possible under different circumstances. Even ostensibly passive observation requires some participation, a point which natural scientists such as Bronowski have emphasized in the point that perception itself is a subjective experience.

> 'The world is not a fixed, solid array of objects, out there, for it cannot be fully separated from our perception of it. It shifts under our gaze, it interacts with us, and the knowledge that it yields has to be interpreted by us. There is no way of exchanging information that does not demand an act of judgement. . . . Every judgement in science stands on the edge of error, and is personal.'
>
> (Bronowski 1973: 364, 374)

But subjectivity also has an active dimension, as Malinowski explicitly recognized. Not only did he 'set nets', he actively drove his ethnographic 'quarry' into them (Malinowski 1922: 8). Anthropology can therefore never be simply a passive cultural translation: good ethnography is the subjective construct of both observation and analysis. We cannot rid ourselves of this subjectivity, nor should we wish to; but we ought, perhaps, to pay it very much more attention, as part of our ontology, than it has attracted in the past. As anthropology changes, we need to understand cognitively (rather than as a slightly embarrassed gut feeling) precisely what this subjectivity is, how it is constructed, and how it affects our performance as anthropological professionals in different situations. Indeed, I would go further, to argue that the current problems of communication among anthropologists, whose subjectivities as citizen-professional and visiting-professional are constituted differently, may be traced to our failure to address these different subjectivities.

Communication

For the citizen anthropologist in the Third World, modes of communication are problematic on two fronts: with fellow-professionals outside his society; and with those whom he teaches in his society.

Our students are an integral part of our social reality, and individually may even be part of our personal research history: so far I have taught five students from the area in which I conducted my first major research project. Two of these five have actually worked as my research assistants in this area. Such students represent one type of engagement of the citizen anthropologist with his own society, and an immediate check on his construction of their reality. They may respect the anthropologist for his status as an intellectual, but this respect does not confer on him a monopoly of the right of interpretation, as may happen when the anthropologist is the only 'expert' on a foreign system.

Many other of our students represent a different kind of communication problem, coming as they do from farms, towns, and cities in which the classical content of anthropology is but a historical relic, of antiquarian interest perhaps, but more often vilified as 'uncivilized' or 'stone age' practices from which they wish to distance themselves as fast as possible. We, rather than their parents, may be their cultural instructors in their rejected past. And even those students who come from rural areas in which some traditions at least survive, often in modified form, share with their urbanized counterparts a prime concern with contemporary reality, which they often have difficulty in recognizing as the anthropologists' 'social change'. After all, how can anyone conceptualize his life as 'social change'? Our problems in communicating with our students, then, may be summarized mainly as those of perceived personal relevance in both the mundane today and the dream world of a developed future.

Yet we do not escape entirely the ritual mode of communication in our search for relevance. Continuing verities such as ethnicity and witchcraft cannot be handled – as in Western textbooks – as if both teacher and student were non-believers, though some indeed may be. The subjective dimension of cultural identity, or part-identity, superimposes on more feeble functional explanations, questions of immediate urgency: do witches really exist? If you say they do not, or that the question is irrelevant, how do I know that witches do exist and are highly relevant? How can I believe your generalized version of a particular ritual when in my area we do it differently? Why do you not pay equal attention to ethnographic examples from my ethnic category? A failure to resolve satisfactorily the subjective referents to being-for-itself and being-for-others which pervade such questions, represents a failure to 'get through to' one's students.

Again, we are confronted here by the issue of equality: the necessity to afford the conceptual frameworks of one's fellow-citizens not merely the status of rationality (as limited and closed systems that are ultimately wrong), but also that of an equal and alternative reality that affects oneself. This is an extremely difficult task, made no easier for the Western-descended intellectual by the requirement that he submit part of his professional life to the authority of a different set of cultural rules. If one fails in this task, in my experience one can expect students to walk out of lectures in protest.

Perforce, then, the conceptual orientation to teaching has to diverge from a situation where a foreign anthropologist relays to foreign students the construction of a socio-cultural reality in an idiom and from an epistemological base which are also strange to the system being explicated.[8] In the shared reality of our own society, when talking of ourselves, scientific anthropology cannot diverge too greatly from subjective experience if teaching is to be effective.[9] In his analytical construction of reality for his students, then, the anthropologist's subjectivity as citizen is involved in a complex combination with his subjectivity as professional, as he operates in two time-frames, the present and the future. For the (visiting) anthropologist teaching foreign students a foreign reality, in contrast, only the professional present, based on past fieldwork experience, is relevant.

While the citizen anthropologist in the Third World seeks to communicate with his students in this mundane mode of subjectivity, then, he must simultaneously conduct a different conversation, in the ritualized mode of objectivity (the mystified ethnographic present), with metropolitan colleagues, assuming, that is, that he wishes to remain within the larger professional discourse. This ritualized mode of communication is specifically exotic and is apparently not interested in the obscure economic, political, historical, and legal details of mundane life in remote corners of the globe. Perhaps it is not even interested in such details of metropolitan society, for they are, after all, already established as the proper preserve of other academic disciplines, which will doubtless present problems other than naïveté to metropolitan citizen anthropologists in the future. The mundane parochialism of the periphery thus finds few publication outlets at the centre. In contrast, the exotic ritual obscurities that find a publication market at the centre, justifying the 'expert' status of metropolitan colleagues, seem to us peripherals largely irrelevant to our lives, our teaching, and our research. The result of these different modes of communication, constructing different social realities and reflecting the current realities of professional power, is not merely that Third World citizen anthropologists feel patronized by and alienated from their Western colleagues. More fundamentally, they feel that there is nothing to talk about that will be of interest and value to themselves as professionals in their own societies: the starting premises are so different as to be irreconcilable. Ahmed (1984) has recently expressed this view regarding Islamic anthropology. I would regard his perfectly valid points as merely one specific instance of a more general problem.

Perhaps these perceptions reflect only the difficulties of a contemporary transition. The West has already lost its former prominence in anthropological research; through no fault of its own it is also losing its capacity to teach at its former volume; and the quantitative market for publication is gradually increasing in the Third World. The locus of domination is, possibly, shifting. But, in the meantime, Western countries dominate the availability of information for our professional discourse, and those of us who find their offerings inadequate, and their criticisms of our own work beyond the points which we regard as important in our own contexts,[10] have little option but to rely on local journals and monograph series which suffer poor distribution even to colleagues similarly placed. We become increasingly divorced from others in comparable situations to our own; and our eccentricities estrange us even from our friends for whom the world has not yet changed with respect to the premise that anthropologists are, by definition, strangers. Nor are we comforted, much less convinced, by the occasional assertion that we are of the centre really, notwithstanding our propensity to be difficult and pretend that we are not.

Citizen anthropologists, especially in the Third World, experience a different subjective professional reality. In my view it is time that we recognized both this difference and the changes in the world of anthropology which have caused it.

We also need to recognize, subjectively as well as professionally, that language itself is not the only barrier to effective communication and the understanding of actors' motives, and that personal linguistic competence will not necessarily overcome the unreliability of interpreters. We know, as professionals, that respondents are prone to mislead anthropologists, regrettably sometimes intentionally, and that such problems are not completely overcome by staying around long enough and asking enough people the same questions. Yet we often overlook the fact that these very problems also plague our professional discourse. Let me take an example from the conference at which this paper was originally presented. Concerning the precise referents of Shalva Weil's (1985) 'dream' (see also this volume, pp. 196–212), among those who heard her original presentation, three opinions were expressed in a later session: that it referred to her original fieldwork; to her subsequent reconstruction of her fieldwork experience for the purposes of writing her paper; and to both, as part of her contemporary experience. Since she was not present to clarify her own intentions when these three opinions were expressed, the conference remained somewhat mystified, some participants expressing reservations about dreams anyway! But the issue is not whether Australian aboriginals should be permitted a monopoly over dreaming: it is instead a problem that goes to the very heart of our construction of anthropology as a professional discipline. If we all speak the same professional language, yet our interpretations *as professionals* of what we hear and read differ, by what fallacy do we presume to construct reality for others?[11]

Nor is language the only barrier to the communication of a social reality with which others can identify. Situational context, occupational role, historical relationship, choice of words, intonation and facial expression, among others, all influence intended and perceived meaning and behaviour constructed on that meaning. Yet how many of us working in foreign societies actually develop our linguistic skills to the level of competence and nuance necessary to account for all the components of communication? And why do so few of us turn such of these skills as we have to their most effective use: to understanding our own linguistic techniques of dissimulation and ambiguity? Why do we, like Weber, lay ourselves open to Schutz's (1972: 8 ff.) criticism that we show too little interest in *how* 'intersubjective agreement' is achieved, especially in fieldwork among strangers, while assuming that it is, indeed, possible? Why have we never even deemed worthy of discussion Kuhn's (1970: 200) point that two people may perceive a situation differently, yet use the same words to describe their different perceptions? Possibly each one of us has personally experienced the point made by Schutz (1972: 19), that the meaning we construct for respondents' behaviour may be apprehended at best dimly by the persons themselves; and worried about how to separate lack of clarity from deliberate haziness and outright lying. Political subtleties of the backstage, including projects to mislead anthropologists, are, as Bailey (1977: 2) emphasizes, the preserve of native speakers.

So why has social anthropology, of all disciplines, persisted in its self-image of studying strangers and translating other cultures and subcultures? What is it about anthropology at home that has been so unattractive? Why do citizen anthropologists have so little of interest to communicate? Do the answers to such questions lie in the distribution of professional power, or over-positivist views of what may reasonably be recognized as 'scientific', or maybe both? Or does the multi-referential answer, perhaps less charitably, not also lie in Bailey's (1977: 17) astringent observation that 'we have a long tradition in anthropology of concealing a void of ideas behind a screen of exotic and bizarre fact, helped out by an appropriate selection of photographs'? And is Bailey's view perhaps supported by the problem of class subjectivities in perception, recently highlighted by Baric (1984)? In short, are we afraid to face the problems of conducting fieldwork among our equals?[12]

Conclusion

I started this paper with two unexplained but obviously contradictory quotations from philosophers, and have used these as general points of reference around which to orient subsequent points which, while they may strike the reader as somewhat disparate, are nonetheless conceptually related.

Basically, my elliptical argument is that Benita Luckmann's view of the fragmentation of identity seems to apply to visiting anthropologists studying foreign societies, who do not, I think, experience the same problems of self-identification and claims on their subjectivity as do those studying their own societies. Should the citizen anthropologist attempt to fragment his self in similar fashion, I suspect the likely outcome would often be mental breakdown. But it is absolutely essential, in my view, that citizen anthropologists attempt to clarify what anthropology has until now left very murky: the subjective base from which social reality is constructed within the anthropological endeavour; the value conflicts; the issues of intervention. For if these difficulties are not resolved – and one view is that they are irresolvable – the citizen anthropologist will continue to face difficulties in his research, teaching, and citizenship responsibilities, that differ from those of acting out a particular professional role among foreigners.

Notes

* The original version of this paper was presented to the 1985 ASA conference held at the University of Keele. I am grateful to Michael Bourdillon for helping to clarify the original presentation of certain ideas, to those who commented on the paper at the conference, and to Raymond Apthorpe, John Clammer, Des Gasper, and Pamela Reynolds for subsequent useful criticism.

1 Unacceptable constructions of reality may ultimately result in the withdrawal of their citizenship rights from offending academics.

2 Perhaps it is their longer historical experience of backyard practice that causes anthropologists in the former colonies to regard as somewhat naïve and simplistic, the more recent ethical agonizings of Westerners only now coming to professional terms with their own backyards.

3 I am aware that Sartre himself later abandoned this particular perspective, but it nonetheless seems to me useful.

4 As Western anthropologists have turned to studying their own societies, they have become notably more concerned about the ethics of data collection and storage, and issues of law (cf. Akeroyd 1983).

5 As John Clammer (personal communication) notes, it is debatable how much any anthropologist transfers from his role-playing during fieldwork to his personal life. Malinowski, for example, was hardly noted for his sensitivity to the feelings of his academic colleagues (Firth 1957: 1, 5, 10–12).

6 My critics have suggested that such role-playing by itself is perhaps inadequate to identify 'bad faith' in the way I have attempted here. Instead, Des Gasper (personal communication) suggests that bad faith inheres in a failure to relate the study of others to the study of self, as interrelated entities; while John Clammer raises the issue of motivation in fieldwork, and the anthropologist's long-term concern for and identity with the subjects (not objects!) of his research. While I agree that these points help to spell out some of the dimensions of bad faith, I would argue that they are both encompassed in my earlier description of the relationship between being-for-itself and being-for-others.

7 The most obvious indication of a resonance between Malinowski and existential philosophers lies in his assertion that 'form is always determined by function, and in so far as we cannot establish such a determinism, elements of form cannot be used in a scientific argument' (1944: 149).

8 Clammer (1983: 1) has noted the difficulties of teaching anthropology and especially anthropological theory to Third World students lacking this epistemological base.

9 This issue is not entirely separate from that of good teaching in the technical sense. There are, admittedly, bad teachers in many universities. However, problems with linguistic idiom, accent, and speed of delivery do not in themselves explain why non-Western students may have great difficulty in grasping concepts explicated by

visiting Western scholars, but experience much less difficulty when taught by a member of their own society.

10 To judge by referees' comments on some of my own papers submitted for metropolitan publication, the centre is distinctly reluctant to envisage alternative conceptual frameworks to its own established ones. For example: 'The most serious criticism is that by concentrating on individual holdings it makes consideration of the issue of class impossible, given that in most theories of social stratification the salient unit is the family not the individual (leaving aside the knotty question of what should be taken as the "family" in this context in African societies).'

11 These problems have long been addressed in other social sciences, and it seems to me that anthropology can no longer afford to ignore such relevant philosophical literature as exists on this topic.

12 As Pamela Reynolds (personal communication) comments: 'Complicity in one's own society causes much more guilt, shame, etc. at both the intrusion and conclusion of research, with the result that citizen anthropologists are in danger of assuming masks; retreating from intimacy in the field (into sociological or psychological techniques); or tipping over into embarrassing self-revelations (psychoanalytic methods), etc.'

References

AHMED, A. S. (1984) Defining Islamic Anthropology. *RAIN* **65**: 2–4.

AKEROYD, A. (1983) Applied Anthropology Training Programmes in the United States. *Annals of the Association of Social Anthropologists of the Commonwealth* **4**: 20–7.

ASAD, T. (ed.) (1973) *Anthropology and the Colonial Encounter*. London: Ithaca Press.

BAILEY, F. G. (1977) *Morality and Expediency*. Oxford: Basil Blackwell.

BARIC, L. (1984) The Puzzle of the Jigsaw. *RAIN* **65**: 6–7.

BRONOWSKI, J. (1973) *The Ascent of Man*. London: BBC Publications.

CHEATER, A. P. (1985) Anthropologists and Policy in Zimbabwe: Design at the Centre and Reactions on the Periphery. In R. Grillo and A. Rew (eds) *Social Anthropology and Development Policy*. London: Tavistock Publications.

CLAMMER, J. (1983) *Modern Anthropological Theory*. New Delhi: Cosmo Publications.

— (1984) Approaches to Ethnographic Research. In R. F. Ellen (ed.) *Ethnographic Research*. London: Academic Press.

FEI HSIAO-TUNG (1983) *Chinese Village Close-Up*. Beijing: New World Press.

FIRTH, R. (ed.) (1957) *Man and Culture*. London: Routledge & Kegan Paul.

— (1967) Themes in Economic Anthropology: A General Comment. In R. Firth (ed.) *Themes in Economic Anthropology*. London: Tavistock Publications.

HORTON, R. (1962) The Kalabari World View: An Outline and Interpretation. *Africa* **32**(3): 197–220.

KUHN, T. (1970) *The Structure of Scientific Revolutions* (2nd edn). Chicago: University of Chicago Press.

LUCKMANN, B. (1978) The Small Life-worlds of Modern Man. In T. Luckmann (ed.) *Phenomenology and Sociology*. Harmondsworth: Penguin.

MALINOWSKI, B. (1922) *Argonauts of the Western Pacific*. London: Routledge & Kegan Paul.

— (1944) *A Scientific Theory of Culture*. New York: Galaxy Books.

— (1967) *A Diary in the Strict Sense of the Term*. New York: Harcourt, Brace & World.

PALUCH, A. K. (1981) The Polish Background to Malinowski's Work. *Man* (NS) **16**(2): 276–85.

SARTRE, J.-P. (1969) *Being and Nothingness* (translated by H. E. Barnes). London: Methuen.

SCHUTZ, A. (1972) *The Phenomenology of the Social World*. London: Heinemann.

— (1978a) Phenomenology and the Social Sciences. In T. Luckmann (ed.) *Phenomenology and Sociology*. Harmondsworth: Penguin.

— (1978b) Some Structures of the Life-world. In T. Luckmann (ed.) *Phenomenology and Sociology*. Harmondsworth: Penguin.

WEIL, S. (in collaboration with M. Weil) (1985) Anthropology Becomes Home; Home Becomes Anthropology. Paper presented to the ASA Conference, University of Keele, 25–29 March (mimeo). See also pp. 196–212 of this volume.

Stella Mascarenhas-Keyes

12 The native anthropologist:
constraints and strategies in research

Introduction

British social anthropologists, at home as well as abroad, usually do fieldwork in 'exotic cultures' (Sarsby 1984: 130). However, for the 'native anthropologist',[1] research occurs within the 'non-exotic' socio-cultural context of primary socialization and requires, as will be shown, a professionally induced schizophrenia between the 'native self' and 'professional self'. This paper addresses itself primarily to the problems of professional access to information and role definition in a context where 'my people' 'do not perceive the investigator as special, exotic or powerful' (Cassell 1977: 413). Section 1 discusses the factors leading to the adoption and the implementation of a multiple-native strategy. Section 2 examines the ways that permanent kinship and associational links affected the legitimation of research, and required strategies to overcome constraints on access to information. In Section 3, I demonstrate the value of using Self as Informant, borrowing the concepts of transference and countertransference developed by psychoanalysts. Since anthropological praxis involves not only fieldwork, but also writing texts, in the final section of this paper I examine some of the issues involved in producing texts destined for both native and academic audiences.

I On becoming a multiple native

Outsiders attempt during fieldwork to become 'marginal natives' (Freilich 1977) and to negotiate a temporary 'social space' within the society. However, the problem is reversed for the native anthropologist who has to transcend an *a priori* ascribed social position in the society in order, like the Outsider, professionally to relate to the whole spectrum of native social categories. The problem is compounded when the native anthropologist is located in a very complex society, such as is found in Goa.

Goa, a tiny region situated on the west coast of India, had been under Portuguese rule for 450 years, with the result that the indigenous population comprises both Catholics and Hindus. Since the mid-nineteenth century, large numbers of Catholics, in comparison to Hindus, have migrated and established globally dispersed satellite communities, with the result that the majority of Catholics in Goa are part of an international Catholic Goan community which transcends geographical boundaries.[2] I was born and brought up within the confines of the Catholic Goan community in Kenya and, on subsequent settlement in Britain fifteen years ago, became an integral member of the Catholic Goan community in London (see Mascarenhas-Keyes 1979). My two previous month-long visits to Goa as a child and teenager had not sensitized me to its social and cultural diversity which was richly manifested in Amora,[3] my focal village, with its population of just under 3,000 persons. From 1979 to 1981 I set up an independent household in the heart of Amora with my European husband, in a bungalow rented from a Catholic Goan living in Bombay.

Apart from a few tribal Kunbis, Amora consisted of equal proportions of indigenous Hindus and Catholics, and there was some residential segregation. The Hindus, who had begun to settle in Amora thirty years previously, were mainly poor low-caste farmers and casual labourers employed by Catholics. The Catholics, who had ancestral links with Amora, were predominantly Brahmins, moderately educated, with good cash incomes derived mainly from current remittances or pensions from technical and white-collar employment outside Goa. They lived in large, moderately furnished houses, usually dressed in Western clothes, ate meat, and drank alcohol, while the Hindus lived in small huts, wore Indian-style clothes, and were largely vegetarian and teetotallers. Konkani (the local vernacular), English, Portuguese, and some Swahili were spoken by different sectors of the society.

Within this heterogeneous society, I was identified by natives in terms of a complement of immutable characteristics: international Catholic, Brahmin, female, married, educated, middle-class (but of recent peasant origins). However, I was extremely reluctant to conform to behavioural patterns and modes of thought culturally expected of my ascribed position because of my respect for cultural diversity cultivated through anthropological training, and my intention to operate as an anthropologist. Although there were some continuing difficulties, described in greater detail below, in legitimizing my research interests and methodological approach, initial verbal acceptance encouraged me to venture into non-stereotypical forays across multiple boundaries. However, I was dismayed to find that I courted considerable criticism and ridicule and it became apparent that, as a neophyte, I was unprepared 'for the more sophisticated task of studying (his) own society' (Srinivas 1966: 157). I longed for an outward sign, such as a large badge, saying 'I am an anthropologist' and therefore should be granted 'diplomatic immunity'. Furthermore, various categories were responding to my overtures with confusion because, although I initially made some cultural concessions, such as sitting cross-legged on the floor eating vegetarian food with Hindus, my specific native identity was still transparent.

The situation was compounded because the nature of the research required periodic visits to other parts of Goa and interviews with government officials and other 'big men'. My first interview with a 'big man' proved fruitless; on greeting me he exclaimed 'You're so young. I expected a man or an older woman', and then proceeded summarily to dismiss all my questions. Furthermore, I did not acquire, as Outsiders usually do, someone to sponsor me or mediate between Self and natives. I had decided against engaging a native research assistant because his/her socio-economic characteristics would circumscribe access to sources of data (see Berreman 1962). I was also reluctant to use key informants (see Casagrande 1960) because of my belief in the necessity of obtaining first-hand rather than socially and personally 'percolated' information. Trapped in a multiple-bind situation, my intuition suggested I wholeheartedly adopt a multiple-native strategy with a chameleon-like virtuosity, in the hope of achieving a higher degree of cultural consonance in different contexts than I had previously managed. This strategy generated different sorts of problems and considerable personal anxiety and anger, which I discuss later in this paper, but for the moment I shall briefly describe how I became a multiple native.

The 'props' used in what was, to a large extent, a 'dramaturgical exercise' (cf. Goffman 1982) were language and the large wardrobe of Western and Indian clothes, footwear, ornaments, and other accessories I felt compelled to acquire. As Pelto points out, because styles of clothing are important signals of social status and role, the 'fieldworker can always influence local attitudes towards him by adopting particular habits of costume' (1970: 227). When visiting 'élites' and 'big men' I wore 'executive' London-style clothes, high-heeled shoes, fashionable accessories, lipstick, a hairstyle that added a few years; I presented my visiting-card and spoke English in 'elaborated code' (see Bernstein 1971). A broadly similar 'scholarly' image was essential when I went to interview sailors in the tavern, which respectable Goan women never enter. With lower-status Catholics, I dressed in clothes tailored in local materials and fashions. I reserved loose sun-dresses, slacks, and other casual wear for research sessions spent with international returnees living in a city beach-side residential area. For periods spent with Hindus, particularly when attending rituals and ceremonies both in Amora and their distant ancestral villages, I dressed in a sari, plastic sandals, smothered my face with white talcum powder, adopted the oiled plaited hairstyle adorned with flowers, and wore gold jewellery and a 'clip-on' nose ring. This evoked favourable comments from Hindus – 'You look like one of us' – and derisive ones from Catholics – 'You look just like a Hindu'.

Outsiders inevitably have to deal with the native language problem and, to some extent, I was confronted by a similar one. Like most international Catholics of my generation, I spoke English, not Konkani, as a first language. However, I did not wish to engage a Konkani-speaking interpreter because, professionally, I was aware of epistemological limitations (Owusu 1978) and, personally, I wanted to redress the effects of cultural imperialism. Consequently, I took an intensive language course in Goa, which considerably improved my previous minimal facility in Konkani.[4] With the overwhelming majority of Hindus, Kunbis, and a smaller number of Catholics, who spoke only Konkani, I conversed in this language, and gradually learned to switch to the dialect of the specific group I was with. Among those who spoke both English and Konkani, I acquiesced in their preference for using English. With traditional Catholic élites, who were multilingual but preferred to speak Portuguese in social gatherings of peers, my limited fluency in Portuguese enabled me to intersperse conversations with token words which often elicited approval. I colluded with Africa returnees by conversing in Swahili, the language they resorted to when transmitting confidential information in mixed company. Language was called on to play a predominant rather than a complementary role when natives dropped in unexpectedly to visit me. Caught, so to speak, in my 'home clothes', usually a plain frock and casual hairstyle, I had to rely on my linguistic repertoire to articulate the multiple-native strategy.

The operation of the multiple-native strategy was considerably facilitated by my residence in an independent household; hence I was exempt from the patronage of a resident native which would probably have circumscribed my autonomy (see Beteille and Madan 1975; Srinivas 1976). Furthermore, by working alone not only did I have the freedom to be psychologically mobile (Powdermaker 1966: 291) but socially mobile too. I did not have to ensure that a 'team performance' was maintained (Goffman 1982: 85–108), and I could continuously and intuitively refine impression management through heightened sensitivity to verbal and non-verbal behavioural nuances. Gender served as a further advantage as cultural elaboration of dress and demeanour was articulated by females. I feel certain that it was only by becoming a multiple native that I was able to achieve a high degree of empathy with respect to each social category. Furthermore, unlike at the beginning of fieldwork, when different natives tended either to 'put on a show' or remain reticent, when my ascribed identity was opaque they relaxed and interacted in a far more 'natural' manner, thus improving the quality of data obtained.

II The significance of permanent kinship and associational links

The Outsider is usually incorporated into native society by acquiring a temporary fictive kinship position (Middleton 1970). However, like a few other anthropologists (Nakleh 1979; Loizos 1981; Stephen and Greer 1981) I was already a permanent component of a web of kinship and associational relationships. These were continually reinforced by visits from my parents (Africa returnees who lived in a nearby town), close kin from my ancestral village, overseas siblings, and international Goan friends holidaying in Goa. Hence Catholics located me within an international kinship and associational network. In contrast to this, Hindus and Kunbis identified me in terms of my husband's foreign status, referring to me as 'hippie's wife'.[5] Both identifications served to obscure the fact that my presence in Goa was for professional purposes. For instance, I was expected by 'relations' as well as villagers to fulfil a host of kinship obligations and I suffered rebuke when I declined. At first I used to regard such visits, particularly to dispersed geographical locations, as a waste of time for anthropological training had socialized me into the 'single village mentality'. To make virtue of necessity I resolved to regard the information gleaned at such events as 'grist to the mill', which facilitated the cultivation of an all-Goa perspective to serve as a backdrop to my focal village.

Kinship and associational links ensured that my past was not a closed book, as is often the case with the Outsider, since many Catholics knew that I had previously held the reputable jobs of secondary school teacher in Kenya and secretary in London. Although educational standards are high, there is little familiarity with the aims and practices of the social sciences. However, a few who 'knew about anthropology' strongly suggested I should study the tribal Kunbis who, because of their different dress, diet, and customs, were regarded as 'exotic' and hence, unlike themselves, the appropriate objects of anthropological study. It was considered strange that an educated, married woman would return from 'modern, advanced Britain' to the 'primitive village' to find out how 'ordinary', let alone 'exotic', people lived. Initially many thought that it was my foreign husband who had come to do research and, at the beginning, invitations were always extended to him to 'show you Goa and how we live'. Not only was I not studying 'exotic' people but the subject of my research was not 'exotic' either, since it focused on the patterns and consequences of international migration, and Catholics saw themselves as much a part of the process as I was. I was made acutely conscious of Agar's comment that 'Ethnography is really quite an arrogant enterprise' (1980: 41) as there were many remarks from Catholics to challenge my claim to special expertise, the implication being that any Goan with time on their hands and the ability to inveigle funds from an agency could do the 'research'.

With the Hindus, the conventional Outsider's excuse of ignorance and curiosity about an alien culture was more acceptable, although perplexing, in gaining entry because the cultural segregation between the two communities was acutely evident. My research interest in the Hindus derived from the fact that their recent settlement in Amora and the agricultural labour force they constituted were directly correlated with the international migration of

Catholics. However, Hindus perceived that it was my ignorance of Hinduism, typical of Catholics, which was the basis of my interest in them. Consequently they always invited me to any religious ceremony taking place in Amora or their distant ancestral homes. They admonished me when I did not take copious notes of their descriptions of deities and explanations of religious events, saying 'Why aren't you writing that in your book?' My real research interest was perceived as tangential to what they discerned as my 'research', and while I was able to broach the issues I was interested in, conspicuous note-taking of such information had to be avoided.

Unlike the Outsider who can become a 'neutral confidant' (Berreman 1962: 11, 19; Goffman 1982: 159), kinship and associational links made it credible that the information I was seeking was not for innocuous 'research' purposes but for personal motives. The Outsider usually has potentially greater access to information because asymmetrical power relations and his ignorance are conspicuous. As Jarvie points out, 'The fieldworker as humble supplicant is obviously not often the case. Many people would not tolerate the white stranger snooping around were it not that he belongs, as far as they are concerned, to the powerful white society which they hesitate to brush with' (1969: 508). While I had considerable success in asking direct questions about migration patterns, the need for extensive questioning on a variety of topics was rarely understood. Even my parents and siblings found such questions exasperating, and often said 'but what has *this* got to do with your research?', and beseeched me not to 'cross-examine our friends'. Questions perceived as peripheral and tangential to my 'research' indicated an unwarranted inquisitiveness, and indeed epitomized the type of Goan who is most feared: the one 'who becomes your friend to get all your news', the one who 'minds everybody's business and not just their own'. Further, even if I could be trusted to keep my promise of confidentiality, there were some fears that other literate natives who dropped in casually at my home would have access to privileged information. I do not wish to imply that 'my people' were excessively paranoid, but intimate knowledge has an ominous and indefinable potency in an environment to which international migration has contributed to making competitiveness, insecurity, and anxiety endemic.

To depersonalize information and alleviate anxiety, I resorted to techniques gained outside anthropological training. I pre-coded quantifiable data in a format suitable for computer analysis, and in the presence of natives recorded data numerically on computer sheets. The significance of the numbers could only be discerned in conjunction with a master sheet specifying what the figures represented. With qualitative information I conspicuously made notes in my personal version of (Pitmans) shorthand, and the nature of the symbolic system employed made it virtually impossible for anyone else but myself to decipher notes.

Like the Outsider, but to a greater degree, I had to resort to covert investigation to get 'back-stage' information. I often had to be seen consciously to be discarding my professional role and operating as an ordinary native. 'Chatting' was invaluable here, and once the art had been mastered, I had access to various arenas of 'private' information. Since I prepared and cooked our own meals, and was genuinely interested in learning to cook traditional dishes, there were numerous occasions when 'cookery lessons' surreptitiously covered a multitude of topics. Cooking and related activities were perceived as legitimate concerns because they attested to my being a 'good Goan wife' who made considerable efforts to provide her foreign husband with the full flavour of Goan cuisine. It also became essential to participate in numerous 'innocuous' activities such as various religious services. Such regular and frequent attendance by an Outsider would have been perceived by natives as conspicuous evidence of professional status and interest in learning 'native ways', but in my case it was seen to testify to my being, unlike most young people, a very 'devout Catholic'. Attendance at novenas at the numerous village chapels and wayside crosses was perceived as a pious measure to remedy my childless condition. Of course, not all natives were 'fooled' and a young teacher remarked, 'You are not concerned about praying; you are going to everything because of your research'.

For the Outsider, as well as the native anthropologist, fieldwork entails the 'balanced reciprocity of relationships and information' (Mayer 1975: 28). However, the demands for reciprocity were different with respect to different social categories. With Hindus, as well as Kunbis and poor Catholics, reciprocity approximated the measures an Outsider would resort to: I wrote official letters, acceded to requests to take photographs, lent money and foodstuffs, paid bus fares, etc. However, with middle- and upper-class Catholics, the fact that I was native, young, and female removed any reticence that older Catholics, and women in particular, had of questioning me about the minutiae of my life. Ablon, who studied middle-class Americans with whom she was culturally identified, points out that the 'diminution of cultural barriers leads to increased personal visibility of the anthropologist' and demands for intimate information (1977: 70). Like the natives, I had little hesitation in divulging impersonal information but was wary of disclosing personal details. Furthermore, since it was obvious that through 'galivanting around the village', as my behaviour was referred to, I had undoubtedly gathered 'salacious information' and there were many attempts to prise it out of me. Hence, with most Catholics, reciprocity led to a heightened vulnerability of Self, and I generally circumvented questions by resorting to evasive answers, lightning and subtle changes of conversation, partial answers, half truths and so forth – the very strategies I tried to steer 'my people' from. While everyday native social interaction, particularly for women, was articulated in the exchange of 'personalized' information, I could only engage partially and cautiously in this activity because had I acceded to their excessive demands, not only would I have epitomized the 'bad native' but also breached professional ethics.

III Self as informant

A belief in naïve empiricism has led anthropologists 'to turn the fieldworker into a self-effacing creature without any reaction other than those of a recording machine' (Nash and Wintrop 1972: 527). However, recent publications have compelled us to recognize the existence of the 'personal equation' (e.g. Malinowski 1967; Beteille and Madan 1975; Okely 1975; Rabinow 1977; Cesara 1982) and that, in a world of already constituted meaning (Rabinow and Sullivan 1979), anthropologists are interpreters, not mere recorders of cultures (Agar 1982; Hammersley and Atkinson 1983; Ellen 1984). Devereux, in his book *From Anxiety to Method in the Behavioural Sciences*, recommends that we must use 'the subjectivity inherent in all observations as the royal road to an authentic, rather than fictitious, objectivity' (1967: xvii). I would further argue that we should incorporate the creative use of emotional reactions of Self and Other as methodological tools in fieldwork. Like Okely (1975: 182) I think social anthropologists should explore analogous methods to psychoanalysts, as I found during fieldwork that I intuitively made methodological use of the concepts 'transference' and 'counter-transference'.[6] Earlier in this paper I described the strategies used in becoming a multiple native and alluded to the hostility directed at me, and the self-anxiety and anger it generated. In the absence of a research assistant and key informants who would have served as social and psychological buffers (Wintrop 1969: 68–9), there was not only a heightened exposure of Self to Others, but correlatively a greater psychological retreat into Self. In the face of stressful experiences in the field, I began to turn 'anxiety to method' but this was an intuitive response, not dictated by any prior training.

Anthropologists continually invite diverse comments as natives try to make sense of their behaviour. However, more so than the Outsider, I became an enduring topic of village comment precisely because I was a native who, by my activities, was constantly challenging multiple norms and values. The most conspicuous areas were non-conventional relations with low-status Catholics and with Hindus, and inappropriate behaviour for a married woman. Women anthropologists (e.g. Golde 1970: 8; Dube 1975: 175) have noted that the behaviour of a female fieldworker is more closely scrutinized than that of a male. Although Catholic Goan women enjoy a considerable degree of autonomy and independence (Mascarenhas-Keyes 1985), nevertheless, my absence from the home and widespread research contact with men provoked numerous snide remarks and jokes from all sectors of society. My husband's Anglo-Saxon reserve and confinement to the private domain of the home engrossed in philosophy books conformed to local expectations of a scholar and served to magnify my enigmatic and public behaviour.

The constant barrage of criticism made me initially very angry and demoralized, and I would self-righteously defend myself by proclaiming my professional status: 'I am an anthropologist; it is my job to mix with all sorts of people; my husband is capable of looking after himself.' Furthermore, initially I told my critics the truth and said I found walking around the village alone and familiar relationships with low-status people very stimulating and enjoyable; not surprisingly, this only served to increase my ostracization. I experienced a great deal of coldness and withholding of information and this in turn increased my anxiety as, by losing rapport with certain sectors of society, my investigation was suffering. Consequently, I adopted a number of strategies.

First of all, I began to regard all comments on Self as valuable sources of information about the society. I recorded the transference reactions (not as systematically as I now wish I had done), analysed them, and used them as methodological tools to indicate areas for investigation. For instance, I would constantly ask myself 'why is criticism made of this aspect of my behaviour and not that; why do some criticize/praise my actions and others do not; when I mention the criticism or comment to another social group, or members of the same social group, why do they respond in the way they do?'

Second, in order to ensure that I maintained rapport with different critics, and was not seen to be unequivocally identified with particular sections, I discreetly and selectively resorted to the manipulation of reality. Hence, for instance, I would return from a few days spent with Hindus in their ancestral villages, and tell Catholics what I had begun to realize they wanted to hear: it was very uncomfortable sleeping on a cowdung floor; toilet facilities were abysmal; I was weak from living on a vegetarian diet; and that to my horror I had discovered nits in my hair. Furthermore, no longer did I rationalize my involvement with Hindus because I had chosen to do such research but because 'my European professor in London would be angry with me if I did not obtain real information on how Hindus lived'. This strategy evoked sympathy and commiseration and, equally importantly, provided a focus for extensive discussions on the nature of Catholic–Hindu relationships. Hence, with various social categories I periodically tried to take the role of Other and this served not only as a diplomatic exercise but also allowed me to 'get into the native's skin' and see things from multiple perspectives.

It was not only criticism of my behaviour which used to anger me but also the views expressed by natives on a variety of topics. The anger stemmed from a conflict of values, and I would agree with Ablon when she states 'the potential of actual value conflicts with our informants becomes more real when we deal with persons who live and interact within our own cultural world' (1977: 70). Initially I would give vent to my anger and argue vehemently, but I was acquiring the reputation of a 'fishwife', particularly because women, even educated ones, do not challenge male views on politics, economics, and religion. Women took me aside and told me to 'stop fighting with the men', and accused me of being inebriated. Consequently, I decided to adopt an approach used by psychoanalysts with respect to counter-transference. I allowed myself to experience the anger but controlled its expression by the adoption of a 'professional attitude' (Winnicott 1960). I noted and analysed my reactions and attempted to use them with equanimity to stimulate further discussion and hence generate data.

Of course, psychoanalysts use transference and counter-transference as therapeutic methods, but I did not see my role during fieldwork as akin to that of a therapist. While I agree with Huizer (1979) and Kielstra (1979) that anthropologists can operate effectively as social activists, my interest in Goa was in 'pure' research rather than research in 'the service of humankind' (Spradley 1980: 16–20). Hence it was important not deliberately to try to change native behaviour, and to adopt strategies that would not prevent access to the whole cross-section of the population. The stresses of fieldwork are legion (see Henry and Saberwal 1969) and anthropologists have resorted to various measures to alleviate stress such as short vacations, excessive eating, social isolation of Self (see Pelto 1970: 223–25). However, since stress seems to be the *sine qua non* of fieldwork (Kobben 1967: 46), rather than escape from it I suggest that we could usefully integrate it into fieldwork methodology. Simultaneously, the strategy helps to maintain emotional balance as it reduces the vulnerability of Self and increases resilience to adverse comments.

IV The implications of writing texts for a native and academic audience

A reflexive awareness of ethnographic writing should also take into account the potential audience for the finished product (Hammersley and Atkinson 1983: 227). For the native anthropologist, it is the academic as well as the native context which significantly affects the writing of anthropological texts. For most Outsiders post-fieldwork contact consists of sporadic correspondence with a few natives, while for the native anthropologist interaction with 'my people' is a life-long engagement. Since my return to London and the Goan community here, letters and personal enquiries have always included the questions 'When will the thesis be finished?' 'When will we be able to read it?' Some have even raised provocative questions about academic verification: 'Who will examine your thesis? Do they know about Goa? If they don't know about Goa, how will they know that you are *right*?' In producing an anthropological text for an audience which includes natives, the native anthropologist shares the concerns of the Outsider about respecting confidentiality, protecting individuals, and keeping the field open for further research (Barnes 1967: 205–12). However, there are additional issues. Natives, like everyone else, want to be portrayed in the most advantageous light and will feel betrayed if this is not done. Furthermore, the demands of science must be finely weighed against those of humanity (Kloos 1969: 511) as publication of certain material may lead to long-term disruption of the anthropologist's personal relationships (Nakleh 1979: 349) as well as those of his kin with other natives (Stephen and Greer 1981: 129).

During the writing up of the thesis, I found myself being somehow compelled, in comparison to other students, to devote a disproportionate amount of time to history. Reflecting on this recently, I have identified three main reasons, apart from a theoretical attraction to a diachronic perspective. First of all, despite the fact that I have always emphasized to natives that I am a social anthropologist whose concern is with contemporary society, it is the minimal historical material contained in my previous writings (Mascarenhas-Keyes 1979, and short articles in the Goan Association (UK) Newsletter), that has aroused greatest interest. Indeed, I am sometimes publicly referred to as 'our *historian*', and Amora natives enquire, 'Have you finished writing the *history* of our village yet?'

Second, my personal reasons for undertaking the research involved a desire to locate an autobiography within a cultural biography. The decision to read social anthropology after graduating in psychology, the choice of ethnographic area and research problem were determined primarily by a quest for self-knowledge. Perhaps anthropological research is inherently autobiographical (Crick 1982: 16) and all academic research is 'really all about the perfection of one's own soul' (Barley 1983: 10). Given this emotional involvement, there is the danger of egocentricism referred to by the native anthropologist, Delmos J. Jones: 'the insider may depend too much on his own background, his own sentiments, his desires for what is good for his people' (1970: 256). However, as Aguilar points out, such dangers 'can be mitigated with relative ease once one is aware of them' (1981: 23).

Third, I have been responding to the demands of the profession, which socializes anthropologists to look for 'exotica'. For a native anthropologist, the 'exoticism' of one's own society is less apparent, and hence I have been beset by an unconscious need to look for 'extraordinariness'. Conscious recognition of this was facilitated by introspection and recent participation in Outsider research. By delving into historical material, particularly Goa's unusual colonial experience, I have sought to draw out its 'uniqueness' and 'exoticism'. I felt compelled to explore the 'exotic' through history in order to highlight the 'exotic' of the ordinary, contemporary situation. Hence the native anthropologist, in order to operate within the conventional model of knowledge generation, has to 'discover' or 'uncover' the exotic by utilizing a different level of reality than that given by the ethnographic situation. Furthermore, the Eurocentric bias persists in the academic pressure to highlight certain features, such as caste, which have 'exotic' appeal to European audiences (Asad 1973).

'When we publish, our eye is more often to our colleagues than on our informants' noted Barnes (1967: 205). However, academic feedback takes place mainly in an ethnographic and methodological vacuum (Crick 1982: 17–18). In addition, the culture of Academia, about which we know only a little (Caplow and McGee 1965; Boissevain 1974; Bailey 1977; Platt 1976), influences the various stages of research, including script production and promotion, in ways which have so far remained invisible, particularly to neophytes. The pursuit of 'objective ethnographic accounts' or the 'definitive ethnography' is illusory (Nash and Wintrop 1972: 531; Agar 1982: 784; Devereux 1967: 207) as evidenced by contrasting accounts of the same culture (e.g. Mead 1935 and Fortune 1939; Redfield 1930 and Lewis 1951). Furthermore, professional natives have criticized a number of texts produced by Outsiders for inaccuracies in the translation of cultures and have suggested a dialogue between native and foreign professionals (Owusu 1978).

However, since cultural phenomena are differently interpreted by anthropologists, native or Outsider, as well as natives, I would go further than Owusu and suggest a continuing dialogue between anthropologists and 'my people', a dialogue which has so far begun and terminated with fieldwork. Although texts have found their way to the field (Barnes 1967: 205), this has been haphazard, and furthermore the asymmetrical power relations that pertained, particularly during the colonial era, probably militated against natives contesting the point of view developed by the powerful Outsider (Nash and Wintrop 1972: 531). I propose that we take seriously Parkin's tentative suggestion that a commitment to reflexivity include native reflection on anthropological texts (1982: xii–xiv). Such reflection should be from a cross-section of natives, not a selected few. In cases where the level of literacy precludes appraisals of written texts, native feedback can be obtained to other mediums of discourse, such as oral accounts (Josselin de Jong 1967) and ethnographic films, whose potential has yet to be exploited (see MacDougall 1978; Henley 1985). I suggest that native feedback be used to complement academic feedback in order to advance our knowledge and understanding of culture and society. Such 'multiple triangulation' (Denzin 1978) would also reduce the dangers of ethnocentrism of Outsiders and egocentrism of native anthropologists.

Conclusion

This paper has provided a case illustration of the conduct of fieldwork and script production by a native anthropologist. Unlike the Outsider, who becomes a marginal native in order to gain access to natives, I have shown that for me it was necessary to become a multiple native in order to transcend the limitations of an *a priori* ascribed position and to deal with the cultural complexities of the field situation. Furthermore, since the native anthropologist, unlike the Outsider, is an intrinsic and permanent part of a complex web of kinship and associational relationships, I have indicated the strategies used to legitimize research, and provide assurance that information collected during fieldwork is for professional and not personal interests. I have shown that fieldwork exposed me to a considerable degree of stress, and argued that anxiety can be turned to method. By using Self as Informant the culturally induced sources of stress can be subjected to systematic analysis and used as a methodological tool in fieldwork. Finally, I have shown that because the dialogue with natives does not terminate with fieldwork for the native anthropologist, as it does for most Outsiders, their demands, as well as those of the profession, influence the production of anthropological texts. I have concluded by suggesting that anthropologists should not only welcome academic feedback, but also systematically solicit and analyse native feedback from a cross-section of natives in order to obtain a more penetrating insight into culture and society.

Acknowledgements

The research on which this paper is based was supported by an SSRC studentship from 1978 to 1981. I would like to thank Lionel Caplan, David Parkin, Shaun Keyes, John Thorne, Teotonio de Souza, Parminder Bachu, members of the Anthropology Research Students Thesis Aid Group and ASA 1985 conference participants, for comments on earlier drafts of this paper.

Notes

1 A plethora of names has emerged to label anthropology at home (see Messerschmidt 1981: 13). There are also different categories of native anthropologists (Stephen and Greer 1981: 124). I use the term to refer to an anthropologist, who through and from birth, is an active and integral member of the society studied.
2 Since Goa was until 1961 a Portuguese enclave within India, the term 'international migration' is used here to refer to migration from Goa to elsewhere in India as well as overseas.
3 Pseudonym.
4 No facilities for learning Konkani are available in London, either at universities or within the Goan community.
5 Goa is the current mecca of Western 'hippies' and while international Catholic Goans differentiate between different categories of Europeans, the Hindus and Kunbis use the generic term 'hippie' to apply to any white person, irrespective of age.
6 The two terms have been defined in a number of ways by psychoanalysts and I am using the broad definitions where transference refers to the patient's emotional attitude to the analyst, while counter-transference refers to the analyst's emotional attitude to the patient (see Heimann 1950; Winnicott 1956, 1960; Rycroft 1968) and by extension of these terms to anthropology, we can substitute anthropologist for psychoanalyst, and native for patient.

References

ABLON, J. (1977) Field Method in Working with Middle-Class Americans. *Human Organization* **36**: 69–72.

AGAR, M. (1980) *The Professional Stranger*. London: Academic Press.
— (1982) Toward an Ethnographic Language. *American Anthropologist* **84**: 779–95.
AGUILAR, J. (1981) Insider Research: An Ethnography of a Debate. In D. Messerschmidt (ed.) *Anthropologists at Home in North America: Methods and Issues in the Study of One's Own Society*. Cambridge: Cambridge University Press.
ASAD, T. (ed.) (1973) Introduction. In *Anthropology and the Colonial Encounter*. London: Ithaca.
BAILEY, F. G. (1977) *Morality and Expediency: The Folklore of Academic Politics*. Oxford: Blackwell.
BARLEY, N. (1983) *The Innocent Anthropologist*. London: British Museum.
BARNES, J. A. (1967) Some Ethical Problems in Modern Fieldwork. In D. G. Jongmans and P. C. W. Gutkind (eds) *Anthropologists in the Field*. Assen: Van Gorcum.
BERNSTEIN, B. (1971) *Class, Codes and Control: Theoretical Studies towards a Sociology of Language*. London: Routledge & Kegan Paul.
BERREMAN, G. D. (1962) Behind Many Masks; Ethnography and Impression Management. In G. D. Berreman (ed.) *Hindus of the Himalayas. Ethnography and Change*. Berkeley, Calif.: University of California Press.
BETEILLE, A. and MADAN, T. N. (1975) Introduction. *Encounter and Experience. Personal Accounts of Fieldwork*. Delhi: Vikas.
BOISSEVAIN, J. (1974) Towards a Sociology of Social Anthropology. *Theory and Society* **1**: 211–30.
CAPLOW, T. and MCGEE, R. J. (1965) *The Academic Marketplace*. New York: Anchor Books.
CASAGRANDE, J. B. (ed.) (1960) *In the Company of Man. Twenty Portraits by Anthropologists*. New York: Harper & Brothers.
CASSELL, J. (1977) Relationship of Observer to Observed in Peer Group Research. *Human Organization* **36**: 412–16.
CESARA, M. (1982) *Reflections of a Woman Anthropologist: No Hiding Place*. London: Academic Press.
CRICK, M. (1982) Anthropological Field Research, Meaning Creation and Knowledge Construction. In D. Parkin (ed.) *Semantic Anthropology*. ASA Monograph 22. London: Academic Press.
DENZIN, N. K. (1978) *The Research Act: A Theoretical Introduction to Social Research*. New York: McGraw-Hill.
DEVEREUX, G. (1967) *From Anxiety to Method in the Behavioural Sciences*. The Hague: Mouton.
DUBE, L. (1975) Woman's World – Three Encounters. In A. Beteille and T. N. Madan (eds) *Encounter and Experience*. Delhi: Vikas.
ELLEN, R. F. (ed.) (1984) *Ethnographic Research: A Guide to General Conduct*. London: Academic Press.
FORTUNE, R. (1939) Arapesh Warfare. *American Anthropologist* **41**: 22–41.
FREILICH, N. (ed.) (1977) *Marginal Natives at Work. Anthropologists in the Field*. New York: Schenkman.
GOFFMAN, E. (1982) *The Presentation of Self in Everyday Life*. Harmondsworth: Penguin.
GOLDE, P. (1970) Introduction. *Women in the Field: Anthropological Experiences*. Chicago: Aldine.
HAMMERSLEY, M. and ATKINSON, P. (1983) *Ethnography: Principles in Practice*. London: Tavistock Publications.
HEIMANN, P. (1950) On Counter Transference. *International Journal of Psychoanalysis* **xxxi**: 81–4.
HENLEY, P. (1985) British Ethnographic Film: Some Recent Developments. *Anthropology Today* **1**: 5–17.

HENRY, F. and SABERWAL, S. (eds) (1969) *Stress and Response in Fieldwork*. New York: Holt, Rinehart & Winston.

HUIZER, G. (1979) Research-through-Action: Some Practical Experiences with Peasant Organizations. In G. Huizer and B. Mannheim (eds) *The Politics of Anthropology*. The Hague: Mouton.

JARVIE, I. C. (1969) The Problem of Ethical Integrity in Participant Observation. *Current Anthropology* 5: 505–8.

JONES, DELMOS J. (1970) Towards a Native Anthropology. *Human Organization* 29: 251–59.

JONGMANS, D. G. and GUTKIND, P. C. W. (eds) (1967) *Anthropologists in the Field*. Assen: Van Gorcum.

JOSSELIN DE JONG, P. E. (1967) The Participants' View of their Culture. In D. G. Jongmans and P. C. W. Gutkind (eds) *Anthropologists in the Field*. Assen: Van Gorcum.

KIELSTRA, N. (1979) Is Useful Action Research Possible? In G. Huizer and B. Mannheim (eds) *The Politics of Anthropology*. The Hague: Mouton.

KLOOS, P. (1969) Role Conflicts in Social Fieldwork. *Current Anthropology* 10: 509–12.

KOBBEN, A. J. F. (1967) Participation and Quantification: Fieldwork among the Djuka (bush negroes of Surinam). In D. G. Jongmans and P. C. W. Gutkind (eds) *Anthropologists in the Field*. Assen: Van Gorcum.

LEWIS, O. (1951) *Life in a Mexican Village: Tepoztlan Restudied*. Champaign: University of Illinois Press.

LOIZOS, P. (1981) *The Heart Grown Bitter: A Chronicle of Cypriot War Refugees*. London: Cambridge University Press.

MACDOUGALL, D. (1978) Ethnographic Film: Failure and Promise. *American Rev. Anthropology* 7(4): 5–25.

MALINOWSKI, B. (1967) *Diary in the Strict Sense of the Term*. London: Routledge & Kegan Paul.

MAQUET, J. J. (1964) Objectivity in Anthropology. *Current Anthropology* 5(1): 47–55.

MASCARENHAS-KEYES, S. (1979) *Goans in London: Portrait of a Catholic Asian Community*. London: Goan Association (UK).

— (1985) The Changing Role of Women in a Migration Oriented Society. Paper presented to Conference on Women and the Household, January, New Delhi.

MAYER, A. C. (1975) Becoming a Participant Observer. In A. Beteille and T. N. Madan (eds) *Encounter and Experience*. Delhi: Vikas.

MEAD, M. (1935) *The Mountain Arapesh. V. The Record of Unabelin with Rorschach Analysis*. Anthropological Papers of the American Museum of Natural History, 41, Part 3.

MESSERSCHMIDT, D. (1981) On Anthropology 'at home'. In D. Messerschmidt (ed.) *Anthropologists at Home in North America: Methods and Issues in the Study of One's Own Society*. Cambridge: Cambridge University Press.

MIDDLETON, J. (1970) *The Study of the Lugbara: Expectation and Paradox in Anthropological Research*. New York: Holt, Rinehart & Winston.

NAKLEH, K. (1979) On being a Native Anthropologist. In G. Huizer and B. Mannheim (eds) *The Politics of Anthropology*. The Hague: Mouton.

NASH, D. and WINTROP, R. (1972) The Emergence of Self-Consciousness in Ethnography. *Current Anthropology* 13: 527–42.

OKELY, J. (1975) The Self and Scientism. *Journal of the Anthropological Society of Oxford* 6: 171–88.

OWUSU, M. (1978) The Ethnography of Africa: The Usefulness of the Useless. *American Anthropologist* 80: 310–34.

PARKIN, D. (ed.) (1982) Introduction. *Semantic Anthropology*. ASA Monograph 22. London: Academic Press.

The native anthropologist 195

PELTO, P. J. (1970) *Anthropological Research: The Structure of Inquiry*. New York: Harper & Row.
PLATT, J. (1976) *Realities of Social Research: An Empirical Study of British Sociologists*. Brighton: University of Sussex Press.
POWDERMAKER, H. (1966) *Stranger and Friend: The Way of an Anthropologist*. London: Secker & Warburg.
RABINOW, P. (1977) *Reflections on Fieldwork in Morocco*. Berkeley, Calif.: University of California Press.
— and SULLIVAN, W. (1979) Introduction: The Interpretative Turn: Emergence of an Approach. *Interpretative Social Science: A Reader*. Berkeley, Calif.: University of California Press.
REDFIELD, R. (1930) *Tepoztlan: A Mexican Village*. Chicago: University of Chicago Press.
RYCROFT, C. (1968) *A Critical Dictionary of Psychoanalysis*. Harmondsworth: Penguin.
SABERWAL, S. and HENRY, F. (1969) Introduction. In F. Henry and S. Saberwal (eds) *Stress and Response in Fieldwork*. New York: Holt, Rinehart & Winston.
SARSBY, J. G. (1984) Special Problems of Fieldwork in Familiar Settings. In R. F. Ellen (ed.) *Ethnographic Research*. London: Academic Press.
SPRADLEY, J. P. (1980) *Participant Observation*. New York: Holt, Rinehart & Winston.
SRINIVAS, M. N. (1966) Some Thoughts on the Study of One's Own Society. *Social Change in Modern India*. Berkeley, Calif.: University of California Press.
— (1976) *The Remembered Village*. Berkeley, Calif.: University of California Press.
STEPHEN, J. B. and GREER, L. S. (1981) Ethnographers in their Own Cultures: Two Appalachian Cases. *Human Organization* 40: 123–30.
WINNICOTT, D. W. (1956) On Transference. *International Journal of Psychoanalysis* 37.
— (1960) Counter Transference. *British Journal of Medical Psychology* 35.
WINTROP, R. (1969) An Inward Focus: A Consideration of Psychological Stress in Fieldwork. In F. Henry and S. Saberwal (eds) *Stress and Response in Fieldwork*. New York: Holt, Rinehart & Winston.

Shalva Weil
in collaboration with Michael Weil

13 Anthropology becomes home; home becomes anthropology[1]

'Let's consider who it was that dreamed it all. This is a serious question. . . .
He was part of my dream, of course – but then I was part of his dream
too! . . .
Which do *you* think it was?'

(Lewis Carroll, *Through The Looking Glass*)

Recollecting fieldwork is like recounting an Indian dream. It is a series of
dreams within dreams, each experienced separately and yet interconnected
with the next; each experienced individually and yet understood
simultaneously.

On one level, the dream is the fieldwork carried out among a group of
people (Indian Jews) living in the country in which I reside (Israel). During
the course of fieldwork, the field can become inseparable from one's home
and one's home, at a certain stage in the process of fieldwork, can become
indistinguishable from the object of one's anthropological preoccupation.

On another level, the confluence of anthropology and home can occur on
the psychological and personal, and not necessarily physical, level.
Anthropology, therefore, no longer becomes the field-site but an all-
embracing intellectual discipline, which interacts with those who constitute
the home, such as family members, co-residents, or friends.

On a phenomenological level, home is the familiar, only becoming
'uncharted territory' when a homecomer returns and finds the basis for the
taken-for-granted changed (Schutz 1962; Jones 1984), while fieldwork can be
the location of others experienced by a stranger in a non-familiar place. The
existential dialectic between these two apparent opposites may be played out
in the unconscious as well as the conscious, as familiar place interacts with
non-familiar to produce stranger-at-home as well as home-with-stranger.

The dream operates on all these levels simultaneously, as do the realities of
fieldwork. Like Russian dolls within dolls, each part exists simultaneously by
and for itself and in relation to other parts, as part of a larger whole. The

problem, however, is both how to describe all these levels individually, and, at the same time, how to fit them together into one complex whole. The difficulty is compounded when one finds oneself as part of that whole: a doll among other, familiar dolls fitted inside a larger doll.

Under such circumstances, how can one, as an ethnographer, objectively capture the reality of the whole? How can one portray adequately that complex process known as fieldwork? In this specific case, how can one describe effectively the staging by which home and field grow together, fuse, and eventually part?

The narration or demonstration of this process requires a process in itself, namely, the translation of the experience into an ethnographic text. This task may be as complicated as the very act of fieldwork and may involve a parallel process, by which the anthropology/home distinction becomes blurred. The illusory yet real problems of construction and reconstruction of the text may come to be but a mirror of the dreamlike yet real experience of fieldwork.

Recounting the fieldwork experience, then, becomes the unfolding of a dream. Suddenly, there is no beginning and no end – just different fragments re-experienced of a larger unity. The question is whether, with such a view of fieldwork, any real, objective account can be obtained?

One of the ways to search for this objectivity and gain validation for the experience is to enter into a dialogue with others in order to verify events and hence produce a text (e.g. Crapanzano 1980; Dumont 1978). Ethnography thus becomes the result of interaction with the other in order to comprehend the self, 'the culturally mediated and historically situated self which finds itself in a continuously changing world of meaning' (Rabinow 1977: 6). Ethnographers become self-reflective and reflexive, conscious that the anthropology of yesteryear blurred the quasi-sacred distinction between ideal and actual models, telling us how it 'ought to be' in the field rather than how 'it really was'.

In the backlash of the last few years and the corresponding surge of interest in hermeneutics and phenomenological anthropology, ethnographers have looked through their 'epistemological windows' (Ward and Werner 1984) and succeeded in debunking the myth of fieldwork. Today, fieldwork can be a drudgery; it may have no guidelines or rules; its construction may be partial. Anthropologists can be natives-as-strangers (Heilman 1980), just as often as they are strangers-as-natives in the traditional phenomenological sense. Life in its complexities presents field situations equally complex. Anthropologists stay on in the field, partially or completely. They either advocate study or study advocacy among informants. They realize identities oft submerged as well as submerging identities already realized – all in the name of anthropology.

However, if the act of fieldwork was once tinted by rose-coloured spectacles, today our 'epistemological windows' are misted. We select facts, acknowledging that our work is interpretive. We show how the construction of ethnography is enacted in interaction with native others, but we do not have the perception to see that the 'reconstruction of a set of encounters' (Rabinow 1977: 6) is itself deplete: it may overcome the blur between ideal and actual but it superimposes in its stead an equally harmful transgression: the non-distinction between prescribed and preferred relations.

In the field, prescribed relations are informants: key informants, and general informants, who are subsumed under the 'native' category. Preferred relations are additional relations, other Others: friends, spouses, girl-friends, natal family, or colleagues. In the process of fieldwork, all these Others come into play, influencing and, at times, dominating the interpretation of the act. And yet, curiously, the role of the latter type of Other is rarely recalled – a brief 'I thank my wife Betty for typing the manuscript' kind of statement, or 'I thank Paul Hyman for his . . . acute and unique insights' (Rabinow 1977). But what role do these Others, present in the field, actually play in the reconstruction of fieldwork and the construction of the ethnographic text? How is it, for example, that Rabinow, so sensitive to the input of 'insider's outsiders' and other Others, does not discuss the influence of his friend beyond the above brief dismissal, despite the fact that Hyman mysteriously photographed every one of Rabinow's informants and therefore must have been *there*? How is it that Rabinow omits to mention the effect upon fieldwork of the Geertzes (and their students) whose house in Sefrou, we have it on good record, Rabinow frequented regularly? It is remarkable that even Evans-Pritchard, one of the last of the valiant anthropologists from what he himself called 'the age of the dodo' (Evans-Pritchard 1973), despite his avowed preference for solitude, never saw fit to examine the influence of discussants on the development of his work and dismissed certain others, like witches, as invisible?[2] In short, the role of selected unmentionable, yet often not untouchable, Others has not been given honest attention by anthropologists in their recollection of the realities of fieldwork and the subsequent writing of ethnography.

Every anthropologist enters into discourse with non-native as well as native Others, be they kin, colleagues, spouse, or friends. In so doing, the anthropologist negotiates a shared reality with these Others and, with them, enters the realm of intersubjectivity. At this point, however, the paradox of intersubjectivity begins to manifest itself for, so long as the non-anthropologist remains apart – objective and Other – a measure of objectivity can be attained. But as soon as the Other becomes an increasingly equal partner in the search for objectivity – a 'We-relation' by which the two (or more) 'grow old together' (Husserl 1970) – that goal recedes. This illusory process, which appears to be the core problem of the ethnographic text and a central difficulty of anthropology as an objective discipline, is but a dream within a dream, paralleling, in my case, the complex interrelationship between home and anthropology in the field.

*   *   *

We arrived in Israel in November 1972 and moved to the immigrant town of Lod in February 1973. My anthropological mission was to conduct fieldwork among a community of Bene Israel (literally: 'Children of Israel') Indian Jews. I have described the situation of the Bene Israel in Israel elsewhere (e.g. Weil 1977a, 1977b, 1977c, 1980, 1981). In Lod, most of the Bene Israel had immigrated to Israel during the 1950s and 1960s. Some were also recent immigrants. They hailed, in the main, from Bombay, but they had also emigrated directly from Karachi (in Pakistan), and from the Konkan villages outside Bombay, to Israel.

Although Lod was often referred to as a 'slum' by middle-class (and even working-class) Israelis, it represented one of the better established Israeli Indian settlements, in Bene Israel terms. This was largely due to its proximity to Ben Gurion airport and to Israel Aircraft Industries, which employed many Indian Jews.

We departed from Lod in February 1975 and stayed on in Israel, moving to Jerusalem, where we live until this day.

Getting there

She: I initiate the idea, like I initiated fieldwork. Michael is enthusiastic; he will share in the creation. I explain how the role of the spouse or the Other present in the field has been ignored. An almost indubitable fact. He will write his section recounting fieldwork from his point of view; I shall write mine. Together, we shall show how anthropology and the home become indistinguishable at a certain stage in fieldwork among the Indian Jews in Israel.

I delegate like I did then. For Michael, writing the article is not his major preoccupation. It is a side issue, to which he will relate in his spare time. A tension arises between us. I, cast in the role of the dedicated anthropologist, am convinced of the missionary importance of writing this article as a reminder to the world of anthropologists that their observations are rarely independent and as such often impaired. He, I claim, is simply doing me a favour. He denies. He will write his part when he can. I must understand that there are other things in life besides anthropology. I wait impatiently. Meanwhile, I read, write, and reflect about the fieldwork experience. Finally, Michael writes down some thoughts about our entry into the field . . .

He: The first interface between myself as a professional and Shalva as an anthropologist lay in the decision as to where we would locate ourselves in Israel. Our investigations began in parallel. I looked for work opportunities, she searched for the ideal fieldwork site where there were concentrations of Bene Israel. The process narrowed down to two sites – the Tel Aviv region and

Beersheba in the south. The final decision was a joint one. I had a preferred posting in Tel Aviv, while Lod, a 'development town' of 30,000 people within commuting distance of Tel Aviv, had the third-largest concentration of Bene Israel in Israel (2,000 out of a total Indian population in Israel of 25,000).

We never actually discussed what our respective roles would be in the field or how we would interact. It was understood that while each would 'do his own thing', some sort of support and assistance would be given to the other.

Upon arrival in Israel, we were temporarily based in a hostel in a North Tel Aviv suburb. I began to work almost immediately as an economist in a large industrial conglomerate in Tel Aviv and Shalva began to arrange her entry into the field.

This was a trying period for two reasons. First, residence in the hostel as a temporary abode gave an unnatural and transient tone to our existence. Second, the preparations for fieldwork and commuting to the field-site proved difficult and unsatisfying. Thus we both felt the need to make our move to live with the Indian community as soon as possible.

She: I remember well being totally frustrated in North Tel Aviv, having arrived in Israel, but not quite living with the Indians. I remember the day we drove for the first time to Lod. I was in a state of shock at the tumbledown dwellings which constituted Lod's 'Old City', and the filth and conformity of the matchboxes which constituted the new part of Lod. Michael turned to me and said: 'Well, this is where you chose to live; this is what you want to do.' I was not at all sure, but somehow or other I forced myself to go through with it; to rent an apartment of sixty-five square metres with Indian neighbours (the head of the household was the President of the Federation of Indian Jews) in a central part of Lod within five minutes' walking distance from practically every Bene Israel in the town, and to live 'just like the natives'.

She: We 'divide and rule' with the article. We both write independently and compare. But the article is mine: the authority to lead, to edit, to rewrite lies with me. Michael 'commutes' with the article, like he commuted to the field.

In order to produce an ethnographic text conveying what *really* took place, She turns to Him for verification. He reluctantly agrees to reconstruct the dream of fieldwork and thereby supply Her with a yardstick of objectivity. He enters temporarily into that dream by writing his impressions – and wakes fitfully to declare it was not his dream. Awake, the relationship between the reality of the fieldwork dream and the reality of the waking life establishes itself. He stands apart from Her, agreeing to enter the dream, but guarding the boundaries of his 'objective' self. Once in the dream, the dreamers – who did the fieldwork – cannot be certain that they have woken up from the last of their dreams. Fieldwork lives on – in the very country in which they reside. The relationship between the dreamers replicates itself in the attempt to construct the text which mirrors the dream.

Settling in

She: *Having gained entry, I set myself some sort of daily routine which consisted of observations in the morning; social contacts and writing; a siesta in the afternoon; census-taking or interviewing in the late afternoon; and attending functions, organization meetings, or celebrations in the evening.*

At first, I confined myself to observations on more 'public' occasions such as shopping, or Indian cultural evenings. Soon the work became cumulative as I developed more and more contacts within the Indian community. I began to be invited to weddings and circumcision ceremonies. Then I began to attend more 'private' rituals, such as pre-wedding mehendi ceremonies, purification ceremonies, or hair-cutting rituals. Parallel to this, I began to discuss in English, Hebrew, or Marathi (with the aid of an informant/friend/translator) more 'private' matters: the questions of religious discrimination (the Bene Israel were not accepted as 'full Jews' until 1964) and racial prejudice; the problems of being a co-wife in a monogamous society; or the difficulties of understanding the attitudes of Moroccan or Polish Jewish neighbours towards Indian Jews. At first, I could write up leisurely notes and the famous 'field diary'. After about a year, when I came to know practically every Bene Israel in Lod — some better, some less — my life became a frenzy of Indian social engagements and I was hard pressed to get through a day's 'work'. I became increasingly dependent upon Michael to help me complete my self-imposed tasks.

He: While we never discussed what my role in the field would be, I think that it was understood that my main function would be one of providing moral support and acting as a 'bouncing-board' for ideas. In practice, I took upon myself additional roles.

First, I acted as research assistant. In this respect, I performed largely technical tasks, such as taping and photography. This division of responsibilities enabled Shalva to concentrate more fully on the intellectual and content aspects of the field research and not to be distracted by technical problems.

I also assisted in carrying out some of the more mundane parts of fieldwork, such as collecting statistical data, and aiding in census-taking. Furthermore, I acted in certain circumstances as the 'male anthropologist' gaining entry to what were solely male domains.

The most obvious example was in the synagogue where I participated actively in the services from the men's section while Shalva sat upstairs in the ladies' gallery. Our joint roles here were interesting. I was acting on Shalva's behalf, investigating and learning for her as an extension of her. On the other hand, she was actually 'present', physically located a few yards from me, yet in a different world, and, at the same time, I was 'anthropologizing' as she was (from the woman's perspective).

She: As we settle in to writing, the routine of fieldwork takes on an even greater reality, as does the division of labour between us in the ethnographic creation.

She hopes that through His increased understanding a clearer, more real, account of the fieldwork experience can be attained. But the dreamers of fieldwork, grasping to recollect accurately, find themselves in what Wendy O'Flaherty has called a 'receding frame'. She writes: 'The dream is what helps us to crash through the frame of apparent reality – the last visible frame – even though the dream, too, is a frame, and not the last frame, either' (O'Flaherty 1984: 202).

The last visible frame at this stage is the division of labour between us in the agreement to collaborate in the production of the text. The reality is the inequality in the endeavour, whereby the ethnographic authority, in Clifford's terms (1983), despite all our endeavours, will rest with me. This reality only reflects the frame of the dream which was fieldwork.

Juggling

He: The to-ing and fro-ing betwixt Lod and Tel Aviv made me live a very schizophrenic existence. My presence in Lod was ethereal, transient and temporary. I would wander in, not quite there, somewhat shadowlike. At times, my presence became stronger. In the synagogue, especially, or during situations that involved Michael and Shalva and not the anthropologist and her spouse, the presence was at its realest.

The commuting nature of my 'fieldwork' led to increase its non-permanency rather than the converse. Thus I was most keen that we would make trips to other places to see our own 'natural' friends, to eat at more Westernized restaurants and visit the cinema, theatre, and concerts, and also to go shopping elsewhere but the *shuk* (market). We also used to spend occasional weekends away, and it was these excursions out of the field that kept me balanced; although in retrospect they may well have had a more destabilizing influence.

She: One of the greatest difficulties I had was 'balancing' the field and the home. During the first year of intense fieldwork, I tried to carry out most of my work during the day when Michael was away. I thus concentrated on shopping in the bazaar, as the Bene Israel called it, talked to non-working women, observed the men in their respective places of work, such as Israel

Aircraft Industries and the national airline, El Al, and drew up a profile of Lod, the 'airport town'. However, after I became familiar with the field, I decided to conduct a census of every Bene Israel household to gain information not readily available by observation. After that, I conducted an in-depth survey of family life among thirty women. It became increasingly clear that in order to keep to a random sample, I had to interview in the afternoons (from 3 p.m. on) and in the evenings after the Bene Israel (and Michael) came home from work. In addition, the invitations to social engagements – weddings, pre-wedding and post-wedding varrath ceremonies, parties and so on – steadily increased as fieldwork progressed. All these were evening commitments, which required my attendance. Michael could either stay at home alone in our shikun (standard apartment) or come along. He usually chose the latter when it came to festivities. I cannot remember that I was willing to compromise, i.e. not attend, having been successful in securing so many social invitations. My only compromise was my agreement to leave Lod occasionally on Saturdays in order to spend the Sabbath with non-Indian friends, an agreement reached only after I felt I knew exactly what happened in Lod on Saturdays and things were beginning to repeat themselves.

She: The same dilemma troubles me now. I try to make my anthropological commitments during the day and attempt to set aside a private life in the evenings for us. But, as I write, I take more and more time out of the 'Home' time: discussions revolve around the writing of the article; I take an evening off here and there to search for more references in the library.

'It is impossible to be inside the dream and outside the dream at the same time,' states O'Flaherty. 'Yet we *are* inside and outside, in another sense, every time we dream. The best way to express this paradox, perhaps, is to imagine what it might be like to live the dream and to tell it at the same time, and this is what the Indian myths attempt to do' (O'Flaherty 1984: 202). This is also what we are attempting to do. We are both inside and outside the dream, even if She is inside more often than outside, while He is outside more often than inside. Today, Kluckhohn's statement about 'stereo vision' (1949) is hopelessly out of date. We are in the age of 'quadrophonic vision' as two or more persons 'see' stereo together.

This pattern replicates itself today, at this stage in the writing of the article. Neither She nor He remains outside the dream; both 'see' from both sides of the fence simultaneously. However, in abandoning reality, even temporarily, it becomes increasingly difficult to walk the tightrope between subjectivity and objectivity, on the one hand, and experiencing the experience and recounting it, on the other. As Silvers has pointed out in a fascinating attempt to understand silence among children and present that narrative as dialectical knowledge, 'This moving back and forth between what the researcher has already said and what must be reflectively said constitutes a tension of discourse – a dialectic of reflective discourse' (Silvers 1983: 106).

The tension is compounded in that the unequally experienced dream may be illusory and yet it exists. It occurs in order to highlight the major action and bracket the narrative. The attempt to separate field and home occurred and occurs at exactly the point when the system is straining in one direction or another: either to burst out of the dream altogether – may be this is the point at which many anthropologists get divorced or split up – or to enter the realm of the shared dream.

Merging

He: Somewhere through fieldwork, anthropology overran our lives. Our social lives became determined by the coming list of weddings, mourning visits, and other occasions, of which there were many. It became most important that we stay in Lod for the festivals so that we witness the various rites and traditions. Shalva developed a detailed plan of action for interviewing and data-gathering. All these dictated a plan of work and play that was Bene Israel-centred. Furthermore, the location of our flat right in the middle of the field meant that it was impossible to expel, however temporarily, anthropology from our home; there was no let-up. A further illustration of this was the fact we possessed neither telephone nor television, so that we had little communication with the outside world or means of escape while in our home.

Gradually, I began to let events take me over. I became absorbed in the Bene Israel community. I attended synagogue every Saturday and if I did not turn up once, I would be missed. I developed my own small circle of friends – synagogue friends, and husbands of women from the Indian Women's Organization which Shalva frequented. I got involved in social activities and surprised even myself at bidding in Marathi at the public auction for *mitzvot* (lit.: commandments; ritual honours) in the synagogue.

She: I managed to develop an incredible rapport with the Indian Jews. Perhaps it was because I was a newcomer to Israel and they either were or felt the same way in Israeli society. Perhaps it was because we shared a common British heritage and I held a common language and culture with most of my informants. Perhaps it was because they were shy and retiring and I felt comfortable with that projected part of me.

She: Michael is supposed to be writing about his experiences in the field. He is more than co-operating. He is involved in the writing between himself and me.

As I write these words, the telephone goes. It is the ex-headmistress of the Sir Elie Kedourie School in Bombay, one of my major informants – and friends – in Israel. Would Michael and I and the kids come to a Marathi drama and Indian dance evening on Saturday night in Lod? I am not doing fieldwork any more; Michael never was. And yet the reality of living on in the field is part of this paper.

We attend the evening. Twelve years have gone by, but little has changed. We are greeted the same, the warmth is still there. The audience of 500 packing the cultural centre in Lod (which never existed in my day) is almost exclusively Indian, like it was then. One or two white faces; the rest chatting away in Hebrew, English, and Marathi. The entertainment is exclusively Indian – songs, music, a dance group, drama. Michael and I feel nostalgic.

He: Lod has grown considerably, there is a ring road skirting the city and a new modern centre has been built moving the centre of gravity away from the dilapidated 'Old City'. But in all other respects, nothing has changed. The concert took place in a recently built cultural centre. The mayor, in typical fashion, failed to turn up for an Indian event. Seats had been reserved for us in the front row. The hall was completely full, a sea of some 500 Indian faces and less than half a dozen non-Indians, who were municipal and other functionaries. Lots of people came up to us before the show and after. They all smiled warmly, shook hands, yet little conversation took place. The expression of warmth and empathy said all.

The Bene Israel looked the same but a bit older; perhaps one or two fewer saris, but otherwise most of the women came in traditional dress. The hall was bare and cold; there was silence, decorum, and lots of warmth.

Then one or two opening remarks from officialdom in Hebrew, longer words of introduction by the Bene Israel leaders (ladies, that is) in English with even an honorary mention of Shalva, and the show began. Dances by an Indian dancer, a girls' dance, a band of men singing and playing traditional instruments and then the climax – a Marathi drama.

The evening was long and enjoyable. We were thrown back ten years into the belly of the Bene Israel community and the same feelings of hospitality and acceptance, complemented by expressions of respect for Shalva, and for me, as her husband. It made us both feel very nostalgic, very warm and grateful to the community that they accepted us and remembered us.

The shared dream is a very Indian creation which links two people experiencing its reality. When the dream is exposed, its truth value is enhanced because two people are or were there. Shared dreams, as O'Flaherty explains (1984), are not mere complementary dreams for, in the shared dream, one lover sees the exact same elements and has the same experiences as the other. At this point, it is illusory to distinguish between the ego and the alter; they are experiencing the same reality.

This is the equivalent of Schutz's 'Pure We-relationship', or Buber's famous 'I–Thou relationship', in which the experience is of being of oneself with the other. 'The I of the basic world I–Thou appears as a person and becomes conscious of itself as subjectivity' (Buber 1970: 111). Through inclusion and lack of differentiation, gone is objectivity.

Although for some ethnographers, such as Jules-Rosette, 'total immersion' poses no obstacle to the attainment of a 'reflexive ethnography' (1978), the involvement of both She and He in the native world constitutes here the negation of sociological or external modes of analysis. There were few other Others during this period, or none to jostle one for more than temporary time out of the complacency of what Husserl calls 'transcendental intersubjectivity' (Husserl 1970).

As we write, we are engaged in a passionate recounting to the other of the shared dream – fieldwork – in order to convince ourselves – and subsequently others – that it really took place. By means of corroboration, the dream of fieldwork is relived as we both share in a reincarnated field-experience with the Indians today.

Wanting 'out'

He: I tired of fieldwork and Lod much earlier than Shalva. After about a year I had had enough. First, it was not too dissimilar from a previous experience I had had in Israel; second, I do not think that I had any really close friends in Lod. My Bene Israel friends were more of a superficial or acquaintance type of friend; Shalva's situation was different.

My feelings towards the Bene Israel were doublefold. On the one hand, I was very fond of them, I felt genuine empathy and warmth which seemed to be reciprocated. They were genuinely 'nice' people and very attractive once one penetrated them and understood what made them tick. I also enjoyed the fact that we shared a common British heritage. On the other hand, they were difficult people to be friends with. Not because they were unfriendly or did not accept me, but rather that I am a fairly verbal person and for me friendship manifests itself in conversations. The Bene Israel, however, are rather unverbal. Much of their conversation and communication is silent and non-verbal, and I was not used to this and felt uncomfortable with it.

[As I write these words I hear the ring of resentment which is strange because I can't remember it from then, though it may have lurked somewhere in the subconscious and explains both the need to make many excursions from the field and my desire to leave Lod after a year or more.]

Thus it was that when I felt that fieldwork had been done, I commenced to put the pressure on Shalva to leave Lod both because I was bored with it and wanted time to devote to my career and second because I wanted Shalva to write-up. I was convinced, like her supervisor, that fieldwork must stop and that she must distance herself from the Bene Israel in order to gain a perspective.

She: My SSRC grant was running out and I was conscious of pressure both from my supervisor, who was interested in the progress of my doctoral thesis, and from my husband, who was fed up with the fieldwork. However, I declared that I wanted to stay and live with the Indians for the rest of my life. I forced myself to try to write up the thesis but the pose of objectivity held little interest for me. I was torn between the ostensible purpose of my fieldwork – to write a doctorate – and writing a 'true' description of things the way the Indians see Israeli society. I was also conscious of my mission to prove to the world that the Bene Israel were 'full Jews', which the Bene Israel had somehow imposed upon me.

My supervisor visited Israel. He gently but firmly advised me to move out of the field.

He: The dilemmas of the whole fieldwork experience were exemplified in the question of the birth of our daughter Ilana. (We have always thought of her as the 'fieldwork child', the product of the total anthropologist.) Prior to her birth and while contemplating the likely turn of events, we considered what we would do should a boy be born and how we would plan the circumcision ceremony. The *Brith Mila* (circumcision) was considered very important to the Bene Israel and it was thus inconceivable that our *Brith* would not take place within the community. However, what concerned me was that the Bene Israel *mohel* (ritual circumcizer) was somewhat inept and inexact in his job, a fact that I, as photographer, was all too aware of, having seen his handiwork from very close and somewhat bloody quarters. To have imported a *mohel* would be most insulting and to have the ceremony away from 'home' was unthinkable. Fortunately (?), a girl was born and the problem pre-empted.

The community was most disappointed on my behalf as a baby boy would have been a more fitting blessing in their eyes. In fact, most members in the synagogue extended condolences to me on the 'sad event'; only one gentleman congratulated me on joining the club – he had seven girls!

She: The birth of Ilana was one of the landmarks of my fieldwork. It signified my acceptance as a complete woman in Bene Israel society. I must confess that prior to the birth I was worried that we would have a boy, but I was prepared to submit to Bene Israel norms of hygiene and ritual demands. I was also worried that we might not have a boy and suffer a loss of face, particularly for a first child.

I could not understand why my Bene Israel friends did not visit me immediately after I gave birth. It turned out that they were disappointed on our behalf. In addition, they thought that I was busy with my own mother, *who had turned up in Lod to help in the post-natal period. However, very soon a delegation of Indian women came to my house with a request to carry out a traditional Indian 'naming ceremony' for my new baby girl. The occasion was wonderful. Over thirty women, ten men and twenty children squashed into our apartment. They dressed me in a sari and presented me with five fruits on my stomach saying 'Better luck next time; may you have five sons!' They sang songs to my daughter in Marathi and swung her on a* hindola *(cradle/swing). I wanted to stay in Lod.*

For Him, epistemological discrepancies – concerning the perception of the reality – began to appear. Reality began to be perceived in an altered state, and disconfirmatory facts – in the form of the absence of 'real' friends, doubts as to the expertise of the ritual circumcizer, and the like – began to appear, confirming for Him that the dream could be interrupted by more 'real' waking moments. For Him, a more 'real' self could be realized, perhaps, without the 'impression-management' he was suddenly aware he was conducting. Delmos calls this state 'culture fatigue' (Delmos 1973) and advocates for the anthropologist greater directness in field relationships and less artificial role-playing. For the non-anthropologist, the end of 'impression-management' meant the end of the shared dream.

For Her, the end of the shared dream is self-evident, but waking to reality requires validation of the ontological reality that the dream was. He becomes a yardstick for that reality of the dream for he stands outside it; She is sometimes still within. He is requested to collaborate to construct proof of their existence in the once-shared dream. She transcends in the illusion 'solitary consciousness' and reaches the realization that 'simultaneous with my lived experience of you, there is your lived experience which belongs to you and *is* part of your stream of consciousness' (Schutz 1967: 108). In the final analysis, as Schutz himself acknowledges, even though a Thou-orientation towards another exists, 'In real life we never experience the pure existence of others; instead we meet real people with their own personal characteristics and traits' (Schutz 1967: 164).

She: In the writing of the article, Michael tires. He wants to finish and 'to get on to the next'. Outside the dream, and yet still perpetuating it, he helps me construct the next stage. Pulling me out of the transcendental intersubjective realm, he provides an 'objective' voice.

Writing-up

She: A few months after the birth of Ilana, I returned to Sussex to report on my fieldwork. A seminar I gave on the Bene Israel in Lod jolted me to see how unobjective I had become. I returned home to Lod intent on gaining a doctorate which would be as faithful as possible to the Bene Israel and yet live up to academic standards of everything an ethnography should be.

The first stages of writing-up were traumatic. I debated every word and wrote and rewrote hundreds of times a chapter (which later became an article (Weil 1977b)) on names and identity among the Bene Israel. I went over its contents both with Michael and with one or two informants. I was extremely worried that they would not like it or disagree with what was written. I recall that the Bene Israel to whom I showed it were puzzled by the academic tone of the article and amazed at the wealth of material I had succeeded in collecting.

The more I wrote, the more I became aware of the lacunae in my research and the more fieldwork I felt I needed to conduct. However, as this process was taking place, I also became aware of the absurdity of carrying out fieldwork perpetually. I let myself be convinced to leave the field-site, if not Israel. We moved to Jersualem, where we reside today.

He: Some time around the summer of 1974, Shalva started preparing draft chapters, further developed ideas, and received feedback from her supervisor. The exit or disengagement from the field and from the client community took place while writing up.

The role of intellectual interchanger or 'bouncing-board' took on a more important colour than we had originally envisaged. Throughout the various stages of fieldwork and writing-up, Shalva would use me in order to discuss ideas, plans, tactics, concepts, and problems. This role became most important during the trying writing-up phase.

The first few chapters (chronologically, that is) took the longest to write by far, and the structure or the central thesis was the hardest to contemplate or develop. Drawing up the thesis and drafting the first couple of chapters was extremely lengthy and arduous. Shalva struggled with every word and expressed feelings of lack of confidence and security in her ability to say anything about her very rich field-experience.

She: The writing-up of this text is extraordinarily difficult, mainly because it is so personal and I am so involved in the subject matter. I have not experienced anything like it since I wrote the doctorate.

The writing-up of the fieldwork process and the writing of this text had and has an illusory quality. In the writing, I dream of Michael as the dreamer – what O'Flaherty calls 'the dreamer dreamt' (1984: 252) – who acts as a reference for me to realize a different level of reality, which is still, however, one level away from 'the most real' world. I oscillate from the rules of ethnography and the mores of academia to the world of Indians and dreams. Pulled by Him, who is at once outside the frame and at the same time reconstructing a new frame, we both recollect the dream of extricating Her from the frame.

In so doing, the dream becomes reflexive. 'Reflexiveness does not leave the subject lost in its own concerns; it pulls one toward the Other and away from isolated attentiveness toward oneself. Reflexiveness requires subject and object, breaking the thrall of self-concern by its very drive toward self-knowledge that inevitably takes into account a surrounding world of events, people and places' (Myerhoff and Ruby 1982: 5). The reflexivity manifests itself through a seemingly contradictory duality; on the one hand, it draws Her towards Him in the search for a greater objectivity; on the other hand, it enhances the subjectivity of the dreamer. In the final analysis, the reflexive dream is looped, twisted in upon itself such that the inside joins the outside in a more real, objective, if you will, dream.

Leaving

He: The process of disinvolvement and disengagement were the most traumatic for Shalva, forcing a real end to the momentum of fieldwork and knowing that she could never return either to the state of participant observer and honorary Bene Israel or to the additional role of adviser, mentor, and friend that had also been conferred on her.

I should add in relation to the writing-up process, that while fieldwork ended in a tangible sense when we drove away from Lod after two-and-a-half years, writing-up only terminated when Shalva formally presented her doctoral thesis to the community at a ceremony in honour of Elijah the Prophet and publicly received heaps of praise for having documented the Bene Israel in a form that they thought was positive.

She: *The removal men came to Lod and transferred our belongings to Jerusalem. It took only forty minutes yesterday to drive on the new motorway from our home in Jerusalem to the Indian evening in Lod. But although I continue to live in Israel – and my thesis, completed in 1977, was as much on Israeli society as on the Bene Israel – the two worlds are miles apart.*

Michael is busy in his job; I work as an anthropologist at the university. Although my anthropology intrudes into our lives, it is not all-consuming. There are barriers.

The dream ends and the objective account is written. And yet the dream lives on and is relived in the very attempt to reconstruct it. In a mood of *déja vu*, the dream today reflecting the dream of then jolts us out of the dream, making the past real. For the very act of recollection provides verification of the dream as

real. Events today, in an illusory manner, prove to us the existence of real
elements in yesteryear.

As they stand apart, She and He exist outside the dream, living their daily
lives in a world cut off from fieldwork. Their waking routines are lived out
separately; they stand 'face to face' as subject and object. Meanwhile, the
realities of fieldwork continue to mark the present, just as the field continues
to exist and they continue to enter into it intermittently. In the moments of
déjà vu, the dream is remembered as real, confirmed by the existence of the
Other. In the process of the reconstruction of the dream, reality is re-created.

She:Our worlds are apart and yet sometimes they merge. Michael offers
me support; I take an interest in his work. We decide to collaborate on
a joint article, on the very real problems of having stayed on in Israel
after fieldwork, on the continuing pervasiveness of the field.

I initiate the idea, like I initiated the fieldwork. Michael is
enthusiastic; he will share in the creation . . .

Notes

1 My sincere thanks go to a non-native Other, Don Handelman, who aided me with
   several drafts of this paper and encouraged me to re-enter the dream. I am also
   grateful to the participants of the ASA conference at Keele (25–29 March 1985),
   who provided stimulating comments on my paper.
2 In Zandeland, for example, Evans-Pritchard notes that he had the company of the
   DC, 'my gallant and dear friend, the late Major Larken (we met for a few hours
   every new moon) and an Anglican Missionary . . . and his wife (both Australians)
   and nobody else in any direction for several days' journey – walking, that is, with
   porters' (Evans-Pritchard 1973: 237).

References

BUBER, M. (1970) *I and Thou* (3rd edn). Edinburgh: T. & T. Clark.
CARROLL, L. (1887) *Through the Looking Glass and What Alice Found There*. London:
Macmillan.
CLIFFORD, J. (1983) On Ethnographic Authority. *Representations* **1**(2): 118–46.
CRAPANZANO, V. (1980) *Tuhami: Portrait of a Moroccan*. Chicago: University of
Chicago Press.
DELMOS, J. (1973) Culture Fatigue: The Results of Role-Playing in Anthropological
Research. *Anthropological Quarterly* **46**(1); 30–7.
DUMONT, J. (1978) *The Headman and I: Ambiguity and Ambivalence in the
Fieldworking Experience*. Austin: University of Texas Press.
EVANS-PRITCHARD, E. (1973) Some Recollections on Fieldwork in the Twenties.
Anthropological Quarterly **46**(4): 235–42.
HEILMAN, S. (1980) Jewish Sociologist: Native-as-Stranger. *The American Sociologist*
15: 100–08.
HUSSERL, E. (1954/1970) *The Crisis of European Sciences and Transcendental
Phenomenology*. Evanston: Northwestern University Press.

JONES, F. (1984) The Provisional Homecomer. *Human Studies* **7**(2): 227–30.

JULES-ROSETTE, B. (1978) Towards a Theory of Ethnography. *Sociological Symposium* **24**: 81–98.

KLUCKHOHN, C. (1949) *Mirror for Man: The Relation of Anthropology to Modern Life.* New York: McGraw Hill.

MYERHOFF, B. and RUBY, J. (1982) *The Crack in the Mirror.* Boston, Mass.: MIT Press.

O'FLAHERTY, W. (1984) *Dreams, Illusion and Other Realities.* Chicago: University of Chicago Press.

RABINOW, P. (1977) *Reflections on Fieldwork in Morocco.* Berkeley, Calif.: University of California Press.

SCHUTZ, A. (1962) *Collected Papers* (edited by Maurice Natanson). The Hague: M. Nijhoff.

— (1967) *The Phenomenology of the Social World* (translated by G. Walsh and P. Lehnert). Chicago: Northwestern University Press.

SILVERS, R. (1983) On the Other Side of Silence. *Human Studies* **6**(1): 91–108.

WARD, J. and WERNER, O. (1984) Difference and Dissonance in Ethnographic Data. *Communication and Cognition* **17**(2/3): 219–43.

WEIL, S. (1977a) The Bene Israel in Lod, Israel: A Study in the Persistence of Ethnicity and Ethnic Identity. Unpublished D.Phil. thesis presented to the University of Sussex.

— (1977b) Names and Identity among the Bene Israel. *Ethnic Groups* **1**(3): 201–19.

— (1977c) Verbal Interaction among the Bene Israel. *International Journal of the Sociology of Language* **13**: 71–85.

— (1980) The State of Research into Bene Israel Indian Jews. *Indian Economic and Social History Review* **17**(4): 397–408.

— (1981) *The Jews from the Konkan: The Bene Israel Community of India.* Tel Aviv: Bet Hatefutsoth.

Name index

Subject index